THE
CARE OF BOOKS

𝕷𝖔𝖓𝖉𝖔𝖓: C. J. CLAY AND SONS,
CAMBRIDGE UNIVERSITY PRESS WAREHOUSE,
AVE MARIA LANE,
𝕲𝖑𝖆𝖘𝖌𝖔𝖜: 50, WELLINGTON STREET.

𝕷𝖊𝖎𝖕𝖟𝖎𝖌: F. A. BROCKHAUS.
𝕹𝖊𝖜 𝖄𝖔𝖗𝖐: THE MACMILLAN COMPANY.
𝕭𝖔𝖒𝖇𝖆𝖞: E. SEYMOUR HALE.

Fig. 15. EZRA WRITING THE LAW.

Frontispiece to the *Codex Amiatinus*.

THE
CARE OF BOOKS

An Essay on the
Development of Libraries and
their Fittings, from the earliest times to
the end of the Eighteenth Century

By

JOHN WILLIS CLARK, M.A., F.S.A.

Registrary of the University
and formerly Fellow of Trinity College, Cambridge

FOLCROFT LIBRARY EDITIONS / 1973

Library of Congress Cataloging in Publication Data

Clark, John Willis, 1833-1910.
  The care of books.

  Reprint of the 1901 ed. published by University
Press, Cambridge.
    1. Libraries—History. 2. Library architecture—
History. 3. Library fittings and supplies—History.
I. Title.
Z721.C59 1973   021'.009   73-15956
ISBN 0-8414-3502-2 (lib. bdg.)

Limited 100 Copies

Manufactured in the United States of America

Folcroft Library Editions
Box 182
Folcroft, Pa. 19032

THE
CARE OF BOOKS

An Essay on the
Development of Libraries and
their Fittings, from the earliest times to
the end of the Eighteenth Century

By

JOHN WILLIS CLARK, M.A., F.S.A.

Registrary of the University
and formerly Fellow of Trinity College, Cambridge

CAMBRIDGE
at the University Press

1909

Cambridge:
PRINTED BY J. AND C. F. CLAY,
AT THE UNIVERSITY PRESS.

FRANCISCO AIDANO GASQUET

MONACHO BENEDICTINO

D.D.

MAGISTRO DISCIPULUS

PREFACE.

WHEN engaged in editing and completing *The Architectural History of the University and Colleges of Cambridge,* I devoted much time and attention to the essay called *The Library.* The subject was entirely new; and the more I looked into it, the more convinced did I become that it would well repay fuller investigation than was then possible. For instance, I felt certain that the Customs affecting monastic libraries would, if one could only discover them, throw considerable light on collegiate statutes relating to the same subject.

The *Architectural History* having been published, I had leisure to study libraries from my new point of view; and, while thus engaged, I fortunately met with the admirable paper by Dom Gasquet which he modestly calls *Some Notes on Medieval Monastic Libraries.* This brief essay—it occupies only 20 pages—opened my eyes to the possibilities that lay before me, and I gladly place on record here the debt I owe to the historian to whom I have dedicated this book.

When I had the honour of delivering the Rede Lecture before the University of Cambridge in June 1894, I attempted a reconstruction of the monastic library, shewing its relationship, through its fittings, to

the collegiate libraries of Oxford and Cambridge ; and
I was also able, following the example set by Dom
Gasquet in the above-mentioned essay, to indicate the
value of illuminated manuscripts as illustrating the life of
a medieval student or scribe. In my lectures as Sandars
Reader in Bibliography, delivered before the University
of Cambridge in 1900, I developed the subject still
further, extending the scope of my enquiries so as to
include the libraries of Greece and Rome.

In writing my present book I have availed myself
freely of the three works above mentioned. At the same
time I have incorporated much fresh material ; and I am
glad to take this opportunity of stating, that, with the
single exception of the Escõrial, I have personally
examined and measured every building which I have
had occasion to describe ; and many of the illustrations
are from my own sketches.

I call my book an *Essay*, because I wish to indicate
that it is only an attempt to deal, in a summary fashion,
with an extremely wide and interesting subject—a subject,
too, which might easily be subdivided into separate heads
each capable of more elaborate treatment. For instance,
with regard to libraries in Religious Houses, I hope to
see a book written, dealing not merely with the way in
which the books were cared for, but with the subjects
most generally studied, as indicated to us by the catalogues which have survived.

A research such as I have had to undertake has
naturally involved the co-operation of numerous librarians
and others both in England and on the Continent. From
all these officials I have experienced unfailing courtesy
and kindness, and I beg them to accept this collective

expression of my gratitude. To some, however, I am under such particular obligations, that I wish to mention them by name.

In the first place I have to thank my friends Dr Jackson of Trinity College, Dr Sandys of S. John's College, Dr James of King's College, and F. J. H. Jenkinson, M.A., University Librarian, for their kind help in reading proofs and making suggestions. Dr Sandys devoted much time to the revision of the first chapter. As my work deals largely with monastic institutions it is almost needless to say that I have consulted and received efficient help from my old friend W. H. St John Hope, M.A., Assistant Secretary to the Society of Antiquaries.

My researches in Rome were made easy to me by the unfailing kindness and ready help accorded on every occasion by Father C. J. Ehrle, S.J., Prefect of the Vatican Library. My best thanks are also due to Signor Rodolfo Lanciani, to Professor Petersen of the German Archeological Institute, Rome, and to Signor Guido Biagi of the Biblioteca Laurenziana, Florence. At Milan Monsignor Ceriani of the Ambrosian Library was so kind as to have the library photographed for my use.

The courteous officials who administer the great libraries of Paris with so much ability, have assisted me in all my researches. I wish specially to thank in this place M. Léopold Delisle and M. Léon Dorez of the Bibliothèque Nationale; M. A. Franklin of the Bibliothèque Mazarine; M. H. Martin of the Bibliothèque de l'Arsenal; and M. A. Peraté, Sous-Conservateur du Château de Versailles.

I have also to thank Señor Ricardo Velasquez for his beautiful elevation of the bookcases in the Escõrial Library; Father J. van den Gheyn, S.J., of the Royal Library, Brussels, for his trouble in shewing me, and allowing me to have photographed, several MSS. from the library under his charge; my friends Mr T. G. Jackson, R.A., Architect, for lending me his section of Bishop Cobham's library at Oxford; E. W. B. Nicholson, M.A., Librarian, and Falconer Madan, M.A., Sub-Librarian, in the Bodleian Library, for information respecting the building and its contents; Mr F. E. Bickley of the British Museum for much help in finding and examining MSS.; and Lionel Cust, M.A., Director of the National Portrait Gallery, for general direction and encouragement.

Messrs Macmillan have allowed me to use three illustrations which appear in the first chapter; Mr Murray has given the same permission for the woodcut of the carrells at Gloucester; and Messrs Blades for the representation of James Leaver's book-press.

Lastly I wish to thank the staff of the University Press for using their best efforts to produce the work rapidly and well, and for many acts of personal kindness to myself.

JOHN WILLIS CLARK.

SCROOPE HOUSE,
   CAMBRIDGE,
     September 23rd, 1901.

CONTENTS.

CHAPTER V.

CHAPTER VI.

CHAPTER VII.

CHAPTER VIII.

CHAPTER IX.

LIST OF ILLUSTRATIONS.

THE CARE OF BOOKS.

CHAPTER I.

INTRODUCTION. ASSYRIAN RECORD-ROOMS. LIBRARIES IN
GREECE, ALEXANDRIA, PERGAMON, ROME. THEIR SIZE,
USE, CONTENTS, AND FITTINGS. ARMARIA OR PRESSES.
THE VATICAN LIBRARY OF SIXTUS V. A TYPE OF AN
ANCIENT ROMAN LIBRARY.

 PROPOSE, in the following Essay, to trace
the methods adopted by man in different ages
and countries to preserve, to use, and to make
accessible to others, those objects, of whatever
material, on which he has recorded his thoughts.
In this investigation I shall include the position,
the size, and the arrangement, of the rooms in which these
treasures were deposited, with the progressive development of
fittings, catalogues, and other appliances, whether defensive, or
to facilitate use. But, though I shall have to trace out these
matters in some detail, I shall try to eschew mere antiquarianism,
and to impart human interest, so far as possible, to a research
which might otherwise exhaust the patience of my readers.
Bibliography, it must be understood, will be wholly excluded.
From my special point of view books are simply things to
be taken care of; even their external features concern me
only so far as they modify the methods adopted for arrangement and preservation. I must dismiss the subject-matter of
the volumes which filled the libraries of former days with a
brevity of which I deeply regret the necessity. I shall point out

the pains taken to sort the books under various comprehensive heads; but I shall not enumerate the authors which fall under this or that division.

The earliest repositories of books were connected with temples or palaces, either because priests under all civilisations have been *par excellence* the learned class, while despots have patronised art and literature; or because such a position was thought to offer greater security.

I will begin with Assyria, where the record-rooms, or we might almost say the library, in the palace of Assur-bani-pal,

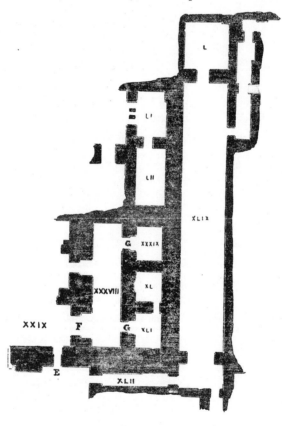

Fig. 1. Plan of the Record-Rooms in the Palace of Assur-bani-pal, King of Nineveh.

King of Nineveh, were discovered by Mr Layard in 1850 at Kouyunjik, on the Tigris, opposite Mosul. The plan (fig. 1), taken from Mr Layard's work[1], will shew, better than a long description, the position of these rooms, and their relation to the rest of the building—which is believed to date from about 700 B.C. The long passage (No. XLIX) is one of the entrances to the palace. Passing thence along the narrower passage (No. XLII) the explorers soon reached a doorway (E), which led them into a large hall (No. XXIX), whence a second doorway (F) brought them into a chamber (No. XXXVIII). On the north side of this room were two doorways (G, G), each "formed by two colossal bas-reliefs of Dagon, the fish-god." "The first doorway," says Mr Layard, "guarded by the fish-gods, led into two small chambers opening into each other, and once panelled with bas-reliefs, the greater part of which had been destroyed. I shall call these chambers 'the chambers of records,' for, like 'the house of the rolls' or records, which Darius ordered to be searched for the decree of Cyrus concerning the building of the Temple of Jerusalem[2], they appear to have contained the decrees of the Assyrian kings, as well as the archives of the empire."

Mr Layard was led to this conclusion by finding, in these rooms, enormous quantities of inscribed tablets and cylinders of baked clay. "To a height of a foot or more from the floor they were entirely filled with them; some entire, but the greater part broken into many fragments, probably by the falling in of the upper part of the building....These documents appear to be of various kinds. Many are historical records of wars, and distant expeditions undertaken by the Assyrians; some seem to be royal decrees, and are stamped with the name of a king, the son of Esarhaddon; others again...contain lists of the gods, and probably a register of offerings made in their temples[3]."

So far Mr Layard. Subsequent researches have shewn that these two small rooms—they were 27 feet and 23 feet long

---

[1] *Discoveries in the Ruins of Nineveh and Babylon.* 2 vols., 8vo. Lond. 1853. Vol. II., p. 343.

[2] Ezra, vi. 1.

[3] Mr Layard gives a view of the interior of one of these rooms (p. 345) after it had been cleared of rubbish.

respectively, with a uniform breadth of 20 feet—contained the literature as well as the official documents of Assyria. The tablets have been sorted under the following heads: History; Law; Science; Magic; Dogma; Legends: and it has been shewn (1) that there was a special functionary to take charge of them; (2) that they were arranged in series, with special precautions for keeping the tablets forming a particular series in their proper sequence; (3) that there was a general catalogue, and probably a class-catalogue as well[1].

Excavations in other parts of Assyria have added valuable information to Layard's first discovery. Dr Wallis Budge, of the British Museum, whom I have to thank for much kind assistance, tells me that "Kouyunjik is hardly a good example of a Mesopotamian library, for it is certain that the tablets were thrown about out of their proper places when the city was captured by the Medes about B.C. 609. The tablets were kept on shelves....When I was digging at Derr some years ago we found the what I call 'Record Chamber,' and we saw the tablets lying *in situ* on slate shelves. There were, however, not many literary tablets there, for the chamber was meant to hold the commercial documents relating to the local temple...." Dr Budge concludes his letter with this very important sentence: "We have no definite proof of what I am going to say now, but I believe that the bilingual[2] lists, which Assur-bani-pal had drawn up for his library at Nineveh, were intended 'for the use of students.'"

To this suggestion I would add the following. Does not the position of these two rooms, easily accessible from the entrance to the palace, shew that their contents might be consulted by persons who were denied admission to the more private apartments? And further, does not the presence of the god Dagon at the entrance indicate that the library was under the protection of the deity as well as of the sovereign?

As a pendant to these Assyrian discoveries I may mention the vague rumour echoed by Athenæus of extensive libraries collected in the sixth century before our era by Polycrates[3],

---

[1] *La Bibliothèque du Palais de Ninive*, par M. Joachim Menant. 8vo. Paris, 1880, p. 32.

[2] The two languages are the ancient Sumerian and the more modern Assyrian.

[3] Athenæus, Book I., Chap. 4.

tyrant of Samos, and Peisistratus, tyrant of Athens, the latter collection, according to Aulus Gellius[1], having been accessible to all who cared to use it. It must be admitted that these stories are of doubtful authenticity; and further, that we have no details of the way in which books were cared for in Greece during the golden age of her literature. This dearth of information is the more tantalizing as it is obvious that private libraries must have existed in a city so cultivated as Athens; and we do, in fact, find a few notices which tell us that such was the case. Xenophon[2], for instance, speaks of the number of volumes in the possession of Euthydemus, a follower of Socrates; and Athenæus records, in the passage to which I have already alluded, the names of several book-collectors, among whom are Euripides and Aristotle.

An allusion to the poet's bibliographical tastes has been detected in the scene of *The Frogs* of Aristophanes, where Æschylus and Euripides are weighing verses against each other in the presence of Dionysus. Æschylus exclaims:

καὶ μηκέτ' ἔμοιγε κατ' ἔπος, ἀλλ' ἐς τὸν σταθμὸν
αὐτός, τὰ παιδί', ἡ γυνή, Κηφισοφῶν,
ἐμβὰς καθήσθω, συλλαβὼν τὰ βιβλία,
ἐγὼ δὲ δύ' ἔπη τῶν ἐμῶν ἐρῶ μόνον.

Come, no more single lines—let him bring all,
His wife, his children, his Cephisophon,
His books and everything, himself to boot—
I'll counterpoise them with a couple of lines[3].

With regard to Aristotle Strabo has preserved a tradition that he "was the first who made a collection of books, and taught the kings of Egypt how to arrange a library[4]"— words which may be taken to mean that Aristotle was the first to work out the arrangement of books on a definite system which was afterwards adopted by the Ptolemies at Alexandria.

These notices are extremely disappointing. They merely serve to shew that collections of books did exist in Greece; but

[1] *Noct. Att.* Book VII., Chap. 17. Libros Athenis disciplinarum liberalium publice ad legendum præbendos primus posuisse dicitur Pisistratus tyrannus.

[2] Xenophon, *Memorabilia*, Book IV., Chap. 2.

[3] Aristoph. *Ranæ*, 1407—1410, translated by J. H. Frere. The passsage has been quoted by Castellani, *Biblioteche nell' Antichità*, 8vo., Bologna, 1884, pp. 7, 8, and many others.

[4] Strabo, ed. Kramer, Berlin, 8vo., 1852, Book XIII., Chap. 1, § 54. πρῶτος ὧν ἴσμεν συναγαγὼν βιβλία, καὶ διδάξας τοὺς ἐν Αἰγύπτῳ βασιλέας βιβλιοθήκης σύνταξιν.

they give us no indication of either their extent or their arrangement. It was left to the Emperor Hadrian to build the first public library at Athens, to which, as it was naturally constructed on a Roman design, I shall return after I have described those from which it was in all probability imitated.

But, if what may be termed Greece in Europe declines to give us information, that other Greece which extended itself to Asia Minor and to Egypt—Greater Greece it would be called in modern times—supplies us with a type of library-organisation which has been of far-reaching influence.

After the death of Alexander the Great (B.C. 323) a Greek dynasty, that of the Ptolemies, established itself at Alexandria, and another Greek dynasty at Pergamon. Both were distinguished —like Italian despots of the Renaissance—for the splendour and the culture of their courts, and they rivalled one another in the extent and richness of their libraries; but, if we are to believe Strabo, the library at Pergamon was not begun until the reign of Eumenes II. (B.C. 197—159), or 126 years after that at Alexandria[1].

The libraries at Alexandria (for there were two)—though far more celebrated and more extensive than the library at Pergamon—need not, from my point of view, detain us for more than a moment, for we are told very little about their position, and nothing about their arrangement. The site of the earliest, the foundation of which is ascribed to Ptolemy the Second (B.C. 285—247), must undoubtedly be sought for within the circuit of the royal palace, which was in the fashionable quarter of the city called Bruchcion. This palace was a vast enceinte, not a separate building, and, as Strabo, who visited Alexandria 24 B.C., says,

Within the precincts of the palace is the Museum. It has a colonnade, a lecture-room, and a vast establishment where the men of letters who share the use of the Museum take their meals together. This College has a common revenue; and is managed by a priest who is over the Museum, an officer formerly appointed by the kings of Egypt, but, at the present time, by the Emperor[2].

---

[1] Book XIII., Chap. 4, § 2.

[2] Book XVII., Chap. 1, § 8. τῶν δὲ βασιλείων μέρος ἐστὶ καὶ τὸ Μουσεῖον, ἔχον περίπατον καὶ ἐξέδραν καὶ οἶκον μέγαν, ἐν ᾧ τὸ συσσίτιον τῶν μετεχόντων τοῦ Μουσείου

That the older of the two libraries must have been in some way connected with these buildings seems to me certain from two considerations. First, a ruler who took so keen an interest in books as Ptolemy, would assuredly have kept his treasures under his own eye; and, secondly, he would hardly have placed them at a distance from the spot where the learned men of Alexandria held their meetings[1].

At some period subsequent to the foundation of Ptolemy's first library, a second, called the daughter of the first[2], was established in connexion with the Temple of Serapis, a magnificent structure in the quarter Rhacôtis, adorned so lavishly with colonnades, statuary, and other architectural enrichments, that the historian Ammianus Marcellinus declares that nothing in the world could equal it, except the Roman Capitol[3].

This brief notice of the libraries of Alexandria shews that the earlier of the two, besides being in a building dedicated to the Muses, was also connected in all probability with a palace, and the second with a temple. If we now turn to Pergamon, we shall find the library associated with the temple and τέμενος of Athena.

The founder selected for the site of his city a lofty and precipitous hill, about a thousand feet above the sea-level. The rocky plateau which forms the summit is divided into three gigantic steps or terraces. On the highest, which occupies the northern end of the hill, the royal palace is believed to have been built. On the next terrace, to the south, was the temple of Athena; and on the third, the altar of Zeus. External to those three groups of buildings, partly on the edge of the hill, partly on its sides, were the rest of the public buildings. The lower slopes were probably occupied in ancient times, as at present, by the houses of the citizens.

φιλολόγων ἀνδρῶν· ἐστὶ δὲ τῇ συνόδῳ ταύτῃ καὶ χρήματα κοινὰ καὶ ἱερεὺς ὁ ἐπὶ τῷ Μουσείῳ, τεταγμένος τότε μὲν ὑπὸ τῶν βασιλέων νῦν δ' ὑπὸ Καίσαρος.

[1] One of the anonymous lives of Apollonius Rhodius states that he presided over the Museum Libraries (τῶν βιβλιοθηκῶν τοῦ Μουσείου).

[2] Epiphanius, *De Pond. et Mens.*, Chap. 12. ἔτι δὲ ὕστερον καὶ ἑτέρα ἐγένετο βιβλιοθήκη ἐν τῷ Σεραπείῳ, μικροτέρα τῆς πρώτης, ἥτις θυγάτηρ ὠνομάσθη αὐτῆς.

[3] Ammianus Marcellinus, Book XXII., Chap. 16, § 12. Atriis columnariis amplissimis et spirantibus signorum figmentis ita est exornatum, ut post Capitolium quo se venerabilis Roma in æternum attollit, nihil orbis terrarum ambitiosius cernat. See also Aphthonius, *Progymn.* c. XII. ed. Walz, *Rhetores Græci*, i. 106.

These magnificent structures, which won for Pergamon the distinction of being "by far the noblest city in Asia minor[1]," were in the main due to Eumenes the Second, who, during his reign of nearly forty years (B.C. 197—159), was enabled, by the wise policy of supporting the Romans, to transform his petty state into a powerful monarchy. The construction of a library is especially referred to him by Strabo[2], and from the statement of Vitruvius that it was built for the delight of the world at large (*in communem delectationem*), we may infer that it was intended to be public[3]. That he was an energetic book-collector, under whose direction a large staff of scribes was perpetually at work, may be gathered from the well-known story that his bibliographical rival at Alexandria, exasperated by his activity and success, conceived the ingenious device of crippling his endeavours by forbidding the exportation of papyrus. Eumenes, however, says the chronicler, was equal to the occasion, and defeated the scheme by inventing parchment[4]. It is probable that Eumenes not only began but completed the library, for in less than a quarter of a century after his death (B.C. 133) the last of his descendants bequeathed the city and state of Pergamon to the Romans. It is improbable that they would do much to increase the library, though they evidently took care of it, for ninety years later, when Mark Antony is said to have given it to Cleopatra, the number of works in it amounted to two hundred thousand[5].

---

[1] Pliny, *Hist. Nat.*, Book v., Chap. 30. Longeque clarissimum Asiæ Pergamum.

[2] Strabo, Book XIII., Chap. 4, § 2. After recounting the successful policy of Eumenes II. towards the Romans, he proceeds: κατεσκεύασε δὲ οὗτος τὴν πόλιν, καὶ τὸ Νικηφόριον ἄλσει κατεφύτευσε, καὶ ἀναθήματα καὶ βιβλιοθήκας καὶ τὴν ἐπὶ τοσόνδε κατοικίαν τοῦ Περγάμου τὴν νῦν οὖσαν ἐκεῖνος προσεφιλοκάλησε.

[3] *De Architectura*, Book VII., Præfatio. The passage is quoted in the next note.

[4] Pliny, *Hist. Nat.*, Book XIII., Chap. 11. Mox æmulatione circa bibliothecas regum Ptolemæi et Eumenis, supprimente chartas Ptolemæo, idem Varro membranas Pergami tradidit repertas. Vitruvius, on the other hand (*ut supra*) makes Ptolemy found the library at Alexandria as a rival to that at Pergamon. Reges Attalici magnis philologiæ dulcedinibus inducti cum egregiam bibliothecam Pergami ad communem delectationem instituissent, tunc item Ptolemæus, infinito zelo cupiditatisque incitatus studio, non minoribus industriis ad eundem modum contenderat Alexandriæ comparare.

[5] Plutarch, *Antonius*, Chap. 57. To a list of accusations against Antony for his subservience to Cleopatra, is added the fact: χαρίσασθαι μὲν αὐτῇ τὰς ἐκ Περγάμου βιβλιοθήκας, ἐν αἷς εἴκοσι μυριάδες βιβλίων ἁπλῶν ἦσαν.

The site of the acropolis of Pergamon was thoroughly explored between 1878 and 1886 at the expense of the German
Government; and in the course of their researches the archeo-
logists employed discovered certain rooms which they believe to
have been originally appropriated to the library. I have had
the accompanying ground-plan (fig. 2) reduced from one of

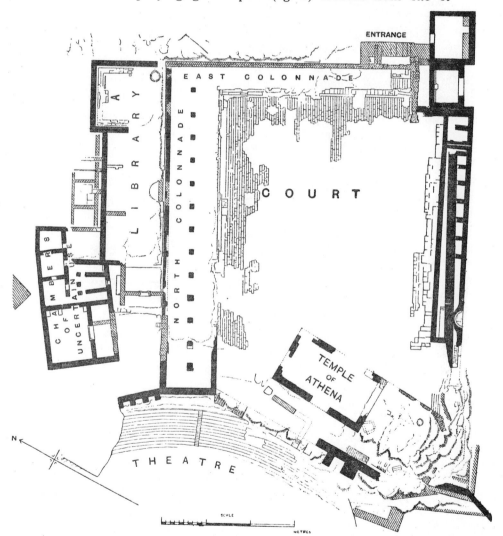

Fig. 2. Plan of the temple and precinct of Athena, Pergamon; with that of the Library
and adjacent buildings.

their plates, and have condensed my description of the locality from that given in their work[1]. I have also derived much valuable information from a paper published by Alexander Conze in 1884[2].

Of the temple of Athena only the foundations remain, but its extent and position can be readily ascertained. The enclosure, paved with slabs of marble, was entered at the south-east corner. It was open to the west and to the south, where the ground falls away precipitously, but on the east and north it was bounded by a cloister in two floors. The pillars of this cloister were Doric on the ground-floor, Ionic above. The height of those in the lower range, measured from base to top of capital, was about 16 feet, of those in the upper range about 9 feet.

This enclosure had a mean length of about 240 feet, with a mean breadth of 162 feet[3]. The north cloister was 37 feet broad, and was divided down the centre by a row of columns. The east cloister was of about half this width, and was undivided.

On the north side of the north cloister, the German explorers found four rooms, which they believe to have been assigned to library purposes. The platform of rock on which these chambers stood was nearly 20 feet above the level of the floor of the enclosure, and they could only be entered from the upper cloister. Of these rooms the easternmost is the largest, being 42 feet long, by 49 feet broad. Westward of it are three others, somewhat narrower, having a uniform width of 39 feet. The easternmost

---

[1] *Altertümer von Pergamon*, Fol., Berlin, 1885, Band II. Das Heiligtum der Athena Polias Nikephoros, von Richard Bohn. The ground-plan (fig. 2) is reduced from Plate III. in that volume.

[2] *Die Pergamenische Bibliothek.* Sitzungsberichte der Königl. Preuss. Akad. der Wiss. zu Berlin, 1884, II. 1259—1270.

[3] In my first lecture as Sandars Reader at Cambridge in the Lent Term, 1900, I pointed out that this enclosure was of about the same size as Nevile's Court at Trinity College, if to the central area there we add the width of one of the cloisters; and that the temple of Athena was of exactly the same width as the Hall, but about 15 feet shorter. Nevile's Court is 230 feet long from the inside of the pillars supporting the Library to the wall of the Hall; and it has a mean breadth of 137 feet. If the width of the cloister, 20 feet, be added to this, we get 157 feet in lieu of the 162 feet at Pergamon.

of these three rooms is also the smallest, being only 23 feet long; while the two next have a uniform length of about 33 feet.

At the south-west corner of this building, but on a lower level, and not accessible from it, other rooms were found, the use of which is uncertain.

We will now return to the eastern room. The foundations of a narrow platform or bench extended along the eastern, northern, and western sides, and in the centre of the northern side there was a mass of stone-work which had evidently formed the base for a statue (fig. 2, A). The discovery of a torso of a statue of Athena[1] in this very room indicated what statue had occupied this commanding position, and also what had probably been the use of the room.

This theory was confirmed by the discovery in the north wall of two rows of holes in the stone-work, one above the other, which had evidently been made for the reception of brackets, or battens, or other supports for shelves[2], or some piece of furniture. The lower of these two rows was carried along the east wall as well as along the north wall. Further, stones were found bearing the names of Herodotus, Alcæus, Timotheus of Miletus, and Homer, evidently the designations of portrait-busts or portrait-medallions ; and also, two titles of comedies.

Lastly, the very position of these rooms in connexion with the colonnade indicates their use. It will be observed that the colonnade on the north side of the area is twice as wide as that on the east side—a peculiarity which is sufficient of itself to prove that it must have been intended for some other purpose than as a mere covered way. But, if it be remembered that libraries in the ancient world were usually connected with colonnades (as was probably the case at the Serapeum at Alexandria, and was certainly the case at Rome, as I shall proceed to shew) a reason is found for this dignified construction, and a strong confirmation is afforded for the theory that the rooms beyond it once contained the famous library.

---

[1] Now in the Royal Museum, Berlin.

[2] Similar sockets have been discovered in the walls of the chambers connected with the Stoa of King Attalus at Athens. These chambers are thought to have been shops, and the sockets to have supported shelves on which wares were exposed for sale. Conze, *ut supra*, p. 1260; Adler. *Die Stoa des Königs Attalos zu Athen*, Berlin, 1874; Murray's *Handbook for Greece*, ed. 1884, 1. p. 255.

When the Romans had taken possession of Pergamon, those who had charge of the city would become familiar with the library; and it seems to me almost certain that, when the necessity for establishing a public library at Rome had been recognised, the splendid structure at Pergamon would be turned to as a model. But, if I mistake not, Roman architecture had received an influence from Pergamon long before this event occurred. What this was I will mention presently.

No public library was established in Rome until the reign of Augustus. Julius Cæsar had intended to build one on the largest possible scale, and had gone so far as to commission Varro to collect books for it[1]; but it was reserved for C. Asinius Pollio, general, lawyer, orator, poet, the friend of Virgil and Horace, to devote to this purpose the spoils he had obtained in his Illyrian campaign, B.C. 39. In the striking words of Pliny "he was the first to make men's talents public property (*ingenia hominum rem publicam fecit*)." The same writer tells us that he also introduced the fashion of decorating libraries with busts of departed authors, and that Varro was the only living writer whose portrait was admitted[2]. Pollio is further credited, by Suetonius, with having built an *atrium libertatis*[3], in which Isidore, a writer of the seventh century, probably quoting a lost work of Suetonius, places the library, with the additional information, that the collection contained Greek as well as Latin books[4].

The work of Pollio is recorded among the acts of generosity which Augustus suggested to others. But before long the emperor turned his own attention to libraries, and enriched his capital with two splendid structures which may be taken as types of Roman libraries,—the library of Apollo on the Palatine Hill, and that in the Campus Martius called after Octavia, sister to the emperor. I will take the latter first.

The *Porticus Octaviæ*, or, as it was sometimes called, the *Opera Octaviæ*, must have been one of the most magnificent structures in Rome (fig. 3). It stood in the Campus Martius, near the Theatre of Marcellus, between the Capitoline Hill and the Tiber. A double colonnade surrounded an area which

---

[1] Suetonius, *Cæsar*, Chap. 44.
[2] Pliny, *Nat. Hist.*, Book VII., Chap. 30; Book XXXV., Chap. 2.
[3] Suetonius, *Augustus*, Chap. 29.   [4] Isidore, *Origines*, Book VI., Chap. 5.

measured 443 feet by 377 feet, with *Jani*, or four-faced arch-
ways, at the four corners, and on the side next the Tiber a

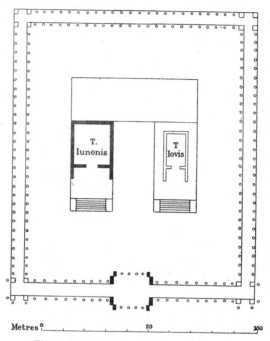

Fig. 3. Plan of the Porticus Octaviæ, Rome.
From *Formæ Urbis Romæ Antiquæ*, Berlin, 1896.

double hexastyle porch, which, with a few fragments of the
colonnade, still exists in a fairly good state of preservation[1].
Within this space were two temples, one of Jupiter, the other
of Juno, a *curia* or hall, in which the Senate frequently met,
a *schola* or "Conversation Hall[2]," and two libraries, the one of
Greek, the other of Latin books. The area and buildings
were crowded with masterpieces in bronze and marble.

This structure was originally built by Quintus Metellus,
about 146 B.C.[3] One of the temples was due to his own liberality,
the other had been erected by Domitius Lepidus, B.C. 179. Now

[1] Lanciani, *Ruins and Excavations of Ancient Rome*, ed. 1897, p. 471. Middleton,
Ancient Rome, 1892, II. 204, 205.

[2] Nibby, *Roma Antica*, p. 601. [Augusto] vi aggiunse un luogo per conversare
chiamato *Schola*.

[3] Vell. Pat., Book I., Chap. II. Hic est Metellus Macedonicus qui porticus quæ
fuere circumdatæ duabus ædibus sine inscriptione positis, quæ nunc Octaviæ porticibus
ambiuntur, fecerat.

twenty years before, Metellus had fought in a successful campaign against Perseus king of Macedonia, in which the Romans had been assisted by Eumenes II.; and in B.C. 148, as Prætor, he received Macedonia as his province. Is it not possible that on one or other of these occasions he may have visited Pergamon, and, when designing his buildings in Rome, have copied what he had seen there? Again, in B.C. 157, Crates of Mallus, a distinguished grammarian, was sent from Pergamon as ambassador to Rome, and, being laid up there by an accident, gave lectures on grammar, in the course of which he could hardly have failed to mention the new library[1].

The buildings of Metellus were altered, if not entirely rebuilt, by Augustus, B.C. 33, out of the proceeds of his victorious campaign against the Dalmatians; with the additional structures above enumerated. The *schola* is believed to have stood behind the temples, and the libraries behind the *schola*, with the *curia* between them[2]. Thus the colonnades, which Metellus had restricted to the two temples, came at last to serve the double purpose for which they were originally intended in connexion with a library as well as with a temple.

The temple and area of Apollo on the Palatine Hill, which Augustus began B.C. 36 and dedicated B.C. 28, exhibit an arrangement precisely similar to that of the Porticus Octaviæ. The size was nearly the same[3], and the structures included in the area were intended to serve the same purposes. The temple stood in the middle of a large open peristyle, connected with which were two libraries, one for Greek, the other for Latin books; and between them, used perhaps as a reading-room or vestibule, was a hall in which Augustus occasionally convened the Senate. It contained a colossal statue of Apollo, made of gilt bronze; and on its walls were portrait-reliefs of celebrated writers, in the form of medallions, in the same material[4].

---

[1] Suet. *De Illustr. Gramm.* c. 2.   [2] Middleton, *Ancient Rome*, 1892, II. 205.

[3] I have taken these dimensions from Middleton's Plan of the Palatine Hill (*ut supra*, p. 156), but until the site has been excavated they must be more or less conjectural.

[4] Middleton, *Ibid.*, I. 185—188. The evidence for the portraits rests on the following passage in the *Annals* of Tacitus ii. 37, where he is relating how Hortalus, grandson of the orator Hortensius, being reduced to poverty, came with his four children to the Senate: "igitur quatuor filiis ante limen curiæ adstantibus, loco sententiæ, cum in Palatio senatus haberetur, modo Hortensii inter oratores sitam imaginem, modo Augusti, intuens, ad hunc modum cœpit."

Of the other public libraries of Rome—of which there are said to have been in all twenty-six—I need mention only three as possessing some peculiarity to which I shall have to draw attention. Of these the first was established by Tiberius in his palace, at no great distance from the library of Apollo; the second and third by Vespasian and Trajan in their Fora, connected in the one with the temple of Peace, and in the other with the temple dedicated in honour of Trajan himself.

Of the first two of these libraries we have no information; but in the case of the third we are more fortunate. The Forum

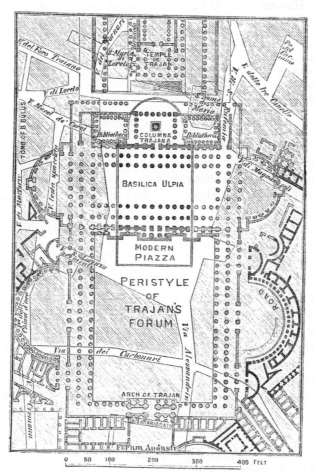

Fig. 4. Plan of the Forum of Trajan; after Nibby.

of Trajan (fig. 4) was excavated by order of Napoleon I., and the extent of its buildings, with their relation to one another, is therefore known with approximate accuracy. The Greek and Latin libraries stood to the right and left of the small court between the *Basilica Ulpia* and the *Templum Divi Trajani*, the centre of which was marked by the existing Column. They were entered from this court, each through a portico of five inter-columniations. The rooms, measured internally, were about 60 feet long, by 45 feet broad.

At this point I must mention, parenthetically, the library built by Hadrian at Athens. Pausanias records it in the following passage:

> Hadrian also built for the Athenians a temple of Hera and Panhellenian Zeus, and a sanctuary common to all the gods. But most splendid of all are one hundred columns; walls and colonnades alike are made of Phrygian marble. Here, too, is a building adorned with a gilded roof and alabaster and also with statues and paintings: books are stored in it. There is also a gymnasium named after Hadrian; it too has one hundred columns from the quarries of Libya[1].

A building called the Stoa of Hadrian, a ground-plan of which (fig. 5) I borrow from Miss Harrison's *Mythology and Monuments of Ancient Athens*, has been identified with part at least of that which Pausanias describes in the above passage. A lofty wall, built of large square blocks of Pentelic marble, faced on the west side by a row of Corinthian columns, enclosed a quadrangular court, measuring 328 feet from east to west, by 250 feet from north to south. This court, entered through a sort of propylæa on the west side (N), was surrounded by a cloister or colonnade 27 feet wide, and containing 100 columns. None of those columns are standing, but their number can be accurately calculated from the marks of the bases still to be seen on the eastern side of the quadrangle.

Within this area are the remains of a building of uncertain use, and at present only partially excavated.

On the east side a row of five chambers, of which that in the centre was the largest, opened off from the colon-nade[2].

---

[1] Pausanias, *Attica*, Book I., Chap. 18, § 9, ed. J. G. Frazer, Vol. I., p. 26.

[2] The above description is derived from Miss Harrison's book, *ut supra*, pp. 195—198; Pausanias, ed. J. G. Frazer, Vol. II., pp. 184, 185.

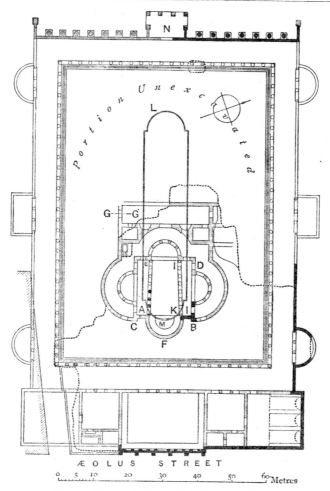

Fig. 5. Plan of the Stoa of Hadrian, at Athens.

AE, KI. Pier-arcade of the medieval church of the Panagia.

B. North-east angle of this church, of Roman work.

B, C, D, F. Portions of the Roman building which preceded the church.

L, M. Reservoirs.

N. Propylæa through which the court was entered.

If the ground plan of this structure (fig. 5) be compared with that of the precinct of Athena and library at Pergamon (fig. 2), a striking similarity between them will at once be

C. L.   2

recognised; and, whatever may have been the destination of the
building within the cloistered area, there can, I think, be little
doubt that the library was contained in the five rooms beyond
its limits to the east. They must have been entered from the
cloister, much as those at Pergamon were. It is possible that
Hadrian may himself have visited Pergamon, for Trajan had
built an imperial residence there; but, even if he did not do
this, he would accept the type from the great libraries built
at Rome by Augustus. It should be mentioned that S. Jerome
specially commemorates this library among Hadrian's works at
Athens, and says that it was of remarkable construction (*miri
operis*)[1].

From this brief digression I return to the public libraries of
Rome. In the first place those built by Augustus had a regular
organisation. There appears to have been a general director
called *Procurator Bibliothecarum Augusti*[2]; and subordinate
officers for each division: that is to say, one for the Greek
books, one for the Latin books. These facts are derived from
inscriptions found in *Columbaria*. Secondly, it may be concluded
that they were used not merely for reading and reference, but as
meeting-places for literary men.

The Palatine libraries evidently contained a large collection
of old and new books; and I think it is quite certain that new
books, as soon as published, were placed there, unless there was
some special reason to the contrary. Otherwise there would be
no point in the lines in which Ovid makes his book—sent
from Pontus after his banishment—deplore its exclusion. The
book is supposed to climb from the Forum to the temple of
Apollo:

> Signa peregrinis ubi sunt alterna columnis
>   Belides et stricto barbarus ense pater
> Quæque viri docto veteres cœpere novique
>   Pectore lecturis inspicienda patent.
> Quærebam fratres exceptis scilicet illis
>   Quos suus optaret non genuisse parens;
> Quærentem frustra custos e sedibus illis
>   Præpositus sancto iussit abire loco[3].

[1] Eusebius, *Chronicon,* ed. Schöne, Vol. II., p. 167.
[2] Middleton, *Ancient Rome,* I. 186.
[3] *Tristia,* III. 59.

Where, set between each pair of columns from some foreign quarry, are statues of the Danaids, and their barbarous father with drawn sword ; and where whatever the minds of men of old or men of to-day have imagined, is laid open for a reader's use. I sought my brethren, save those of course whom their father would fain have never begotten ; and, while I was seeking for them in vain, he who was set over the room bade me leave that holy ground.

The second couplet can only mean that old books and new books were alike to be found there. The general nature of the collection, and its extent, may be further gathered from the advice which Horace gives to his friend Celsus :

> Quid mihi Celsus agit? monitus multumque monendus
> Privatas ut quærat opes, et tangere vitet
> Scripta Palatinus quæcunque recepit Apollo[1].

What is my friend Celsus about? he who has been reminded, and must still be reminded again and again, that he should draw upon his own resources, and be careful to avoid the multifarious writings which Palatine Apollo has taken under his charge.

A man might say now-a-days, " Trust to your own wits, and don't go so often to the library of the British Museum."

Aulus Gellius, who lived A.D. 117—180, speaks of "sitting with a party of friends in the library of the palace of Tiberius, when a book happened to be taken down with the title M. Catonis Nepotis," and they began asking one another who this M. Cato Nepos might be[2]. This library contained also public records[3].

The same writer tells a story of a grammatical difficulty which was to be settled by reference to a book *in templo Pacis*, in the forum of Vespasian ; and again, when a particular book was wanted, "we hunted for it diligently," he says, "and, when we had found it in the temple of Peace, we read it[4]."

The library in the forum of Trajan, often called *Bibliotheca Ulpia*, was apparently the Public Record Office of Rome. Aulus Gellius mentions that some decrees of former prætors had fallen in his way there when he was looking for something else, and that he had been allowed to read them[5]; and a statement of Vopiscus is still more conclusive as to the nature of its contents. It tells us, moreover, something about the arrangement. In

---

[1] *Epist.*, I. 3. 17.   [2] *Noctes Atticæ*, v. 21. 9.
[3] Vopiscus, *Hist. Aug. Script.*, II. 637.
[4] Aulus Gellius, *ut supra*, XVI. 8. 2.   [5] *Ibid.*, XI. 17. 1.

his life of the Emperor Tacitus (Sept. A.D. 275—Apr. 276)
Vopiscus says:

> And lest anybody should think that I have given too hasty a
> credence to a Greek or Latin author, the Ulpian Library has in its
> sixth press (*armarium*) an ivory volume (*librum elephantinum*) in which
> the following decree of the Senate, signed by Tacitus with his own
> hand, is recorded, etc.[1]

Again, in his life of the Emperor Aurelian, the same writer
records how his friend Junius Tiberianus, prefect of the city, had
urged him to undertake the task, and had assured him that:
"even the linen-books (*libri lintei*) shall be brought out of the
Ulpian library for your use[2]."

Books could occasionally be borrowed from a public library,
but whether from one of those in the city of Rome, I cannot say.
The scene of the story which proves this is laid by Aulus Gellius
at Tibur (Tivoli), where the library was in the temple of Hercules
—another instance of the care of a library being entrusted to a
temple. Aulus Gellius and some friends of his were assembled
in a rich man's villa there at the hottest season of the year.
They were drinking melted snow, a proceeding against which
one of the party, a peripatetic philosopher, vehemently pro-
tested, urging against the practice the authority of numerous
physicians and of Aristotle himself. But none the less the
party went on drinking snow-water. Whereupon "he fetched
a treatise by Aristotle out of the library of Tibur, which was
then very conveniently accommodated in the temple of Hercules, and brought it to us, saying—[3]." But I need not finish the
quotation, as it has no bearing on my special subject.

It is probable that numerous collections of books had been
got together by individuals in Rome, before it occurred to
Augustus and his friends to erect public libraries. One such
library, that belonging to the rich and luxurious Lucullus, has
been noticed as follows by Plutarch[4]:

---

[1] Flavii Vopisci *Tacitus*, c. 8.   [2] Id., *Aurelianus*, c. 1.

[3] *Noctes Atticæ*, XIX. 5.

[4] Plutarch, *Lucullus*, Chap. XLII. Σπουδῆς δ' ἄξια καὶ λόγου τὰ περὶ τὴν τῶν βιβλίων
κατασκευήν. καὶ γὰρ πολλά, καὶ γεγραμμένα καλῶς, συνῆγε, ἥ τε χρῆσις ἦν φιλοτιμοτέρα
τῆς κτήσεως, ἀνειμένων πᾶσι τῶν βιβλιοθηκῶν, καὶ τῶν περὶ αὐτὰς περιπάτων καὶ σχολα-
στηρίων ἀκωλύτως ὑποδεχομένων τοὺς Ἕλληνας, ὥσπερ εἰς Μουσῶν τι καταγώγιον ἐκεῖσε
φοιτῶντας καὶ συνδιημερεύοντας ἀλλήλοις, ἀπὸ τῶν ἄλλων χρειῶν ἀσμένως ἀποτρέχοντας.

His procedure in regard to books was interesting and remarkable. He collected fine copies in large numbers; and if he was splendid in their acquisition, he was more so in their use. His libraries were accessible to all, and the adjoining colonnades and reading-rooms were freely open to Greeks, who, gladly escaping from the routine of business, resorted thither for familiar converse, as to a shelter presided over by the Muses.

The Romans were not slow in following the example set by Lucullus; and a library presently became indispensable in every house, whether the owner cared for reading or not. This fashionable craze is denounced by Seneca (writing about A.D. 49) in a vehement outburst of indignation, which contains so many valuable facts about library arrangement, that I will give a free translation of it.

Outlay upon studies, best of all outlays, is reasonable so long only as it is kept within certain limits. What is the use of books and libraries innumerable, if scarce in a lifetime the master reads the titles? A student is burdened by a crowd of authors, not instructed; and it is far better to devote yourself to a few, than to lose your way among a multitude.

Forty thousand books were burnt at Alexandria. I leave others to praise this splendid monument of royal opulence, as for example Livy, who regards it as "a noble work of royal taste and royal thoughtfulness." It was not taste, it was not thoughtfulness, it was learned extravagance —nay not even learned, for they had bought their books for the sake of show, not for the sake of learning—just as with many who are ignorant even of the lowest branches of learning books are not instruments of study, but ornaments of dining-rooms. Procure then as many books as will suffice for use; but not a single one for show. You will reply: "Outlay on such objects is preferable to extravagance on plate or paintings." Excess in all directions is bad. Why should you excuse a man who wishes to possess book-presses inlaid with *arbor-vitæ* wood or ivory; who gathers together masses of authors either unknown or discredited; who yawns among his thousands of books; and who derives his chief delight from their edges and their tickets?

You will find then in the libraries of the most arrant idlers all that orators or historians have written--book-cases built up as high as the ceiling. Nowadays a library takes rank with a bathroom as a necessary ornament of a house. I could forgive such ideas, if they were due to extravagant desire for learning. As it is, these productions of men whose genius we revere, paid for at a high price, with their portraits ranged in line above them, are got together to adorn and beautify a wall[1].

---

[1] *De Tranquillitate Animi*, Chap. IX. Studiorum quoque quæ liberalissima impensa est, tamdiu rationem habet quamdiu modum. Quo innumerabiles libros et

A library was discovered in Rome by Signor Lanciani in 1883 while excavating a house of the 4th century on the Esquiline in the modern Via dello Statuto. I will narrate the discovery in his own words.

I was struck, one afternoon, with the appearance of a rather spacious hall [it was about 23 feet long by 15 feet broad], the walls of which were plain and unornamented up to a certain height, but beautifully decorated above in stucco-work. The decoration consisted of fluted pilasters, five feet apart from centre to centre, enclosing a plain square surface, in the middle of which there were medallions, also in stucco-work, two feet in diameter. As always happens in these cases, the frame was the only well-preserved portion of the medallions. Of the images surrounded by the frames, of the medallions themselves, absolutely nothing was left *in situ*, except a few fragments piled up at the foot of the wall, which, however, could be identified as having been representations of human faces. My hope that, at last, after fifteen years of excavations, I had succeeded in discovering a library, was confirmed beyond any doubt by a legend, written, or rather painted, in bright red colour on one of the frames. There was but one name POLONIVS THYAN..., but this name told more plainly the purpose of the apartment than if I had discovered there the actual book-shelves and their contents[1].

When I had the pleasure of meeting Signor Lanciani in Rome in April, 1898, he most kindly gave me his own sketch

bibliothecas quarum dominus vix tota vita indices perlegit? onerat discentem turba, non instruit, multoque satius est paucis te auctoribus tradere, quam errare per multos. Quadraginta milia librorum Alexandriæ arserunt: pulcherrimum regiæ opulentiæ monumentum alius laudaverit, sicut et Livius, qui *elegantiæ regum curæque egregium id opus* ait *fuisse*: non fuit elegantia illud aut cura, sed studiosa luxuria, immo ne studiosa quidem, quoniam non in studium sed in spectaculum comparaverant sicut plerisque ignaris etiam servilium literarum libri non studiorum instrumenta sed cœnationum ornamenta sunt. Paretur itaque librorum quantum satis sit, nihil in adparatum. "Honestius" inquis "hoc impensis quas in Corinthia pictasque tabulas effuderim." Vitiosum est ubique quod nimium est. Quid habes cur ignoscas homini armaria citro atque ebore captanti, corpora conquirenti aut ignotorum auctorum aut improbatorum et inter tot milia librorum oscitanti, cui voluminum suorum frontes maxime placent titulique? Apud desidiosissimos ergo videbis quicquid orationum historiarumque est, tecto tenus exstructa loculamenta. Iam enim inter balnearia et thermas bibliotheca quoque ut necessarium domus ornamentum expolitur. Ignoscerem plane, si studiorum nimia cupidine oriretur: nunc ista conquisita, cum imaginibus suis descripta, sacrorum opera ingeniorum in speciem et cultum parietum comparantur. With this passage may be compared Lucian's tract: Πρὸς ἀπαίδευτον καὶ πολλὰ βιβλία ὠνούμενον. My friend Mr F. Darwin informs me that the Latin citrus, or Greek κέδρος, is the coniferous tree called *Thuia articulata* = *Callitris quadrivalvis*. See Hehn, *Kulturpflanzen*, Berl. 1894. Engl. Trans. p. 431.

[1] Lanciani, *Ancient Rome*, 8vo. 1888, p. 193.

of the pilasters and medallion, taken at the moment of discovery.
I am therefore able to reproduce exactly (fig. 6) one compartment of the wall of the library above described. The height

Fig. 6. Elevation of a single compartment of the wall of the Library discovered
in Rome, 1883.

From notes and measurements made by Signor Lanciani and Prof. Middleton.

of the blank wall below the stucco-work, against which the
furniture containing the books stood, has been laid down as
about 3 feet 6 inches, on the authority of Professor Middleton[1].
The remains of the medallion are still to be seen in the Museo
del Orto Botanico, Rome. The person commemorated is obviously Apollonius Tyaneus, a Pythagorean philosopher and
wonderworker, said to have been born about four years before
the Christian era.

A similar room was discovered at Herculaneum in 1754.
A full account of the discovery was drawn up at once by
Signor Paderni, keeper of the Herculaneum Museum, and ad-
dressed to Thomas Hollis, Esq., by whom it was submitted to
the Royal Society. I will extract, from this and subsequent
letters, the passages that bear upon my subject.

[1] *Ancient Rome*, ed. 1892, II. 254.

Naples, 27 April, 1754.

...The place where they are digging, at present, is under *Il Bosco di Sant'Agostino*....All the buildings discover'd in this site are noble ;...in one there has been found an entire library, compos'd of volumes of the Egyptian Papyrus, of which there have been taken out about 250....[1]

To the same.

18 October, 1754.

...As yet we have only entered into one room, the floor of which is formed of mosaic work, not unelegant. It appears to have been a library, adorned with presses, inlaid with different sorts of wood, disposed in rows ; at the top of which were cornices, as in our own times.

I was buried in this spot more than twelve days, to carry off the volumes found there ; many of which were so perished, that it was impossible to remove them. Those which I took away amounted to the number of three hundred and thirty-seven, all of them at present uncapable of being opened. These are all written in Greek characters. While I was busy in this work I observed a large bundle, which, from the size, I imagined must contain more than a single volume. I tried with the utmost care to get it out, but could not, from the damp and weight of it. However I perceived that it consisted of about 18 volumes, each of which was in length a palm and three Neapolitan inches, being the largest hitherto discovered. They were wrapped about with the bark of a tree and covered at each end with a piece of wood. All these were written in Latin, as appears by a few words which broke off from them. I was in hopes to have got something out of them, but they are in a worse condition than the Greek[2]....

From Sir J. Gray, Bart.

29 October, 1754.

...They have lately met with more rolls of *Papyri* of different lengths and sizes, some with the *Umbilicus* remaining in them : the greater part are Greek in small capitals....The Epicurean Philosophy is the subject of another fragment.

A small bust of Epicurus, with his name in Greek characters, was found in the same room, and was possibly the ornament of that part of the library where the writings in favour of his principles were kept ; and it may also be supposed that some other heads of philosophers found in the same room were placed with the same taste and propriety[3].

 Between 1758 and 1763, the place was visited by Winckelmann, who wrote long letters in Italian, describing what he saw, to Consigliere Bianconi, Physician to the King of Saxony. One of these, dated 1762, gives the following account of the library :

---

[1] *Phil. Trans.*, Vol. XLVIII., Pt 2, p. 634.   [2] *Ibid.*, p. 821.
[3] *Ibid.*, p. 825.

Il luogo in cui per la prima volta caddero sott' occhio, fu una piccola stanza nella villa d' Ercolano di cui parlammo sopra, la cui lunghezza due uomini colle braccia distese potevano misurare. Tutto all' intorno del muro vi erano degli scaffali quali si vedono ordinariamente negli archivi ad altezza d' uomo, e nel mezzo della stanza v' era un altro scaffale simile o tavola per tenervi scritture, e tale da potervi girare intorno. Il legno di questa tavola era ridotto a carboni, e cadde, come è facile ad imaginarselo, tutta in pezzi quando si toccò. Alcuni di questi rotoli di papiri si trovarono involti insieme con carta più grossolana, di quella qualità che gli antichi chiamavano *emporetica*, e questi probabilmente formavano le parti ed i libri d' un' opera intiera[1]....

The place in which they [the rolls] were first seen was a small room in the villa at Herculaneum of which we spoke above, the length of which could be covered by two men with their arms extended. All round the wall there were book-cases such as are commonly seen in record-rooms, of a man's height, and in the middle of the room there was another similar book-case or table to hold writings, of such a size that one could go round it. The wood of this table was reduced to charcoal, and, as may easily be imagined, fell all to pieces when it was touched. Some of these papyrus rolls were found fastened together with paper of coarser texture, of that quality which the ancients called *emporetica*, and these probably formed the parts and books of an entire work.

The information which these observers have given us amounts to this: the room was about 12 feet long, with a floor of mosaic. Against the walls stood presses, of a man's height, inlaid with different sorts of wood, disposed in rows, with cornices at the top; and there was also a table, or press, in the centre of the room. Most of the rolls were separate, but a bundle of eighteen was found "wrapped about with the bark of a tree, and covered at each end with a piece of wood." A room so small as this could hardly have been intended for study. It must rather have been the place where the books were put away after they had been read elsewhere.

Before I quit this part of my subject, I should like to mention one other building, as its arrangements throw light on the question of fitting up libraries and record-offices. I allude to the structure built by Vespasian, A.D. 78, to contain the documents relating to his restoration of the city of Rome. It stood at the south-west corner of the Forum of Peace, and what now exists of it is known as the Church of SS. Cosma e Damiano.

[1] *Opere di G. G. Winckelmann*, Prato, 1831, VII. 197.

The general arrangement and relation to adjoining structures will be understood from the plan (fig. 7). The room was about

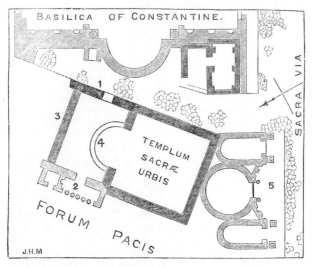

Fig. 7. Plan of the Record-House of Vespasian, with the adjoining structures.

125 feet long by 65 feet broad, with two entrances, one on the north-west, from the *Forum Pacis*, through a hexastyle portico (fig. 7. 2), the other on the north-east, through a square-headed doorway of travertine which still exists (*ibid.* 1) together with a considerable portion of a massive wall of Vespasian's time. After a restoration by Caracalla the building came to be called *Templum Sacræ Urbis*. It was first consecrated as a church by pope Felix IV. (526—530), but he did little more than connect it with the *Heroon Romuli* (*ibid.* 5), and build the apse (*ibid.* 4).

The whole building was mercilessly mutilated by pope Urban VIII. in 1632; but fortunately a drawing of the interior had been made by Pirro Ligorio in the second half of the sixteenth century, when the original treatment of the walls was practically intact.

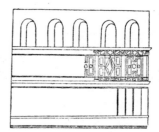

Fig. 8. Part of the internal wall of the Record-House of Vespasian.

Reduced from a sketch taken in the 16th century by Pirro Ligorio.

I give a reduced copy of a small portion of this drawing (fig. 8). As Lanciani says:

The walls were divided into three horizontal bands by finely cut cornices. The upper band was occupied by the windows; the lower was simply lined with marble slabs covered by the bookcases...which contained the...records...; the middle one was incrusted with tarsia-work of the rarest kinds of marble with panels representing panoplies, the wolf with the infant founders of Rome, and other allegorical scenes[1].

I explained at the beginning of this chapter that my subject is the care of books, not books themselves; but, at the point which we have now reached in regard to Roman libraries, it is necessary to make a few remarks about their contents. It must be remembered, in the first place, that those who fitted them up had to deal with rolls (*volumina*), probably of papyrus, but possibly of parchment; and that a book, as we understand the word, the Latin equivalent for which was *codex*, did not come into general use until long after the Christian era. Some points about these rolls require notice.

The length and the width of the roll depended on the taste or convenience of the writer[2]. The contents were written in columns, the lines of which ran parallel to the long dimension[3], and the reader, holding the roll in both hands, rolled up the part he had finished with his left hand, and unrolled the unread portion with his right. This way of dealing with the roll is well shewn in the accompanying illustration (fig. 9) reduced from a fresco at Pompeii[4]. In most examples the two halves of the roll are turned inwards, as for instance in the well-known statue of Demosthenes in the Vatican[5]. The end of the roll was fastened

---

[1] Lanciani, *Ruins of Ancient Rome*, pp. 213—217. He describes and figures Ligorio's elevation, from MS. Vat. 3439, in *Commissione Archeologica Comunale di Roma*, Ann. X. Ser. II., 1882, pp. 29—54. See also Middleton, *Ancient Rome*, 1892, II. 15.—19. The plan of Rome called the Capitoline Plan, because it is now preserved in the Museum of the Capitol, was fixed to the north-east wall (fig. 7. 3).

[2] The average length of a roll may be taken at 20—30 ft.; the width at 9—11 in. See *The Palæography of Greek Papyri*, by F. G. Kenyon, Oxf. 1899, Chap. II.

[3] The breadth of these columns from left to right was not great, and their length was considerably shorter than the width of the roll, as a margin was left at the top and bottom.

[4] *Antichità di Ercolano.* Fol. Napoli, 1779. Vol. v., Tavola 55, p. 243.

[5] In this statue the roll is a restoration, but a perfectly correct one. It is original, and slightly different, in the replica of the statue at Knowle Park, Sevenoaks, Kent. See a paper on this statue by J. E. Sandys, Litt.D., in *Mélanges Weil*, 1898, pp. 423—428.

to a stick (usually referred to as *umbilicus* or *umbilici*). It is
obvious that this word ought properly to denote the ends of the

Fig. 9. A reader with a roll: from a fresco at Pompeii.

stick only, but it was constantly applied to the whole stick, and
not to a part of it, as for instance in the following lines :

> ...deus nam me vetat
> Inceptos olim promissum carmen iambos
> Ad umbilicum adducere[1].

...for heaven forbids me to cover the scroll down to the stick
with the iambic lines I had begun—a song promised long ago to the
world.

These sticks were sometimes painted or gilt, and furnished
with projecting knobs (*cornua*) similarly decorated, intended to
serve both as an ornament, and as a contrivance to keep the
ends of the roll even, while it was being rolled up. The sides of
the long dimension of the roll (*frontes*) were carefully cut, so
as to be perfectly symmetrical, and afterwards smoothed with
pumice-stone and coloured. A ticket (*index* or *titulus*, in Greek

---

[1] Horace, *Epodes*, XIV. 5—8. Comp. Martial, *Epigrams*, IV. 89. Ohe ! libelle,
Iam pervenimus usque ad umbilicos.

σίλλυβος or σίττυβος), made of a piece of papyrus or parchment, was fastened to the edge of the roll in such a way that it hung out over one or other of the ends. As Ovid says:

> Cetera turba palam titulos ostendet apertos
> Et sua detecta nomina fronte geret[1].

The others will flaunt their titles openly, and carry their names on an uncovered edge.

The roll was kept closed by strings or straps (*lora*), usually of some bright colour[2]; and if it was specially precious, an envelope which the Greeks called a jacket (διφθέρα[3]), made of parchment or some other substance, was provided. Says Martial:

> Perfer Atestinæ nondum vulgata Sabinæ
> Carmina, purpurea sed modo culta toga[4].

Convey to Sabina at Ateste these verses. They have not yet been published, and have been but lately dressed in a purple garment.

Martial has combined in a single epigram most of the ornaments with which rolls could be decorated. This I will quote next, premising that the oil of cedar, or *arbor-vitæ*, mentioned in the second line not only imparted an agreeable yellow colour, but was held to be an antiseptic[5].

> Faustini fugis in sinum? sapisti.
> Cedro nunc licet ambules perunctus
> Et frontis gemino decens honore
> Pictis luxurieris umbilicis,
> Et te purpura delicata velet,
> Et cocco rubeat superbus index[6].

His book had selected the bibliomaniac Faustinus as a patron. Now, says the poet, you shall be anointed with oil of

---

[1] *Tristia*, I. i. 109.

[2] Catullus (xxii. 7) says of a roll which had been got up with special smartness:
> Novi umbilici, lora rubra, membrana
> Directa plumbo, et pumice omnia æquata.

[3] Lucian, *Adv. Indoct.*, Chap. 16.   [4] *Epigrams*, X. 93.

[5] My friend M. R. James, Litt.D., of King's College, has kindly given me the following note: In the apocryphal Assumption of Moses Joshua is told to 'cedar' Moses' words (=rolls), and to lay them up in Jerusalem: "quos ordinabis et chedriabis et repones in vasis fictilibus in loco quem fecit [Deus] ab initio creaturæ orbis terrarum." Assump. Mos., ed. Charles, I. 17. See also Ducange, s.v. Cedria. Vitruvius (II. ix. 13) says: "ex cedro oleum quod cedreum dicitur nascitur, quo reliquæ res cum sint unctæ, uti etiam libri, a tineis et carie non læduntur." See above, p. 22.   [6] *Epigrams*, III. ii. 6.

cedar; you shall revel in the decoration of both your sets of edges; your sticks shall be painted; your covering shall be purple, and your ticket scarlet.

When a number of rolls had to be carried from one place to another, they were put into a box (*scrinium* or *capsa*). This receptacle was cylindrical in shape, not unlike a modern hat-box[1]. It was carried by a flexible handle, attached to a ring on each side; and the lid was held down by what looks very like a modern lock. The eighteen rolls, found in a bundle at Herculaneum, had doubtless been kept in a similar receptacle.

My illustration (fig. 10) is from a fresco at Herculaneum. It will be noticed that each roll is furnished with a ticket (*titulus*). At the feet of the statue of Demosthenes already referred to, and of that of Sophocles, are *capsæ*, both of which show the flexible handles.

Fig. 10. Book-box or capsa.

I will next collect the information available respecting the fittings used in Roman libraries. I admit that it is scattered and imperfect; but legitimate deductions may, I think, be arrived at from it, which will give us tolerably certain ideas of the appearance of one of those collections.

The words used to designate such fittings are: *nidus*; *forulus*, or more usually *foruli*; *loculamenta*; *pluteus*; *pegmata*.

Nidus needs no explanation. It can only mean a pigeon-hole. Martial uses it of a bookseller, at whose shop his own poems may be bought.

> De primo dabit alterove *nido*
> Rasum pumice purpuraque cultum
> Denaris tibi quinque Martialem[2].

---

[1] Ovid (*Tristia*, 1. i. 105) addressing his book, says:
> Cum tamen in nostrum fueris penetrale receptus
> Contigerisque tuam, scrinia curva, domum.

[2] *Epigrams*, 1. 117.

Out of his first or second pigeon-hole, polished with pumice stone, and smart with a purple covering, for five denarii he will give you Martial.

In a subsequent epigram the word occurs with reference to a private library, to which the poet is sending a copy of his works.

> Ruris bibliotheca delicati,
> Vicinam videt unde lector urbem,
> Inter carmina sanctiora si quis
> Lascivæ fuerit locus Thaliæ,
> Hos *nido* licet inseras vel imo
> Septem quos tibi misimus libellos[1].

O library of that well-appointed villa whence a reader can see the City near at hand—if among more serious poems there be any room for the wanton Muse of Comedy, you may place these seven little books I send you even in your lowest pigeon-hole.

Forulus or *foruli* occurs in the following passages. Suetonius, after describing the building of the temple of the Palatine Apollo by Augustus, adds, "he placed the Sibylline books in two gilt receptacles (*forulis*) under the base of the statue of Palatine Apollo"[2]; and Juvenal, enumerating the gifts that a rich man is sure to receive if burnt out of house and home, says,

> Hic libros dabit, et *forulos*, mediamque Minervam[3].

The word is of uncertain derivation, but *forus*, of which it is clearly the diminutive, is used by Virgil for the cells of bees:

> Complebuntque *foros* et floribus horrea texent[4].

The above-quoted passage of Juvenal may therefore be rendered: "Another will give books, and cells to put them in, and a statue of Minerva for the middle of the room."

The word *loculamentum* is explained in a passage of Columella, in which he gives directions for the making of dovecotes:

Let small stakes be placed close together, with planks laid across them to carry cells (*loculamenta*) for the birds to build their nests in, or sets of pigeon-holes made of earthenware[5].

---

[1] *Epigrams*, VII. 17.

[2] Suet. *Aug.* 31. Libros Sibyllinos condidit duobus *forulis* auratis sub Palatini Apollinis basi.

[3] *Sat.* III. 219.   [4] *Georg.* IV. 250.

[5] *De Re Rustica*, VIII. 8. Paxillis adactis tabulæ superponantur; quæ vel loculamenta quibus nidificent aves, vel fictilia columbaria, recipiant.

In a second passage he uses the same word for a beehive[1]; Vegetius, a writer on veterinary surgery, uses it for the socket of a horse's tooth[2]; and Vitruvius, in a more general way, for a case to contain a small piece of machinery[3]. Generally, the word may be taken to signify a long narrow box, open at one end, and, like *nidus* and *forulus*, may be translated "pigeon-hole." Seneca, again, applies the word to books in the passage I have already translated, and in a singularly instructive manner. "You will find," he says, "in the libraries of the most arrant idlers all that orators or historians have written—bookcases (*loculamenta*) built up as high as the ceiling[4]."

Pegmata, for the word generally occurs in the plural, are, as the name implies, things fixed together, usually planks of wood framed into a platform, and used in theatres to carry pieces of scenery or performers up and down. As applied to books "shelves" are probably meant: an interpretation borne out by the *Digest*, in which it is stated that "window-frames and *pegmata* are included in the purchase of a house[5]." They were therefore what we should call "fixtures."

A *pluteus* was a machine used by infantry for protection in the field: and hence the word is applied to any fence, or boarding to form the limit or edge of anything, as a table or a bed. *Plutei* were not attached so closely to the walls as *pegmata*, for in the *Digest* they are classed with nets to keep out birds, mats, awnings, and the like, and are not to be

---

[1] *Ibid.*, IX. 12. 2. The writer, having described bees swarming, proceeds: protinus custos novum loculamentum in hoc præparatum perlinat intrinsecus prædictis herbis...tum manibus aut etiam trulla congregatas apes recondat, atque... diligenter compositum et illitum vas...patiatur in eodem loco esse dum advesperascat. Primo deinde crepusculo transferat et reponat in ordinem reliquarum alvorum.

[2] Vegetius, *Art. Vet.*, III. 32. Si iumento loculamenta dentium vel dentes doluerint.

[3] Vitruvius, *De Arch.*, ed. Schneider, X. 9. Insuper autem ad capsum redæ loculamentum firmiter figatur habens tympanum versatile in cultro collocatum, etc.

[4] Dr Sandys, in his edition of Aristotle's *Constitution of Athens*, 1893, p. 174, has shewn that in the office of the public clerk a similar contrivance was used, called ἐπιστύλιον: "a shelf supporting a series of pigeon-holes, and itself supported by wooden pedestals."

[5] Ulpian, *Digest*, 33. 7. 12. In emptionem domus et specularia et pegmata cedere solent, sive in ædificiis sint posita, sive ad tempus detracta.

regarded as part and parcel of a house[1]. Juvenal uses the word for a shelf in his second Satire, where he is denouncing pretenders to knowledge:

> Indocti primum, quamquam plena omnia gypso
> Chrysippi invenias, nam perfectissimus horum est   /
> Si quis Aristotelem similem vel Pittacon emit
> Et iubet archetypos pluteum servare Cleanthas[2].

In the first place they are dunces, though you find their houses full of plaster figures of Chrysippus; for a man of this sort is not fully equipped until he buys a likeness of Aristotle or Pittacus, and bids a shelf take care of original portraits of Cleanthes.

This investigation has shewn that three of the words applied to the preservation of books, namely, *nidus*, *forulus*, and *loculamentum*, may be rendered by the English "pigeon-hole"; and that *pegma* and *pluteus* mean contrivances of wood which may be rendered by the English "shelving." It is quite clear that *pegmata* could be run up with great rapidity, from a very graphic account in Cicero's letters of the rearrangement of his library. He begins by writing to his friend Atticus as follows:

I wish you would send me any two fellows out of your library, for Tyrannio to make use of as pasters, and assistants in other matters. Remind them to bring some vellum with them to make those titles (*indices*) which you Greeks, I believe, call σίλλυβοι. You are not to do this if it is inconvenient to you[3]....

In the next letter he says:

Your men have made my library gay with their carpentry-work and their titles (*constructione et sillybis*). I wish you would commend them[4].

When all is completed he writes:

Now that Tyrannio has arranged my books, a new spirit has been infused into my house. In this matter the help of your men Dionysius and Menophilus has been invaluable. Nothing could look neater than those shelves of yours (*illa tua pegmata*), since they smartened up my books with their titles[5].

---

[1] *Ibid.*, 29. 1. 17. Reticuli circa columnas, plutei circa parietes, item cilicia, vela, ædium non sunt.

[2] *Sat.* 11. 4. I do not think that these lines refer to a library. The whole house, not a single room in it, is full of plaster busts of philosophers.

[3] *Ep.* cv. (ed. Billerbeck); *Ad Att.* IV. 4, p. 2.

[4] *Ep.* cvi. (*ibid.*); *Ad Att.* IV. 5.

[5] *Ep.* cxi. (*ibid.*); *Ad Att.* IV. 8.

No other words than those I have been discussing are, so far as I know, applied by the best writers to the storage of books ; and, after a careful study of the passages in which they occur, I conclude that, so long as rolls only had to be accommodated, private libraries in Rome were fitted with rows of shelves standing against the walls (*plutei*), or fixed to them (*pegmata*). The space between these horizontal shelves was subdivided by vertical divisions into pigeon-holes (*nidi, foruli, loculamenta*), and it may be conjectured that the width of these pigeon-holes would vary in accordance with the number of rolls included in a single work. That such receptacles were the common furniture of a library is proved, I think, by such evidence as the epigram of Martial quoted above, in which he tells his friend that if he will accept his poems, he may "put them even in the lowest pigeon-hole (*nido vel imo*)," as we should say, "on the bottom shelf"; and by the language of Seneca when he sneers at the "pigeon-holes (*loculamenta*) carried up to the ceiling."

The height of the woodwork varied, of course, with individual taste. In the library on the Esquiline the height was only three feet six inches ; at Herculaneum about six feet.

I can find no hint of any doors, or curtains, in front of the pigeon-holes. That the ends of the rolls (*frontes*) were visible, is, I think, quite clear from what Cicero says of his own library after the construction of his shelves (*pegmata*) ; and the various devices for making rolls attractive seem to me to prove that they were intended to be seen.

A representation of rolls arranged on the system which I have attempted to describe, occurs on a piece of sculpture (fig. 11) found at Neumagen near Trèves in the seventeenth century, among the ruins of a fortified camp attributed to Constantine the Great[1]. Two divisions, full of rolls, are shewn,

---

[1] This cut is given in *Antiquitatum et Annalium Trevirensium libri* xxv. Auctoribus RR. PP. Soc. Jesu P. Christophoro Browero, et P. Jacobo Masenio. 2 v. fol. Leodii, 1670. It is headed : Schema voluminum in bibliothecam (sic) ordine olim digestorum Noviomagi in loco Castrorum Constantini M. hodiedum in lapide reperto excisum. See also C. G. Schwarz, *De Ornamentis Librorum*, 4to, Lips. 1756, pp. 86, 172, 231, and Tab. II., fig. 4. I learnt this reference from Sir E. M. Thompson's *Handbook of Greek and Latin Palæography*, ed. 2, 1894, p. 57, *note*. The Director of the Museum at Trèves informs me that all the antiquities discovered at Neumagen were destroyed in the seventeenth century.

from which a man, presumably the librarian, is selecting one. The ends of the rolls are furnished with tickets.

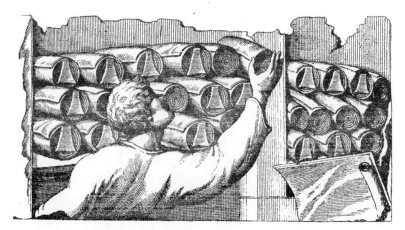

Fig. 11.   A Roman taking down a roll from its place in a library.

The system of pigeon-holes terminated, in all probability, in a cornice. The explorers of Herculaneum depose to the discovery of such an ornament there.

The wall-space above the book-cases was decorated with the likenesses of celebrated authors—either philosophers, if the owner of the library wished to bring into prominence his adhesion to one of the fashionable systems—or authors, dead and living, or personal friends. This obvious form of decoration was, in all probability, used at Pergamon[1]; Pollio, as we have seen, introduced it into Rome; and Pliny, who calls it a novelty (*novitium inventum*), deposes to its general adoption[2]. We are not told how these portraits were commonly treated—whether they were busts standing clear of the wall on the book-cases; or bracketed against the wall; or forming part of its decoration, in plaster-work or distemper. A suitable inscription accompanied them. Martial has preserved for us a charming specimen of one of these complimentary stanzas—for such they undoubtedly would be in the case of a contemporary—to be placed beneath his own portrait in a friend's library:

> Hoc tibi sub nostra breve carmen imagine vivat
> Quam non obscuris iungis, Avite, viris:

[1] See above, p. 11.   [2] *Ibid.*, p. 12.

Ille ego sum nulli nugarum laude secundus,
  Quem non miraris, sed puto, lector, amas.
Maiores maiora sonent: mihi parva locuto
  Sufficit in vestras sæpe redire manus[1].

Placed, with my betters, on your study-wall
Let these few lines, Avitus, me recall:
To foremost rank in trifles I was raised;
I think men loved me, though they never praised.
Let greater poets greater themes profess:
My modest lines seek but the hand's caress
That tells me, reader, of thy tenderness.

The beautiful alto-relievo in the Lateran Museum, Rome, representing an actor selecting a mask, contains a contrivance for reading a roll (fig. 12) which may have been usual in libraries and elsewhere, though I have not met with another instance of it. A vertical support attached to the table on which two masks and a MS. are lying, carries a desk with a rim along its lower edge and one of its sides. The roll is partially opened, the closed portion lying towards the left side of the desk, next the rim. The roll may be supposed to contain the actor's part[2].

Fig. 12. Desk to support a roll while it is being read.

It is much to be regretted that we have no definite information as to the way in which the great public libraries built by Augustus were fitted up; but I see no reason for supposing that their fittings differed from those of private libraries.

When books (*codices*), of a shape similar to that with which

---

[1] *Epigrams*, Lib. IX. *Introduction.*

[2] The whole relief is figured in Seyffert, *Dictionary of Classical Antiquities*, ed. Nettleship and Sandys, p. 649.

modern librarians have to deal, had to be accommodated as
well as rolls, it is manifest that rectangular spaces not more
than a few inches wide would be singularly inconvenient. They
were therefore discarded in favour of a press (*armarium*), a
piece of furniture which would hold rolls (*volumina*) as well
as books (*codices*), and was in fact, as I shall shew, used for both
purposes. The word (*armarium*) occurs commonly in Cicero,
and other writers of the best period, for a piece of furniture in
which valuables of all kinds, and household gear, were stowed
away; and Vitruvius[1] uses it for a book-case. A critic, he says,
" produced from certain presses an infinite number of rolls." In
later Latin writers—that is from the middle of the first century
A.D.—no other word, speaking generally, occurs.

The jurist Ulpian, who died A.D. 228, in a discussion as to
what is comprised under the term *liber*, decides in favour of
including all rolls (*volumina*) of whatever material, and then
considers the question whether *codices* come under the same
category or not—thereby shewing that in his day both forms of
books were in use. Again, when a library (*bibliotheca*) has been
bequeathed, it is questioned whether the bequest includes merely
the press or presses (*armarium vel armaria*), or the books as well[2].

The Ulpian Library, or rather Libraries, in Trajan's Forum,
built about 114 A.D.[3], were fitted up with presses, as we learn
from the passage in Vopiscus which I have already quoted;
and when the ruins of the section of that library which stood
next to the Quirinal Hill were excavated by the French, a
very interesting trace of one of these presses was discovered.
Nibby, the Roman antiquary, thus describes it:

Beyond the above-mentioned bases [of the columns in the portico]
some remains of the inside of the room became visible on the right.
They consisted of a piece of curtain-wall, admirably constructed of brick,
part of the side-wall, with a rectangular niche of large size in the form
of a press (*in foggia di armadio*). One ascended to this by three steps,
with a landing-place in front of them, on which it was possible to stand
with ease. On the sides of this niche there still exist traces of

---

[1] *De Architectura*, Lib. VII. Pref. [Aristophanes] e certis armariis infinita volumina eduxit.

[2] *Digesta Justiniani Augusti*, ed. Mommsen. 8vo. Berlin, 1870. Vol. II. p. 88.
Book XXXII. 52.

[3] This is the date of the *Columna cochlis*. Middleton's *Rome*, II. 24 *note*.

the hinges, on which the panels and the wickets, probably of bronze, rested[1].

It seems to me that we have here an early instance, perhaps the earliest, of those presses in the thickness of the wall which were so common afterwards in the monasteries and in private libraries also. A similar press, on a smaller scale, is described by the younger Pliny: "My bedroom," he says, "has a press let into the wall which does duty as a library, and holds books not merely to be read, but read over and over again[2]."

It must not, however, be supposed that cupboards were always, or even usually, sunk into the wall in Roman times. They were detached pieces of furniture, not unlike the wardrobes in which ladies hang their dresses at the present day, except that they were fitted with a certain number of horizontal shelves, and were used for various purposes according to the requirements of their owners. For instance, there is a sarcophagus in the Museo Nazionale at Rome, on which is represented a shoemaker at work. In front of him is a cupboard, exactly like those I am about to describe, on the top of which several pairs of shoes are set out.

I can, however, produce three representations of such presses being used by the Romans to contain books.

The first occurs on a marble sarcophagus (fig. 13), now in the garden of the Villa Balestra, Rome, where I had the good fortune to find it in 1898[3]; and Professor Petersen, of the German Archaeological School, was so kind as to have it photographed for me. He assigns the work to about 200 A.D.

In the central portion, 21 in. high, by $15\frac{1}{2}$ in. wide, is a seated figure, reading a roll. In front of him is a cupboard, the doors of which are open. It is fitted with two shelves, on the uppermost of which are eight rolls, the ends of which are turned to the spectator. On the next shelf is something which looks like a dish or shallow cup. The lower part of the press is solid. Perhaps a second cupboard is intended. Above, it is finished

---

[1] Nibby, *Roma Antica*, 8vo. Roma, 1839, p. 188.

[2] *Epist.* II. 17. 8. Parieti eius [cubiculi mei] in bibliothecæ speciem armarium insertum est quod non legendos libros sed lectitandos capit.

[3] I should not have known of the existence of this sarcophagus had it not been figured, accurately enough on the whole, in *Le Palais de Scaurus*, by Mazois, published at Paris in 1822. The sarcophagus had passed through the hands of several collectors since Mazois figured it, and I had a long and amusing search for it.

Fig. 13. A Roman reading a roll in front of a press *(armarium)*.

From a photograph of a sarcophagus in the garden of the Villa Balestra, Rome.

off with a cornice, on which rests a very puzzling object. There are a few faint lines on the marble, which Professor Petersen believes are intended to represent surgical instruments, and so to indicate the profession of the seated figure[1]. There is a Greek inscription on the sarcophagus, but it merely warns posterity not to disturb the bones of the deceased[2].

The second representation (fig. 14) is from the tomb of Galla Placidia, at Ra-venna. It occurs in a mosaic on the wall of the chapel in which she was buried, A.D. 449[3]; and was presumably ex-ecuted before that date. The press closely re-sembles the one on the Roman sarcophagus, but it is evidently intended to indicate a taller piece of furniture, and it ter-minates in a pediment. There are two shelves, on which lie the four Gospels, each as a sepa-rate *codex*, indicated by the name of the Evan-gelist above it. This press rests upon a stout frame, the legs of which are kept in position by a cross-piece nearly as thick as themselves.

Fig. 14. Press containing the four Gospels.
From a mosaic above the tomb of the Empress Galla Placidia at Ravenna.

[1] *Mittheilungen des K. D. Archaeologischen Instituts Rom*, 1900, Band XV. p. 171. Der Sarkophag eines Arztes.

[2] The inscription is printed in full in *Antike Bilderwerke in Rom...beschrieben von Friedrich Matz...und F. von Duhn*, 3 vols., 8vo. Leipzig, 1881, Vol. II. p. 346, No. 3127[a].

[3] Garrucci, *Arte Christiana*, Vol. IV. p. 39. It would appear from some curious drawings on glass figured by Garrucci, *ut supra* Pl. 490, that the Jews used presses of similar design in their synagogues to contain the rolls of the law.

The third representation of an *armarium* (fig. 15) occurs in the manuscript of the Vulgate now in the Laurentian Library at Florence, known as the *Codex Amiatinus*, from the Cistercian convent of Monte Amiata in Tuscany, where it was preserved for several centuries[1]. The thorough investigation to which this manuscript has lately been subjected shews that it was written in England, at Wearmouth or Jarrow, but possibly by an Italian scribe, before A.D. 716, in which year it was taken to Rome, as a present to the Pope. The first quaternion, however, on one of the leaves of which the above representation occurs, is probably older; and it may have belonged to a certain *Codex grandior* mentioned by Cassiodorus, and possibly written under his direction[2].

The picture (fig. 15), which appears as the frontispiece to this work, shews Ezra writing the law. On the margin of the vellum, in a hand which is considered to be later than that of the MS., are the words:

CODICIBUS SACRIS HOSTILI CLADE PERVSTIS
ESDRA DEO FERVENS HOC REPARAVIT OPUS.

Behind him is a press (*armarium*) with open doors. The lower portion, below these doors, is filled in with panels which are either inlaid or painted, so that the frame on which it is supported is not visible, as in the Ravenna example. The bottom of the press proper is used as a shelf, on which lie a volume and two objects, one of which probably represents a case for pens, while the other is certainly an inkhorn. Above this are four shelves, on each of which lie two volumes. These volumes have their titles written on their backs, but they are difficult to make out, and my artist has not cared to risk mistakes by attempting to reproduce them. The words, beginning at the left hand corner of the top-shelf, are:

[1] The original of this picture is 18 in. high by 9¾ in. broad, including the border. It could not be photographed, and therefore, through the kind offices of Miss G. Dixon, and Signor Biagi, Librarian of the Laurentian Library, the services of a thoroughly capable artist, Professor Attilio Formilli, were secured to make an exact copy in water colours. This he has done with singular taste and skill. My figure has been reduced from this copy. The press has also been figured in outline by Garrucci, *Arte Christiana*, Vol. III., Pl. 126.

[2] The romantic story of the *Codex Amiatinus* is fully narrated by Mr H. J. White in *Studia Biblica et Ecclesiastica*, 8vo. Oxf. 1890, II. pp. 273—308.

OCT.[1] LIB.	REG.
HIST. LIB.	PSALM. LIB.
SALOMON.	PROPH.
EVANG. IIII.	EPIST. XXI.
ACT. APOSTOL.	

The frame-work of the press above the doors is ornamented in the same style as the panels below, and the whole is surmounted by a low pyramid, on the side of which facing the spectator is a cross, beneath which are two peacocks drinking from a water-trough.

I regret that I could not place this remarkable drawing before my readers in the rich colouring of the original. The press is of a reddish brown; the books are bound in crimson. Ezra is clad in green, with a crimson robe. The background is gold. The border is blue, between an inner and outer band of silver. The outermost band of all is vermilion.

I formerly thought that this book-press might represent those in use in England at the beginning of the eighth century; but, if the above attribution to Cassiodorus be accurate, it must be accounted another Italian example. It bears a general similarity to the Ravenna book-press, as might be expected, when it is remembered that Cassiodorus held office under Theodoric and his successors, and resided at Ravenna till he was nearly seventy years old.

The foundation of Christianity did not alter what I may call the Roman conception of a library in any essential particular. The philosophers and authors of Greece and Rome may have occasionally found themselves in company with, or even supplanted by, the doctors of the Church; but in other respects, for the first seven centuries, at least, of our era, the learned furnished their libraries according to the old fashion, though with an ever increasing luxury of material. Boethius, whose *Consolation of Philosophy* was written A.D. 525, makes Philosophy speak of the "walls of a library adorned with ivory and glass[2]"; and Isidore, Bishop of Seville A.D. 600—636,

---

[1] The *Octateuch*, or, the five books of Moses, with the addition of Joshua, Judges, and Ruth.

[2] *Consol. Philosoph.*, Book I. Ch. 5. Nec bibliothecæ potius comptos ebore ac vitro parietes quam tuæ mentis sedem requiro.

records that "the best architects object to gilded ceilings in libraries, and to any other marble than *cipollino* for the floor, because the glitter of gold is hurtful to the eyes, while the green of *cipollino* is restful to them[1]."

A few examples of such libraries may be cited ; but, before doing so, I must mention the Record-Office (*Archivum*), erected by Pope Damasus (366—384). It was connected with the Basilica of S. Lawrence, which Damasus built in the Campus Martius, near the theatre of Pompey. On the front of the Basilica, over the main entrance, was an inscription, which ended with the three following lines :

ARCHIVIS FATEOR VOLUI NOVA CONDERE TECTA
ADDERE PRÆTEREA DEXTRA LÆVAQUE COLUMNAS
QUÆ DAMASI TENEANT PROPRIUM PER SÆCULA NOMEN.

I confess that I have wished to build a new abode for Archives ; and to add columns on the right and left to preserve the name of Damasus for ever.

These enigmatical verses contain all that we know, or are ever likely to know, respecting this building, which is called *chartarium ecclesiæ Romanæ* by S. Jerome[2], and unquestionably held the official documents of the Latin Church until they were removed to the Lateran in the seventh century. The whole building, or group of buildings, was destroyed in 1486 by Cardinal Raphael Riario, the dissolute nephew of Sixtus IV., to make room for his new palace, now called Palazzo della Cancelleria, and the church was rebuilt on a new site. The connexion with Pope Damasus is maintained by the name, S. Lorenzo in Damaso. No plan of the old buildings, or contemporary record of their arrangement, appears to exist. My only reason for drawing attention to a structure which has no real connexion with my subject is that the illustrious De Rossi considers that in the second line of the above quotation the word column signifies colonnades ; and that Damasus took as his model one of the great pagan libraries of Rome which, in

---

[1] *Origines*, Book VI. Ch. ii. Cum peritiores architecti neque aurea lacunaria ponenda in bibliothecis putent neque pavimenta alia quam a Carysteo marmore, quod auri fulgor hebetat et Carystei viriditas reficiat oculos.

[2] *Apol. adv. Rufinum*, ii. 20 : Opera, ed. Vallarsi, II. 549.

its turn, had been derived from the typical library at Pergamon[1]. According to this view he began by building, in the centre of the area selected, a basilica, or hall of basilican type, dedicated to S. Lawrence ; and then added, on the north and south sides, a colonnade or loggia from which the rooms occupied by the records would be readily accessible. This opinion is also held by Signor Lanciani, who follows De Rossi without hesitation. I am unwilling to accept a theory which seems to me to have no facts to support it ; and find it safer to believe that the line in question refers either to the aisles of the basilica, or to such a portico in front of it as may be seen at San Clemente and other early churches.

A letter to Eucherius, Bishop of Lyons in A.D. 441, from a correspondent named Rusticus, gives a charming picture of a library which he had visited in his young days, say about A.D. 400 :

I am reminded of what I read years ago, hastily, as a boy does, in the library of a man who was learned in secular literature. There were there portraits of Orators and also of Poets worked in mosaic, or in wax of different colours, or in plaster, and under each the master of the house had placed inscriptions noting their characteristics ; but, when he came to a poet of acknowledged merit, as for instance, Virgil, he began as follows :

> Virgilium vatem melius sua carmina laudant ;
> In freta dum fluvii current, dum montibus umbræ
> Lustrabunt convexa, polus dum sidera pascet,
> Semper honos nomenque tuum laudesque manebunt.

> Virgil's own lines most fitly Virgil praise :
> As long as rivers run into the deep,
> As long as shadows o'er the hillside sweep,
> As long as stars in heaven's fair pastures graze,
> So long shall live your honour, name, and praise[2].

---

[1] *De Origine Historia Indicibus scrinii et bibliothecæ Sedis Apostolicæ commentatio Ioannis Baptistæ de Rossi....* 4to. Romæ, 1886, Chapter v. A brief, but accurate, summary of his account will be found in Lanciani's *Ancient Rome*, 8vo. 1888, pp. 187—190. Father C. J. Ehrle has given me much help on this difficult question.

[2] *Sidonii Apollinaris Opera*, ed. Sirmondi. 4to. Paris, 1652. Notes, p. 33. The words of this letter, which I have translated very freely, are as follows:

Sed dum hæc tacitus mecum revolvo, occurrit mihi quod in Bibliotheca studiosi sæcularium litterarum puer quondam, ut se ætatis illius curiositas habet, prætereundo legissem. Nam cum supra memoratæ ædis ordinator ac dominus, inter expressas lapillis aut ceris discoloribus, formatasque effigies vel Oratorum vel etiam Poetarum

Agapetus, who was chosen Pope in 535, and lived for barely a year, had intended, in conjunction with Cassiodorus, to found a college for teachers of Christian doctrine. He selected for this purpose a house on the Cælian Hill, afterwards occupied by S. Gregory, and by him turned into a monastery. Agapetus had made some progress with the scheme, so far as the library attached to the house was concerned, for the author of the Einsiedlen MS., who visited Rome in the ninth century, saw the following inscription "in the library of S. Gregory"—i.e. in the library attached to the Church of San Gregorio Magno.

SANCTORVM VENERANDA COHORS SEDET ORDINE LONGO
    DIVINAE LEGIS MYSTICA DICTA DOCENS
HOS INTER RESIDENS AGAPETVS IVRE SACERDOS
    CODICIBVS PVLCHRVM CONDIDIT ARTE LOCVM
GRATIA PAR CVNCTIS SANCTVS LABOR OMNIBVS VNVS
    DISSONA VERBA QVIDEM SED TAMEN VNA FIDES

> Here sits in long array a reverend troop
> Teaching the mystic truths of law divine:
> 'Mid these by right takes Agapetus place
> Who built to guard his books this fair abode.
> All toil alike, all equal grace enjoy—
> Their words are different, but their faith the same.

These lines undoubtedly imply that there was on the walls a long series of portraits of the Fathers of the Church, including that of Agapetus himself, who had won his right to a place among them by building a sumptuous home for their works[1].

The design of Agapetus, interrupted by death, was carried forward by his friend Cassiodorus, at a place in South Italy called Vivarium, near his own native town Squillace. Shortly after his final retirement from court, A.D. 538, Cassiodorus established there a brotherhood, which, for a time at least, must have been a formidable rival to that of S. Benedict. A library held a prominent place in his conception of what

---

specialia singulorum autotypis epigrammata subdidisset ; ubi ad præiudicati eloquii venit poetam, hoc modo orsus est.

The last three lines of the inscription are from the *Æneid*, Book I. 607. I owe the most important part of the translation of Rusticus to Lanciani, *ut supra*, p. 196: that of Virgil is by Professor Conington.

[1] I have taken the text of the inscription, and my account of Agapetus and his work, from De Rossi, *ut supra*, Chap. VII. p. lv.

was needed for their common life. He says little about its size or composition, but much rhetoric is expended on the contrivances by which its usefulness and attractiveness were to be increased. A staff of bookbinders was to clothe the manuscripts in decorous attire; self-supplying lamps were to light nocturnal workers; sundials by day, and water-clocks by night, enabled them to regulate their hours. Here also was a *scriptorium*, and it appears probable that between the exertions of Cassiodorus and his friend Eugippius, South Italy was well supplied with manuscripts[1].

These attempts to snatch from oblivion libraries which, though probably according to our ideas insignificant, were centres of culture in the darkest of dark ages, will be illustrated by the fuller information that has come down to us respecting the library of Isidore, Bishop of Seville 600—636. The "verses composed by himself for his own presses," to quote the oldest manuscript containing them[2], have been preserved, with the names of the writers under whose portraits they were inscribed.

There were fourteen presses, arranged as follows :

I.	Origen.	VIII.	Prudentius.
II.	Hilary.	IX.	Avitus, Juvencus, Sedulius.
III.	Ambrose.	X.	Eusebius, Orosius.
IV.	Augustine.	XI.	Gregory.
V.	Jerome.	XII.	Leander.
VI.	Chrysostom.	XIII.	Theodosius, Paulus, Gaius.
VII.	Cyprian.	XIV.	Cosmas, Damian, Hippocrates, Galen.

These writers are probably those whom Isidore specially admired, or had some particular reason for commemorating. The first seven are obvious types of theologians, and the presses over which they presided were doubtless filled not merely with their own works, but with bibles, commentaries, and works on Divinity in general. Eusebius and Orosius are types of ecclesiastical historians; Theodosius, Paulus, and Gaius, of jurists; Cosmas, Damian, etc. of physicians. But the Christian poets Prudentius to Sedulius could hardly have needed two presses to contain their works; nor Gregory the Great the whole of one. Lastly, Leander, Isidore's elder brother, could

[1] Cassiodorus, *De Inst. Div. Litt.* Chap. XXX. pp. 1145, 46. Ed. Migne. De Rossi, *ut supra*.

[2] Versus qui scripti sunt in armaria sua ab ipso [Isidoro] compositi. *Cod. Vat. Pal.* 1877, a MS. which came from Lorch in Germany. De Rossi, *ut supra*, Chap. VII.

only owe his place in the series to fraternal affection. I conjecture that these portraits were simply commemorative; and
that the presses beneath them contained the books on subjects
not suggested by the rest of the portraits, as for example, secular
literature, in which Isidore was a proficient.

The sets of verses[1] begin with three elegiac couplets headed
Titulus Bibliothece, probably placed over the door of entrance.

> Sunt hic plura sacra, sunt hic mundalia plura:
>   Ex his si qua placent carmina, tolle, lege.
> Prata vides, plena spinis, et copia florum;
>   Si non vis spinas sumere, sume rosas.
> Hic geminæ radiant veneranda volumina legis;
>   Condita sunt pariter hic nova cum veteri.

> Here sacred books with worldly books combine;
> If poets please you, read them; they are thine.
> My meads are full of thorns, but flowers are there;
> If thorns displease, let roses be your share.
> Here both the Laws in tomes revered behold;
> Here what is new is stored, and what is old.

The authors selected are disposed of either in a single
couplet, or in several couplets, according to the writer's taste.
I will quote the lines on S. Augustine:

> Mentitur qui [te] totum legisse fatetur;
>   An quis cuncta tua lector habere potest?
> Namque voluminibus mille, Augustine, refulges,
>   Testantur libri, quod loquor ipse, tui.
> Quamvis multorum placeat prudentia libris,
>   Si Augustinus adest, sufficit ipse tibi.

> They lie who to have read thee through profess;
> Could any reader all thy works possess?
> A thousand scrolls thy ample gifts display;
> Thy own books prove, Augustine, what I say.
> Though other writers charm with varied lore,
> Who hath Augustine need have nothing more.

The series concludes with some lines "To an Intruder (*ad Inter-
ventorem*)," the last couplet of which is too good to be omitted:

> Non patitur quenquam coram se scriba loquentem;
>   Non est hic quod agas, garrule, perge foras.

> A writer and a talker can't agree:
> Hence, idle chatterer; 'tis no place for thee.

---

[1] *Isidori Opera Omnia*, 4to. Rome, 1803. Vol. VII. p. 179.

Fig. 15. Great Hall of the Vatican Library, looking west.

With these three examples I conclude the section of my work which deals with what may be called the pagan conception of a library in the fulness of its later development. Unfortunately, no enthusiast of those distant times has handed down to us a complete description of his library, and we are obliged to take a detail from one account, and a detail from another, and so piece the picture together for ourselves. What I may call "the pigeon-hole system," suitable for rolls only, was replaced by presses which could contain rolls if required, and certainly did (as shewn (fig. 13) on the sarcophagus of the Villa Balestra), but which were specially designed for *codices.* These presses were sometimes plain, sometimes richly ornamented, according to the taste or the means of the owner. With the same limitations the floor, the walls, and possibly the roof also were decorated. Further, it was evidently intended that the room selected for books should be used for no other purpose ; and, as the books were hidden from view in their presses, the library-note, if I may be allowed the expression, was struck by numerous inscriptions, and by portraits in various materials, representing either authors whose works were on the shelves, or men distinguished in other ways, or friends and relations of the owner of the house.

The Roman conception of a library was realised by Pope Sixtus V., in 1587[1], when the present Vatican Library was commenced from the design of the architect Fontana. I am not aware that there is any contemporary record to prove that either the Pope or his advisers contemplated this direct imitation ; but it is evident, from the most cursory inspection of the large room (fig. 16), that the main features of a Roman library are before us[2]; and perhaps, having regard to the tendency of the Renaissance, especially in Italy, it would be unreasonable to expect a different design in such a place, and at such a period.

This noble hall—probably the most splendid apartment ever assigned to library-purposes—spans the Cortile del Belvedere

---

[1] See Hen. Stevenson, *Topografia e Monumenti di Roma nelle Pitture a fresco di Sisto V. della Biblioteca Vaticana,* p. 7 ; in *Al Sommo Pontefice Leone XIII. Omaggio Giubilare della Biblioteca Vaticana,* Fol. Rome, 1881.

[2] Signor Lanciani (*Ancient Rome,* p. 195) was the first to suggest a comparison between the Vatican Library and those of ancient Rome.

from east to west, and is entered at each end from the galleries connecting the Belvedere with the Vatican palace. It is 184 feet long, and 57 feet wide, divided into two by six piers, on which rest simple quadripartite vaults. The north and south walls are each pierced with seven large windows. No books are visible. They are contained in plain wooden presses 7 feet high and 2 feet deep, set round the piers, and against the walls between the windows. The arrangement of these presses will be understood from the general view (fig. 16), and from the view of a single press open (fig. 17).

In the decoration, with which every portion of the walls and vaults is covered, Roman methods are reproduced, but with a difference. The great writers of antiquity are conspicuous by their absence; but the development of the human race is commemorated by the presence of those to whom the invention of letters is traditionally ascribed; the walls are covered with frescoes representing the foundation of the great libraries which instructed the world, and the assemblies of the Councils which established the Church; the vaults record the benefits conferred on Rome by Sixtus V., in a series of historical views, one above each window; and over these again are stately figures, each embodying some sacred abstraction—"Thrones, dominations, princedoms, virtues, powers"—with angels swinging censers, and graceful nymphs, and laughing satyrs—a strange combination of paganism and Christianity—amid wreaths of flowers, and arabesques twining round the groups and over every vacant space, partly framing, partly hiding, the heraldic devices which commemorate Sixtus and his family:—a web of lovely forms and brilliant colours, combined in an intricate and yet orderly confusion.

It may be questioned whether such a room as this was ever intended for study. The marble floor, the gorgeous decoration, the absence of all appliances for work in the shape of desks, tables, chairs, suggest a place for show rather than for use. The great libraries of the Augustan age, on the other hand, seem, so far as we can judge, to have been used as meeting-places and reading-rooms for learned and unlearned alike. In general arrangement and appearance, however, the Vatican Library must closely resemble its imperial predecessors.

Fig. 17. A single press in the Vatican Library, open.

From a photograph.

APPENDIX TO CHAPTER I.

DECORATION OF THE VATICAN LIBRARY.

THE system of decoration carried out in this Library, of which I have just given a summary description, is so interesting, and bears evidence of so much care and thought, that I subjoin a detailed account of it, which, by the kindness of Father Ehrle, prefect of the Library, I was enabled to draw up during my late visits to Rome. The diagrammatic ground-plan (fig. 18) which accompanies this description, if studied in conjunction with the general view (fig. 16), will make the relation of the subjects to each other perfectly clear. The visitor is supposed to enter the Library from the vestibule at the east end ; and the notation of the piers, windows, wall-frescoes, etc., begins from the same end. Further, the visitor is supposed to examine the east face of each pier first, and then to turn to the left.

I will begin with the figures on the central piers and half-piers. These figures are painted in fresco, of heroic size: and over their heads are the letters which they are supposed to have invented.

1. PILASTER AGAINST EAST WALL.

ADAM.

A tall stalwart figure dressed in short chiton. He holds an apple in his left hand, and a mattock in his right.

Adam divinitus edoctus primus scientiarum et litterarum inventor.

2. FIRST PIER.

(*a*) ABRAHAM.

Abraham Syras et Chaldaicas litteras invenit.

(*b*) THE SONS OF SETH.

Filii Seth columnis duabus rerum cœlestium disciplinam inscribunt.

C. L.   4

(*c*) ESDRAS.

Esdras novas Hebraeorum litteras invenit.

(*d*) MOSES.

Moyses antiquas Hebraicas litteras invenit.

On the cornice of the presses round this pier are the following inscriptions :

(*a*) Doctrina bona dabit gratiam. Prov. xiii. 15.
(*b*) Volo vos sapientes esse in bono. Rom. xvi. 19.
(*c*) Impius ignorat scientiam. Prov. xxix. 7.
(*d*) Cor sapientis quærit doctrinam. Prov. xv. 14.

3. SECOND PIER.

(*a*) MERCURY.

Mercurius Thovt Ægyptiis sacras litteras conscripsit.

(*b*) ISIS.

Isis regina Ægyptiarum litterarum inventrix.

(*c*) MENON.

Menon Phoroneo æqualis litteras in Ægypto invenit.

(*d*) HERCULES.

Hercules ægyptius Phrygias litteras invenit.

On the cornice of the presses :

(*a*) Recedere a malo intelligentia. Job xxviii. 28.
(*b*) Timere Deum ipsa est sapientia. Job xxviii. 22.
(*c*) Faciendi plures libros nullus est finis. Eccl. xii. 12.
(*d*) Dat scientiam intelligentibus disciplinam. Dan. xi. 12.

4. THIRD PIER.

(*a*) PHOENIX.

Phoenix litteras Phoenicibus tradidit.

(*b*) CECROPS.

Cecrops Diphyes primus Atheniensium rex Græcarum litterarum auctor.

(*c*) LINUS.

Linus Thebanus litterarum Græcarum inventor.

(*d*) CADMUS.

Cadmus Phœnicis frater litteras XVI in Græciam intulit.

On the cornice of the presses :

(*a*) In malevolam animam non introibit sapientia. Sap. i. 4.
(*b*) Habentes solatio sanctos libros. 1 Mach. xii. 9.
(*c*) Cor rectum inquirit scientiam. Prov. xxvii. 12.
(*d*) Sapientiam qui abiicit infelix est. Sap. iii. 14.

5. FOURTH PIER.

(*a*) PYTHAGORAS.
Pythagoras . Y . litteram ad humanæ vitæ exemplum invenit.

(*b*) PALAMEDES.
Palamedes bello Troiano Græcis litteris quattuor adiecit.

(*c*) SIMONIDES.
Simonides Melicus quattuor Græcarum litterarum inventor.

(*d*) EPICHARMUS.
Epicharmus Siculus duas Græcas addidit litteras.

On the cornice of the presses:

(*a*) Qui evitat discere incidet in mala. Prov. vii. 16.
(*b*) Non glorietur sapiens in sapientia sua. Ier. ix. 23.
(*c*) Si quis indiget sapientia postulet a Deo. Iac. i. 15.
(*d*) Melior est sapientia cunctis pretiosissimis. Prov. viii. 11.

6. FIFTH PIER.

(*a*) EVANDER.
Evander Carment . F . aborigines litteras docuit.

(*b*) NICOSTRATA.
Nicostrata Carmenta latinarum litterarum inventrix.

(*c*) DEMARATUS.
Demaratus Corinthius etruscarum litterarum auctor.

(*d*) CLAUDIUS.
Claudius imperator tres novas litteras adinvenit.

On the cornice of the presses:

(*a*) Non erudietur qui non est sapiens in bono. Eccl. xxi. 24.
(*b*) Viri intelligentes loquantur mihi. Iac. xxxiv. 34.
(*c*) Non peribit consilium a sapienti. Ier. xviii. 18.
(*d*) Sapientiam atque doctrinam stulti despiciunt. Prov. i. 17.

7. SIXTH PIER.

(*a*) CHRYSOSTOM.
S. Io. Chrysostomus litterarum Armenicarum auctor.

(*b*) VLPHILAS.
Vlphilas Episcopus Gothorum litteras invenit.

4—2

(c) CYRIL.

    S. Cyrillus aliarum Illyricarum litterarum auctor.

(d) JEROME.

    S. Hieronymus litterarum Illyricarum inventor.

On the cornice of the presses :

(a) Scientia inflat charitas vero ædificat. Cor. viii. 1.

(b) Sapere ad sobrietatem. Rom. xii. 3.

(c) Vir sapiens fortis et vir doctus robustus. Prov. xxiv. 5.

(d) Ubi non est scientia animæ non est bonum. Prov. xix. 2.

8. PILASTER AGAINST WEST WALL.

CHRIST.

Our Lord is seated. Over His Head A, Ω; in His Hand an open book :
Ego sum A et Ω; principium et finis. At His Feet : Iesus Christus
summus magister, cælestis doctrinæ auctor.

On Christ's right hand is a POPE, standing, with triple cross and tiara.

    Christi Domini vicarius.

On Christ's left hand is an EMPEROR, also standing, with crown, sword, blue mantle.

    Ecclesiæ defensor.

I will now pass to the decoration of the walls. On the south wall, between the windows, are representations of famous libraries ; on the north wall, of the eight general Councils of the Church. Each space is ornamented with a broad border, like a picture-frame. In the centre above is the general title of the subject or subjects below : e.g. *Bibliotheca Romanorum* ; and beneath each picture is an inscription describing the special subject. Above each window, on the vault, is a large picture, to commemorate the benefits conferred by Sixtus V. on Rome and on the world. I will describe the libraries first, beginning as before at the east end of the room.

I. SIXTUS V. AND THE ARCHITECT FONTANA.

(Right of Entrance.)

Sixtus V. Pont. M. Bibliothecæ Vaticanæ aedificationem prescribit.

The Pope is seated. Fontana, a pair of compasses in his right hand, is on one knee, exhibiting the plan of the intended library.

II. MOSES ENTRUSTS THE TABLES OF THE LAW TO THE LEVITES.

(Left of Entrance.)

Moyses librum legis Levitis in tabernaculo reponendum tradit.

Moses hands a large folio to a Levite, behind whom more Levites are standing. Soldiers, etc., stand behind Moses. Tents in background.

III. BIBLIOTHECA HEBRÆA.

(On first wall-space south side.)

Esdras sacerdos et scriba Bibliothecam sacram restituit.

Ezra, attired in a costume that is almost Roman, stands in the centre of the picture, his back half turned to the spectator. An official is pointing to a press full of books. Porters are bringing in others.

IV. BIBLIOTHECA BABYLONICA.

(Two pictures.)

(a) *The education of Daniel in Babylon.*

Daniel et socii linguam scientiamque Chaldæorum ediscunt.

Daniel and other young men are writing and reading at a table on the right of the picture. A group of elderly men in front of them to the left. Behind these is a lofty chair and desk, beneath which is a table at which a group of boys are reading and writing. In the background a set of book-shelves with a desk, quite modern in style.

(*b*)   *The search for the decree of Cyrus.*

Cyri decretum de templi restauratione Darii iussu perquiritur.

Darius, crowned, his back half turned to the spectator, is giving orders to several young men, who are taking books out of an *armarium* —evidently copied from one of the Vatican book-cupboards.

V.   BIBLIOTHECA ATHENIENSIS.

(Two pictures.)

(*a*)   *Pisistratus arranges a library at Athens.*

Pisistratus primus apud Græcos publicam bibliothecam instituit.

Pisistratus, in armour, over which is a blue mantle, is giving orders to an old man who kneels before him, holding an open book.   Behind the old man attendants are placing books on desks—others are reading. Behind Pisistratus is a group of officers, and behind them again a book-press without doors, and a row of open books on the top.

(*b*)   *Restoration of the library by Seleucus.*

Seleucus bibliothecam a Xerxe asportatam referendam curat.

Servants are bringing in books which are being hastily packed into cases.   In the background is seen the sea, with a ship ; and the door of the palace.   A picture full of life and movement.

VI.   BIBLIOTHECA ALEXANDRINA.

(Two pictures.)

(*a*)   *Ptolemy organises the library at Alexandria.*

Ptolemæus ingenti bibliotheca instructa Hebreorum libros concupiscit.

Ptolemy, a dignified figure in a royal habit, stands in the centre. He is addressing an elderly man who stands on his right.   Behind him are three porches, within which are seen desks and readers.   In the central porch are closed presses, with rows of folios on the top.   Below are desks, at which readers are seated, their backs turned to the presses.

(*b*)   *The Seventy Translators bring their work to Ptolemy.*

LXXII interpretes ab Eleazaro missi sacros libros Ptolemæo reddunt.

Ptolemy is seated on a throne to right of spectator with courtiers on his right and left.   The messengers kneel before him, and hand him volumes.

VII. BIBLIOTHECA ROMANORUM.

(a) *Tarquin receives the Sibylline Books.*

> Tarquinius Superbus libros Sibyllinos tres aliis a muliere incensis tantidem emit.

Tarquin, seated in the centre of the picture, receives three volumes from an aged and dignified woman. In front a lighted brazier in which the other books are burning.

(b) *Augustus opens the Palatine library.*

> Augustus Cæs. Palatina Bibliotheca magnifice ornata viros litteratos fovet.

Augustus, in armour, with imperial mantle, crown and sceptre, stands left of centre. An old man seated at his feet is writing from his dictation. Left of the Emperor are five desks ; with five closed books lying on the top of each. These desks are very probably intended to represent those of the Vatican Library as arranged by Sixtus IV. Two men, crowned with laurel, are standing behind the last desk, conversing. Behind them again is a book-case of three shelves between a pair of columns. Books are lying on their sides on these shelves. Beneath the shelves is a desk, with books open upon it, and others on their sides beneath it.

VIII. BIBLIOTHECA HIEROSOLIMITANA.

Alexander, Bishop and Martyr, collects a library at Jerusalem.

> S. Alexander Episc. et Mart. Decio Imp. in magna temporum acerbitate sacrorum scriptorum libros Hierosolymis congregat.

A picture full of movement, occupying the whole space between two windows. The saint is in the centre of the picture, seated. Young men are bringing in the books, and placing them on shelves.

IX. BIBLIOTHECA CÆSARIENSIS.

Pamphilus, Priest and Martyr, collects a library at Cæsarea.

> S. Pamphilus Presb. et Mart. admirandæ sanctitatis et doctrinæ Cæsareæ sacram bibliothecam conficit multos libros sua manu describit.

Pamphilus, in centre of picture, is giving orders to porters who are bringing in a basket of books. On his left a large table at which a scribe is writing. S. Jerome, seated in right corner of picture, is apparently dictating to the scribe. Behind them is a large book-case on the shelves of which books lie on their sides ; others are being laid on the top by a man standing on a ladder. In the left of the picture is a table covered with a green cloth, on which book-binders are at work. In front of this table a carpenter is preparing boards. In background, seen through a large window, is a view of Cæsarea.

X. BIBLIOTHECA APOSTOLORUM.

S. Peter orders the safe-keeping of books.

> S. Petrus sacrorum librorum thesaurum in Romana ecclesia perpetuo asservari jubet.

S. Peter is standing before an altar on which are books and a cross. In front doctors are writing at a low table.

[A small picture between window and west wall.]

XI. BIBLIOTHECA PONTIFICUM.

The successors of S. Peter carry on the library-tradition.

> Romani pontifices apostolicam bibliothecam magno studio amplificant atque illustrant.

A pope, his left hand resting on a book, is earnestly conversing with a cardinal, whose back is half turned to the spectator. Another pope, with three aged men, in background.

[A small picture on west wall.]

We will now return to the east end of the room, and take the representations of Councils, painted on the east and north walls, in chronological order.

I. II.   CONCILIUM NICAENUM I.

(On east wall.)

The first Council held at Nicæa, A.D. 325.

> S. Silvestro PP. Constantino Mag. imp. Christus dei Filius patri consubstantialis declaratur Arii impietas condemnatur.

The burning of the books of Arius.

> Ex decreto concilii Constantinus Imp. libros Arianorum comburi iubet.

III.   CONCILIUM CONSTANTINOPOLITANUM I.

The first Council held at Constantinople, A.D. 381.

> S. Damaso PP. et Theodosio sen. imp. Spiritus Sancti divinitas propugnatur nefaria Macedonii hæresis extinguitur.

IV. CONCILIUM EPHESINUM.

The Council held at Ephesus, A.D. 431.

> S. Cælestino PP. et Theodosio Jun. Imp. Nestorius Christum dividens damnatur, B. Maria Virgo dei genetrix prædicatur.

V. CONCILIUM CHALCEDONENSE.

The Council held at Chalcedon, A.D. 451.

> S. Leone magno PP. et Marciano Imp. infelix Eutyches vnam tantum in Christo post incarnationem naturam asserens confutatur.

VI. CONCILIUM CONSTANTINOPOLITANUM II.

The second Council held at Constantinople, A.D. 553.

> Vigilio Papa et Iustiniano Imp. contentiones de tribus capitibus sedantur Origenis errores refelluntur.

VII. CONCILIUM CONSTANTINOPOLITANUM III.

The third Council held at Constantinople, A.D. 680.

> S. Agathone Papa Constantino pogonato Imp. monothelitæ hæretici vnam tantum in Christo voluntatem docentes exploduntur.

VIII. CONCILIUM NICAENUM II.

The second Council held at Nicæa, A.D. 787.

> Hadriano papa Constantino Irenes F. imp. impii iconomachi reiiciuntur sacrarum imaginum veneratio confirmatur.

IX. X. CONCILIUM CONSTANTINOPOLITANUM IV.

The fourth Council held at Constantinople, A.D. 869.

> Hadriano papa et Basilio imp. S. Ignatius patriarcha Constant. in suam sedem pulso Photio restituitur.

The burning of the books of Photius.

> Ex decreto concilii Basilius Imp. chirographa Photii et conciliab. acta comburi iubet.

In conclusion I will enumerate the series of eighteen large pictures on the side-walls and in the lunettes at each end of the room, representing, with some few exceptions, the benefits conferred on Rome by Sixtus. The most important of these pictures are above the windows (fig. 16), of which there are seven on each side-wall. A Latin couplet above the picture records the subject, and allegorical figures of heroic size, one on each side, further indicate the idea which it is intended to convey.

The series begins at the east end of the room, over the door.

I. *Procession of Sixtus to his coronation.*

Hic tria Sixte tuo capiti diademata dantur
Sed quantum in cœlis te diadema manet.
ELECTIO SACRA.   MANIFESTATIO.

On the left of this, over the First Nicene Council, is

II. *Coronation of Sixtus, with façade of old S. Peter's.*

Ad templum antipodes Sixtum comitantur euntem
Jamque novus Pastor pascit ovile novum.
HONOR.   DIGNITAS.

With the following picture the series on the south wall begins, above the windows :

III. *An allegorical tableau.   A lion with a human face, and a thunder-bolt in his right paw, stands on a green hill.   A flock of sheep is feeding around.*

Alcides partem Italiæ prædone redemit
Sed totam Sixtus: dic mihi major uter.
JUSTITIA.   CASTIGATIO.

IV. *The obelisk in front of old S. Peter's.   The dome rising behind.*

Dum stabit motus nullis Obeliscus ab Euris
Sixte tuum stabit nomen honosque tuus.
RELIGIO.   MUNIFICENTIA.

V. *An allegorical tableau.   A tree loaded with fruits, up which a lion is trying to climb.   A flock of sheep beneath.*

Temporibus Sixti redeunt Saturnia regna
Et pleno cornu copia fundit opes.
CHARITAS.   LIBERALITAS.

VI. *A Columna Cochlis surmounted by a statue.*

Ut vinclis tenuit Petrum sic alta columna
Sustinet; hinc decus est dedecus unde fuit.
SUBLIMATIO. MUTATIO.

VII. *A crowd assembled in front of a church.*

Sixtus regnum iniens indicit publica vota
Ponderis o quanti vota fuisse vides.
SALUS GENERIS HUMANI. PIETAS RELIGIONIS.

VIII. *The Lateran Palace, with the Baptistery and Obelisk.*

Quintus restituit Laterana palatia Sixtus
Atque obelum medias transtulit ante foras.
SANATIO. PURGATIO.

IX. *A fountain erected by Sixtus.*

Fons felix celebri notus super æthera versu
Romulea passim jugis in urbe fuit.
MISERATIO. BENIGNITAS.

The next two pictures are above the arches leading from the west end of the library into the corridor:

X. *Panorama of Rome as altered by Sixtus.*

Dum rectas ad templa vias sanctissima pandit
Ipse sibi Sixtus pandit ad astra viam.
LÆTIFICATIO. NOBILITAS.

XI. *An allegorical representation of the Tiara, with adoring worshippers.*

Virgo intacta manet nec vivit adultera conjux
Castaque nunc Roma est quæ fuit ante salax.
CASTITAS. DEFENSIO.

With the following picture the series on the north wall begins:

XII. *Section of S. Peter's, with the dome.*

Virginis absistit mirari templa Dianæ
Qui fanum hoc intrat Virgo Maria tuum.
ÆQUIPARATIO. POTESTAS.

XIII. *The Obelisk in the Circus of Nero.*

Maximus est obelus circus quem maximus olim
Condidit et Sixtus maximus inde trahit.
REÆDIFICATIO. COGNITIO VERI DEI.

XIV.   *The Tiber, with the Ponte Sisto, and the Ospedale di Santo Spirito.*

Quæris cur tota non sit mendicus in Urbe:
Tecta parat Sixtus suppeditatque cibos.
CLEMENTIA.   OPERATIO BONA.

XV.   *A similar view.*

Jure Antoninum paulo vis Sixte subesse
Nam vere hic pius est impius ille pius.
ELECTIO SACRA.   VERA GLORIA.

XVI.   *A similar view, with the Obelisk.*

Transfers Sixte pium transferre an dignior alter
Transferri an vero dignior alter erat.
RECOGNITIO.   GRATITUDO.

XVII.   *The Obelisk, now in front of S. Peter's, before it was removed.*

Qui Regum tumulis obeliscus serviit olim
Ad cunas Christi tu pie Sixte locas.
OBLATIO.   DEVOTIO.

XVIII.   *A fleet at sea.*

Instruit hic Sixtus classes quibus æquora purget
Et Solymos victos sub sua jura trahat.
PROVIDENTIA.   SECURITAS.

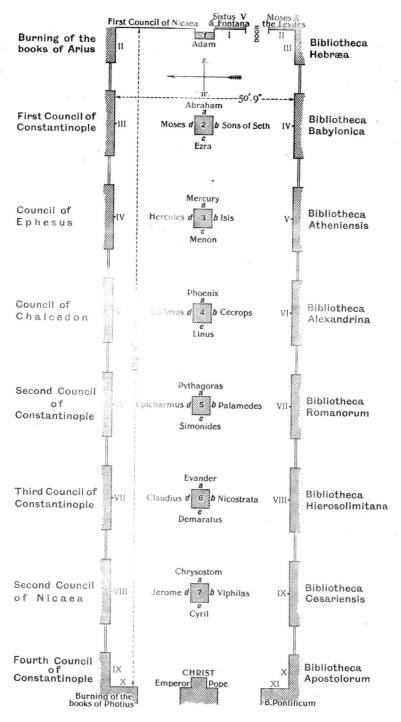

Fig. 18. Rough groundplan of the great hall of the Vatican Library, to illustrate the account of the decoration.

CHAPTER II.

THE evidence collected in the last chapter shews that what I have there called the Roman conception of a library was maintained, even by Christian ecclesiastics, during many centuries of our era. I have next to trace the beginning and the development of another class of libraries, directly connected with Christianity. We shall find that the books intended for the use of the new communities were stored in or near the places where they met for service, just as in the most ancient times the safe-keeping of similar treasures had been entrusted to temples.

It is easy to see how this came about. The necessary service-books would be placed in the hands of the ecclesiastic who had charge of the building in which the congregation assembled. To these volumes—which at first were doubtless regarded in the same light as vestments or sacred vessels— treatises intended for edification or instruction would be gradually added, and so the nucleus of a library would be formed.

The existence of such libraries does not rest on inference only. There are numerous allusions to them in the Fathers

and other writers; S. Jerome, for instance, advises a correspondent
to consult church-libraries, as though every church possessed one[1].
As however the allusions to them are general, and say nothing
about extent or arrangement, this part of my subject need not
detain us long[2].

The earliest collection of which I have discovered any record
is that got together at Jerusalem, by Bishop Alexander, who
died A.D. 250. Eusebius, when writing his Ecclesiastical History
some eighty years later, describes this library as a storehouse of
historical records, which he had himself used with advantage
in the composition of his work[3]. A still more important collection existed at Cæsarea in Palestine. S. Jerome says distinctly
that it was founded by Pamphilus, "a man who in zeal for the
acquisition of a library wished to take rank with Demetrius
Phalereus and Pisistratus[4]." As Pamphilus suffered martyrdom
in A.D. 309, this library must have been got together soon after
that at Jerusalem. It is described as not only extensive, but
remarkable for the importance of the manuscripts it contained.
Here was the supposed Hebrew original of S. Matthew's Gospel[5],
and most of the works of Origen, got together by the pious care
of Pamphilus, who had been his pupil and devoted admirer.
S. Jerome himself worked in this library, and collated there
the manuscripts which Origen had used when preparing his
Hexapla[6]. At Cirta the church and the library were evidently

---

[1] *Epist.* XLIX. § 3. Ad Pammachium. Revolve omnium quos supra memoravi
commentarios, et ecclesiarum bibliothecis fruere et magis concito gradu ad optata
coeptaque pervenies.

[2] I have to acknowledge my indebtedness to the article "Libraries," in the
Dictionary of Christian Antiquities, and to the references there given.

[3] *Hist. Eccl.* VI. 20. ἤκμαζον δὲ κατὰ τοῦτο πλείους λόγιοι καὶ ἐκκλησιαστικοὶ
ἄνδρες ὧν καὶ ἐπιστολὰς ἃς πρὸς ἀλλήλους διεχάραττον ἔτι νῦν σωζομένας εὑρεῖν εὔπορον,
αἳ καὶ εἰς ἡμᾶς ἐφυλάχθησαν ἐν τῇ κατὰ τὴν Αἰλίαν βιβλιοθήκῃ πρὸς τοῦ τηνικάδε τὴν
αὐτόθι διέποντος παροικίαν Ἀλεξάνδρου ἐπισκευασθείσῃ, ἀφ' ἧς καὶ αὐτοὶ τὰς ὕλας τῆς
μετὰ χεῖρας ὑποθέσεως ἐπὶ ταὐτὸ συναγάγειν δεδυνήμεθα.

[4] *Epist.* XXXIV., *Ad Marcellum.* De aliquot locis Psalmi cxxvi. Migne, Vol. XXII.
448.

[5] *Ibid. De Viris Illustribus*, Chap. 3. Migne, Vol. XXIII. 613. Porro ipsum
Hebraicum habetur usque hodie in Cæsariensi bibliotheca quam Pamphilus martyr
studiose confecit.

[6] *Comment. in Titum*, Chap. 3, v. 9. Unde et nobis curæ fuit omnes Veteris Legis
libros quos vir doctus Adamantius in Hexapla digesserat de Cæsariensi bibliotheca
descriptos ex ipsis authenticis emendare.

in the same building, from the way in which they are spoken of in the account of the persecution of A.D. 303—304. "The officers," we are told, "went into the building (*domus*) where the Christians were in the habit of meeting." There they took an inventory of the plate and vestments. "But," proceeds the narrative, "when they came to the library, the presses there were found empty[1]." Augustine, on his deathbed, A.D. 430, gave directions that "the library of the church [at Hippo], and all the manuscripts, should be carefully preserved by those who came after him[2]."

Further, there appears to be good reason for believing that when a church had a triple apse, the lateral apses were separated off by a curtain or a door, the one to contain the sacred vessels, the other the books. This view, which has been elaborated by De Rossi in explanation of three recesses in the thickness of the wall of the apse of a small private oratory discovered in Rome in 1876[3], is chiefly supported by the language of Paulinus, Bishop of Nola, who lived from about A.D. 353 to A.D. 431. He describes a basilica erected by himself at Nola in honour of S. Felix, martyr, as having "an apse divided into three (*apsidem trichoram*)[4]"; and in a subsequent passage, after stating that there are to be two recesses, one to the right, the other to the left of the apse, he adds, "these verses indicate the use of each[5]," and gives the following couplets, with their headings :

On the right of the Apse.

Hic locus est veneranda penus qua conditur, et qua
  Ponitur alma sacri pompa ministerii.

Here are the sacred vessels stored, and here
The peaceful trappings of our holy rites.

---

[1] Optatus : *De schismate Donatistarum.*   Fol. Paris, 1702.   App. p. 167.

[2] *Augustini Opera,* Paris, 1838, XI. p. 102.

[3] *Bullettino di Archeologia Christiana,* Serie terza, 1876, p. 48.

[4] *Epist.* XXXII. § 10 (ed. Migne, Vol. LXI. p. 335).   Basilica igitur illa...reliquiis apostolorum et martyrum intra apsidem trichoram sub altaria sacratis.

[5] *Ibid.* § 13.   Cum duabus dextra lævaque conchulis intra spatiosum sui ambitum apsis sinuata laxetur, una earum immolanti hostias jubilationis antistiti parat ; altera post sacerdotem capaci sinu receptat orantes... § 16.   In secretariis vero duobus quæ supra dixi circa apsidem esse hi versus indicant officia singulorum.

On the left of the same.

Si quem sancta tenet meditandi in lege voluntas
Hic poterit residens sacris intendere libris.

Here he whose thoughts are on the laws of God
May sit and ponder over holy books.

As De Rossi explains, the first of the two niches was intended to contain the vessels and furniture of the altar; the second was reserved for the safe-keeping of the sacred books. The word *trichora*, in Greek τρίχω, is used by later writers to designate a three-fold division of any object—as for instance, by Dioscorides, of the seed-pod of the acacia[1].

Whether this theory of the use of the apse be accurate or fanciful, the purely Christian libraries to which I have alluded were undoubtedly connected, more or less closely, with churches; and I submit that the libraries which in the Middle Ages were connected with cathedrals and collegiate churches are their lineal descendants.

I have next to consider the libraries formed by monastic communities, the origin of which may be traced to very early times. Among the Christians of the first three centuries there were enthusiasts who, discontented with the luxurious life they led in the populous cities along the coasts of Africa and Syria, fled into the Egyptian deserts, there to lead a life of rigorous self-denial and religious contemplation. These hermits were presently joined by other hermits, and small communities were gradually formed, with a regular organization that foreshadowed the Rules and Customs of the later monastic life. Those who governed these primitive monasteries soon realised the fact that without books their inmates would relapse into barbarism, and libraries were got together. The Rule of S. Pachomius (A.D. 292—345), whose monastery was at Tabennisi near Denderah in Upper Egypt, provides that the books of the House are to be kept in a cupboard (*fenestra*) in the thickness of the wall. Any brother who wanted a book might have one for a week, at the end of which he was bound to return it. No brother might

---

[1] Book I. Chap. 2. *De Acacia.* φέρει σπέρμα ἐν θυλάκοις συνεζευγμένοις τριχώροις ἢ τετραχώροις. Comp. also Book IV. Chap. 167. The use of the apse is discussed by Lenoir, *Architecture Monastique*, 4to. Paris, 1852, Vol. I. p. 111.

leave a book open when he went to church or to meals.   In the evening the officer called "the Second," that is, the second in command, was to take charge of the books, count them, and lock them up[1].

These provisions, insisted upon at a very early date, form a suitable introduction to the most important section of my subject—the care of books by the Monastic Orders.   With them book-preserving and book-producing were reduced to a system, and in their libraries—the public libraries of the Middle Ages—literature found a home, until the invention of printing handed over to the world at large the duties which had been so well discharged by special communities.   This investigation is full of difficulty ; and, though I hope to arrive at some definite conclusions respecting the position, size, dimensions, and fittings of monastic libraries, I must admit that my results depend to a certain extent on analogy and inference.   It should be remembered that in England the monasteries were swept away more than three centuries ago by a sudden catastrophe, and that those who destroyed them were far too busy with their own affairs to place on record the aspect or the plan of what they were wrecking.   In France again, though little more than a century has elapsed since her monasteries were over-whelmed by the Revolution, and though descriptions and views of many of her great religious houses have been preserved, and much has been done in the way of editing catalogues of their manuscripts, there is still a lamentable dearth of infor-mation on my particular subject.

I shall begin by quoting some passages from the Rules and Customs of the different Orders, which shew (1) that reading

---

[1] Holsten, *Codex Regularum*, fol. 1759, I. Regula S. Pachomii, No. c. p. 31. Nemo vadens ad collectam aut ad vescendum dimittat codicem non ligatum.   Codices qui in fenestra id est intrinsecus parietis reponuntur ad vesperum erunt sub manu secundi qui numerabit eos et ex more concludet.   The word fenestra is illustrated by a previous section of the Rule, No. LXXXII. p. 30.   Nullus habebit separatim mordacem pavulam ad evellendas spinas si forte calcaverit absque Præposito domus et secundo : pendeatque in fenestra in qua codices collocantur.   Ducange says that the word is used for the small cupboard in which the Sacrament was reserved.   Here it is evidently a recess in the wall closed by a door—like one of the later armaria.   On Pachomius and his foundation see *The Lausiac History of Palladius*, by Dom Cuthbert Butler, Camb. 1898, and esp. p. 234.

C. L.   5

was encouraged and enforced by S. Benedict himself, with whom the monastic life, as we conceive it, may be said to have originated ; (2) that subsequently, as Order after Order was founded, a steady development of feeling with regard to books, and an ever-increasing care for their safe-keeping, can be traced.

The Rule of S. Benedict was made public early in the sixth century ; and the later Orders were but offshoots of the Benedictine tree, either using his Rule or basing their own statutes upon it. It will therefore be desirable to begin this research by examining what S. Benedict said on the subject of study, and I will translate a few lines from the 48th chapter of his Rule, *Of daily manual labour.*

> Idleness is the enemy of the soul ; hence brethren ought, at certain seasons, to occupy themselves with manual labour, and again, at certain hours, with holy reading....
>
> Between Easter and the calends of October let them apply themselves to reading from the fourth hour till near the sixth hour.
>
> From the calends of October to the beginning of Lent let them apply themselves to reading until the second hour....   During Lent, let them apply themselves to reading from morning until the end of the third hour...and, in these days of Lent, let them receive a book apiece from the library, and read it straight through.   These books are to be given out at the beginning of Lent[1].

In this passage the *library*—by which a book-press is probably to be understood—is specially mentioned.   In other words, at that early date the formation of a collection of books was contemplated, large enough to supply the community with a volume apiece, without counting the service-books required for use in the church.

The Benedictine Order flourished and increased abundantly for more than four centuries, until, about A.D. 912, the order of Cluni was established.   It was so called from the celebrated abbey near Mâcon in Burgundy, which, though not the first house of the Order in point of date, became subsequently the first in extent, wealth, and reputation.   As a stricter observance of the Rule of S. Benedict was the main object which the founder of this Order had in view, the Benedictine directions

---

[1] *Benedicti Regula Monachorum*, ed. E. Woelfflin, Leipzig, Teubner, 1895.

respecting study are maintained and developed. The Customs prescribe the following regulations for books :

On the second day of Lent the only passage of the Rule to be read in Chapter is that concerning the observance of Lent.

Then shall be read aloud a note (*brevis*) of the books which a year before had been given out to brethren for their reading. When a brother's name is called, he rises, and returns the book that had been given to him ; and if it should happen that he has not read it through, he is to ask forgiveness for his want of diligence.

A carpet on which those books are to be laid out is to be put down in the Chapter-House ; and the titles of those which are distributed to brethren afresh are to be noted, for which purpose a tablet is to be made of somewhat larger size than usual[1].

In a subsequent chapter it is directed that the books are to be entrusted to the official "who is called Precentor and *Armarius*, because he usually has charge of the library, which is also called the *armarium* (press)[2]. This arrangement shews that up to this date all the books, whether service-books or not, were regarded as belonging to the church.

I come next to the decrees given to the English Benedictines by Archbishop Lanfranc in or about 1070. "We send you" he says "the Customs of our Order in writing, selected from the Customs of those houses (*cœnobia*) which are in our day of the highest authority in the monastic order[3]." The section relating to books is so interesting that I will translate it.

On the Monday after the first Sunday in Lent...before the brethren go in to Chapter, the librarian (*custos librorum*) ought to have all the

---

[1] *De secunda feria quadragesimæ.* In capitulo nequaquam alia Regulæ sententia legitur quam quæ est de quadragesimâ. Recitatur quoque *Brevis* librorum qui anno præterito sunt ad legendum fratribus erogati. Cum quilibet frater nominatur, surgit, et librum sibi datum reddit : et si eum forte non perlegerit, pro indiligentiâ veniam petit. Est autem unus tapes ibi constratus super quem illi libri ponuntur, de quibus iterum quanti dantur, dantur cum *Brevi* ; et ad hoc est una tabula aliquantulum major facta. *Antiquiores Consuetudines Cluniacensis Monasterii.* Lib. I. Cap. LII. D'Achery, *Spicilegium*, ed. 1723, I. 667.

[2] *Ibid.* Lib. III. Cap. X. *Ibid.* 690. *De Præcentore et Armario.* Præcentor et Armarius Armarii nomen obtinuit eo quod in ejus manu solet esse Bibliotheca quæ et in alio nomine Armarium appellatur.

[3] Reyner, *Apostolatus Benedictinorum in Anglia*, fol. 1626. App. Part III. p. 211. As Lanfranc styles himself in the prologue Bishop of Rouen, these decrees must have been issued between August 1067 and August 1070, when he was made Archbishop of Canterbury.

books brought together into the Chapter-House and laid out on a carpet, except those which had been given out for reading during the past year : these the brethren ought to bring with them as they come into Chapter, each carrying his book in his hand.   Of this they ought to have had notice given to them by the aforesaid librarian on the preceding day in Chapter.   Then let the passage in the Rule of S. Benedict about the observance of Lent be read, and a discourse be preached upon it.   Next let the librarian read a document (*breve*) setting forth the names of the brethren who have had books during the past year ; and let each brother, when he hears his own name pronounced, return the book which had been entrusted to him for reading ; and let him who is conscious of not having read the book through which he had received, fall down on his face, confess his fault, and pray for forgiveness.

Then let the aforesaid librarian hand to each brother another book for reading ; and when the books have been distributed in order, let the aforesaid librarian in the same Chapter put on record the names of the books, and of those who receive them[1].

It is, I think, certain that when Lanfranc was writing this passage the Cluniac Customs must have been before him[2].   It should be noted that the librarian is not defined otherwise than as "keeper of the books," but we learn from the Customs of Benedictine houses subsequent to Lanfranc's time that this duty was discharged by the Precentor, as in the Cluniac Customs. For instance, in the Customs of the Benedictine house at Abingdon, in Berkshire, drawn up near the end of the twelfth century, we read:

The precentor shall keep clean the presses belonging to the boys and the novices, and all others in which the books of the convent are stored, repair them when they are broken, provide coverings for the books in the library, and make good any damage done to them[3].

The precentor cannot sell, or give away, or pledge any books ; nor can he lend any except on deposit of a pledge, of equal or greater value than the book itself.   It is safer to fall back on a pledge, than to

---

[1] Reyner, *Apostolatus Benedictinorum in Anglia*, fol. 1626. App. Part III. p. 216.

[2] I am aware that the Customs printed by D'Achery are dated 1110 ; but it need not be assumed that they were written in that year. Similar directions are to be found among the Veteres Consuetudines of the Benedictine Abbey of S. Benoit sur Loire, or Fleury, founded A.D. 625. *Floriacensis vetus Bibliotheca*, 8vo. Lyons, 1605, p. 394.

[3] Cantor almaria puerorum juvenum et alia in quibus libri conventus reponentur innovabit fracta præparabit [reparabit ?] pannos librorum bibliothecæ reperiet fracturas librorum reficiet. *Chronicon monasterii de Abingdon* (De obedientariis Abbendoniæ). Rolls Series, II. 371.

proceed against an individual. Moreover he may not lend except to neighbouring churches, or to persons of conspicuous worth[1].

The Customs of the Abbey of Evesham in Worcestershire give the same directions in a slightly different form.

It is part of the precentor's duty to entrust to the younger monks the care of the presses, and to keep them in repair; whenever the convent is sitting in cloister, he is to go round the cloister as soon as the bell has sounded, and replace the books, in case any brother through carelessness should have forgotten to do so.

He is to take charge of all the books in the monastery, and have them in his keeping, provided his carefulness and knowledge be such that they may be entrusted to him. No one is to take a book out unless it be entered on his roll; nor is any book to be lent to any one without a proper and sufficient voucher, and this too is to be set down on his roll[2].

The Carthusians—the second offshoot of the Benedictine tree (1084)—also preserved the primitive tradition of study. They not only read themselves, but were actively employed in writing books for others. In the chapter of their statutes which deals with the furniture allowed to each "tenant of a cell (*incola celle*)"—(for in this community each brother lived apart, with his sitting-room, bed-room, and plot of garden-ground)—all the articles needful for writing are enumerated, "for nearly all those whom we adopt we teach, if possible, to write," and then the writer passes on to books.

Moreover he—[the tenant of the cell]—receives two books out of the press for reading. He is admonished to take the utmost care and pains that they be not soiled by smoke or dust or dirt of any kind; for it is our wish that books, as being the perpetual food of our souls, should be most jealously guarded, and most carefully produced, that we, who cannot preach the word of God with our lips, may preach it with our hands[3].

---

[1] Cantor non potest libros vendere dare vel impignorare. Cantor non potest libros accommodare nisi pignore, quod tanti vel majoris fuerit, reposito. Tutius est pignori incumbere quam in personam agere. Hoc autem licet facere tantum vicinis ecclesiis vel excellentibus personis. *Ibid.* pp. 373, 374.

[2] *Mon. Angl.* II. 39. The last sentence runs as follows in the original: Nullus librum capiat nisi scribatur in rotulo ejus; nec alicui liber aliquis mutuo tradatur absque competenti et sufficienti memoriali, et hoc ponatur in rotulo ipsius. I owe this quotation and the last to Father Gasquet's *Some Notes on Medieval Monastic Libraries*, 1891, p. 10.

[3] Adhuc etiam libros ad legendum de armario accipit duos quibus omnem diligentiam curamque prebere monetur ne fumo ne puluere vel alia qualibet sorde

They did, however, on occasion lend books, for it is provided that when books are lent no one shall retain them contrary to the will of the lenders[1]. It would be interesting to know how this rule was enforced.

The Cistercian Order—founded 1128—adopted the Benedictine Rule, and with it the obligation of study and writing. Moreover, in their anxiety to take due care of their books, they went further than their predecessors; for they entrusted them to a special officer, instead of to the precentor, and they admitted a special room to contain them into the ground-plan of their houses.

At a later point I shall return to the interesting subject of the Cistercian book-room. For the present I must content myself with translating from their Customs the passage relating to books. It occurs in Chapter CXV., *Of the precentor and his assistant.* After describing his various duties, the writer proceeds:

With regard to the production and safe-keeping of charters and books, the abbat is to consider to whom he shall entrust this duty.

The officer so appointed may go as far as the doors of the writing-rooms when he wants to hand in or to take out a book, but he may not go inside. In the same way for books in common use, as for instance antiphoners, hymnals, graduals, lectionaries [etc.], and those which are read in the Frater and at Collation, he may go as far as the door of the novices, and of the sick, and of the writers, and then ask for what he wants by a sign, but he may not go further unless he have been commanded by the abbat. When Collation is over it is his duty to close the press, and during the period of labour, of sleep, and of meals, and while vespers are being sung, to keep it locked[2].

The Customs of the Augustinian Order are exceedingly full on the subject of books. I will translate part of the 14th chapter of the Customs in use at Barnwell[3], near Cambridge.

maculentur; Libros quippe tanquam sempiternum animarum nostrarum cibum cautissime custodiri et studiosissime volumus fieri vt qui ore non possumus dei verbum manibus predicemus. Guigonis, Prioris Carthusiæ, *Statuta.* Fol. Basle, 1510. *Statuta Antiqua*, Part 2, Cap. XVI. § 9.

[1] Libros cum commodantur nullus contra commodantium retineat voluntatem. *Ibid.* Cap. XXXII. § 16.

[2] *Les Monuments primitifs de la Règle Cistercienne*, par Ph. Guignard, 8vo. Dijon, 1878, p. 237.

[3] *The Observances in use at the Augustinian Priory of S. Giles and S. Andrew at Barnwell*: ed. J. W. Clark. 8vo. Camb., 1897, p. 15. This passage also occurs in the Customs of the Augustinian House at Grönendaal near Brussels. MS. in the Royal Library, Brussels, fol. 53, vo. *De Armario.*

It is headed: *Of the safe keeping of the books, and of the office of Librarian* (*armarius*). As the passage occurs also in the Customs as observed in France and in Belgium, it may be taken, I presume, to represent the general practice of the Order.

The Librarian, who is called also Precentor, is to take charge of the books of the church; all which he ought to keep and to know under their separate titles; and he should frequently examine them carefully to prevent any damage or injury from insects or decay. He ought also, at the beginning of Lent, in each year, to shew them to the convent in Chapter, when the souls of those who have given them to the church, or of the brethren who have written them, and laboured over them, ought to be absolved, and a service in convent be held over them. He ought also to hand to the brethren the books which they see occasion to use, and to enter on his roll the titles of the books, and the names of those who receive them. These, when required, are bound to give surety for the volumes they receive; nor may they lend them to others, whether known or unknown, without having first obtained permission from the Librarian. Nor ought the Librarian himself to lend books unless he receive a pledge of equal value; and then he ought to enter on his roll the name of the borrower, the title of the book lent, and the pledge taken. The larger and more valuable books he ought not to lend to anyone, known or unknown, without permission of the Prelate....

Books which are to be kept at hand for daily use, whether for singing or reading, ought to be in some common place, to which all the brethren can have easy access for inspection, and selection of anything which seems to them suitable. The books, therefore, ought not to be carried away into chambers, or into corners outside the Cloister or the Church. The Librarian ought frequently to dust the books carefully, to repair them, and to point them, lest brethren should find any error or hindrance in the daily service of the church, whether in singing or in reading. No other brother ought to erase or change anything in the books unless he have obtained the consent of the Librarian....

The press in which the books are kept ought to be lined inside with wood, that the damp of the walls may not moisten or stain the books. This press should be divided vertically as well as horizontally by sundry shelves on which the books may be ranged so as to be separated from one another; for fear they be packed so close as to injure each other or delay those who want them[1].

Further, as the books ought to be mended, pointed, and taken care of by the Librarian, so ought they to be properly bound by him.

---

[1] As I know of no other passage in a medieval writer which describes an *armarium*, I transcribe the original text: Armarium, in quo libri reponuntur, intrinsecus ligno vestitum esse debet ne humor parietum libros humectet vel inficiat. In quo eciam diversi ordines seorsum et deorsum distincti esse debent, in quibus libri separatim collocari possint, et distingui abinvicem, ne nimia compressio ipsis libris noceat, vel querenti moram inuectat.

The Order of Prémontré—better known as the Premonstratensians, or reformed Augustinians—repeat the essential part
of these directions in their statute, *Of the Librarian (armarius)*,
with this addition, that it is to be part of the librarian's duty to
provide for the borrowing of books for the use of the House, as
well as for lending[1].

Lastly, the Friars, though property was forbidden, and
S. Francis would not allow his disciples to own so much as a
psalter or a breviary[2], soon found that books were a necessity,
and the severity of early discipline was relaxed in favour of a
library. S. Francis died in 1226, and only thirty-four years
afterwards, among the constitutions adopted by a General
Chapter of the Order held at Narbonne 10 June, 1260, are
several provisions relating to books. They are of no great
importance, taken by themselves, but their appearance at so
early a date proves that books had become indispensable. It is
enacted that no brother may write books, or have them written,
for sale; nor may the chief officer of a province venture to keep
books without leave obtained from the chief officer of the whole
Order; no brother may keep the books assigned to him, unless
they are altogether the property of the Order—and so forth[3].
A century later, when Richard de Bury, Bishop of Durham, was
writing his *Philobiblon* (completed 24 January, 1344—45), he
could say of them and the other friars—whom, be it remembered,
he, as a regular, would regard with scant favour—

But whenever it happened that we turned aside to the cities and
places where the Mendicants had their convents we did not disdain to
visit their libraries and any other repositories of books; nay there we
found heaped up amidst the utmost poverty the utmost riches of wisdom.

[1] Statuta primaria Præmonstratensis Ordinis, Cap. VII. ap. Le Paige, *Bibliotheca
Præm. Ord.* fol. Paris, 1633, p. 803. The words are : Ad Armarium pertinet libros
custodire, et si sciverit emendare ; Armarium librorum, cum necesse fuerit, claudere et
aperire…libros mutuo accipere cum necesse fuerit et nostros quærentibus commodare
sed non sine licentia Abbatis vel Prioris absente Abbate et non sine memoriali
competenti.

[2] The delightful story of S. Francis and the brother who wished for a psalter of
his own is told in the *Speculum Perfectionis*, ed. Sabatier, 8vo. Paris, 1898, p. 11.

[3] These Constitutions have been printed by Father F. Ehrle in a paper called
Die ältesten Redactionen der Generalconstitutionen des Franziskanerordens, in "Archiv
für Literatur und Kirchengeschichte des Mittelalters," Band VI. pp. 1—138. The
passages cited above will be found on p. 111.

We discovered in their fardels and baskets not only crumbs falling from the master's table for the dogs, but the shewbread without leaven and the bread of angels having in it all that is delicious; and indeed the garners of Joseph full of corn, and all the spoil of the Egyptians and the very precious gifts which Queen Sheba brought to Solomon.

These men are as ants ever preparing their meat in the summer, and ingenious bees continually fabricating cells of honey... And to pay due regard to truth...although they lately at the eleventh hour have entered the Lord's vineyard..., they have added more in this brief hour to the stock of the sacred books than all the other vinedressers; following in the footsteps of Paul, the last to be called but the first in preaching, who spread the gospel of Christ more widely than all others[1].

At Assisi, the parent house of the Franciscan Order, there was a library of considerable extent, many volumes of which still exist, with a catalogue drawn up in 1381.

At this point I will resume the conclusions which may be deduced from this examination of the Benedictine Rule and the Customs founded upon it.

In the first place they all assume the existence of a library. S. Benedict contents himself with general directions about study. The Cluniacs put the books in charge of the precentor, who is to be called also *armarius*, and they prescribe an annual audit of them, with the assignment of a single volume to each brother, on the security of a written attestation of the fact. These regulations were adopted by the Benedictines, with fuller rules for the librarian, who is still precentor also. He is to keep both presses and books in repair, and personally to supervise the daily use of the manuscripts, restoring to their proper places those that brethren may have been reading. Among these rules permission to lend books on receipt of a pledge first makes its appearance. The Carthusians maintain the principle of lending. Each brother might have two books, and he is to be specially careful to keep them clean. The Cistercians appoint a special officer to have charge of the books, about the safety of which great care is to be taken, and at certain times of the day he is to lock the press. The Augustinians and the Premonstratensians follow the Cluniacs and Benedictines; but the Premonstratensians direct their librarian to take note of the books that the House borrows as well as of those that it lends; and they adopt the Cistercian precaution about his opening and locking the press.

[1] *The Philobiblon of Richard de Bury*, ed. E. C. Thomas, 8vo. Lond. 1888, p. 203.

Secondly, by the time that Lanfranc was writing his statutes for English Benedictines, it was evidently contemplated that the number of books would have exceeded the number of brethren, for the keeper of the books is directed to bring all the books of the House into Chapter, and after that the brethren, one by one, are to bring in the books which they have borrowed[1]. Among the books belonging to the House there were probably some service-books; but, from the language used, it appears to me that we may fairly conclude that by the end of the eleventh century Benedictine Houses had two sets of books: (1) those which were distributed among the brethren; (2) those which were kept in some safe place, as part of the possessions of the House: or, to adopt modern phrases, that they had a lending library and a library of reference.

Thirdly, it is evident that the loan of books to persons in general, on adequate security, began at a very early date. On this account I have already ventured to call monastic libraries the public libraries of the Middle Ages. As time went on, the practice was developed, and at last became general. It was even enjoined upon monks as a duty by their ecclesiastical superiors. In 1212 a Council which met at Paris made the following decree, but I am not able to say whether it was accepted out of France:

We forbid those who belong to a religious Order, to formulate any vow against lending their books to those who are in need of them; seeing that to lend is enumerated among the principal works of mercy.

After careful consideration, let some books be kept in the House for the use of brethren; others, according to the decision of the abbat, be lent to those who are in need of them, the rights of the House being safe-guarded.

From the present date no book is to be retained under pain of incurring a curse [for its alienation], and we declare all such curses to be of no effect[2].

---

[1] In the Cluniac Customs those volumes only which had been assigned to particular brethren are to be laid on the carpet. It is difficult to understand the reason for this formal assignment of a book to each brother who chose to ask for one. As brethren in those early times had no separate cubicles or cells, it could hardly imply more than a precaution against the difficulty of two brethren requiring the use of the same volume. Possibly the whole intention was disciplinary, to ensure study as prescribed by the Rule.

[2] Delisle, *Bibl. de l'École des Chartes*, Ser. 3, Vol. I. p. 225. Interdicimus inter alia viris religiosis, ne emittant juramentum de non commodando libros suos indigentibus, cum commodare inter præcipua misericordiæ opera computetur. Sed, adhibita

In the same century many volumes were bequeathed to the Augustinian House of S. Victor, Paris, on the express condition that they should be so lent[1]. It is almost needless to add that one abbey was continually lending to another, either for reading or for copying[2].

Houses which lent liberally would probably be the first to relax discipline so far as to admit strangers to their libraries ; and in the sixteenth and following centuries the libraries of the Benedictine House of S. Germain des Près, Paris, as well as the already mentioned House of S. Victor, were open to all comers on certain days in the week.

When we try to realise the feelings with which monastic communities regarded books, it must always be remembered that they had a paternal interest in them. In many cases they had been written in the very House in which they were afterwards read from generation to generation ; and if not, they had probably been procured by the exchange of some work so written. In fact, if a book was not a son of the House, it was at least a nephew.

The conviction that books were a possession with which no convent could dispense, appears in many medieval writers. The whole matter is summed up in the phrase, written about 1170, "claustrum sine armario, castrum sine armamentario[3]," an epigram which I will not spoil by trying to translate it ; and even more clearly in the passionate utterances of Thomas à Kempis on the desolate condition of priest and convent without books[4]. The "round of creation" is explored for similes to enforce this truth. A priest so situated is like a horse without bridle, a ship without oars, a writer without pens, a bird without wings, etc. ; while the House is like a kitchen without stewpans,

consideratione diligenti, alii in domo ad opus fratrum retineantur ; alii secundum providentiam abbatis, cum indemnitate domus, indigentibus commodentur. Et a modo nullus liber sub anathemate teneatur, et omnia predicta anathemata absolvimus. Labbe, *Concilia*, XI. 69.

[1] Delisle, *Cab. des Manuscrits*, II. 226.

[2] M. Delisle (*ut supra*, II. 124) cites an inscription in one of the MSS. of the Bibliothèque Nationale, Paris : "Liber iste de Corbeia : sed prestaverunt nobis usque Pascha."

[3] Mabillon, *Thesaurus Anecdotorum*, Vol. I. p. 151.

[4] *Opera Thomæ a Campis*, fol. 1523. Fol. XLVII. 7. The passage occurs in his *Doctrinale Juvenum*, Cap. V.

a table without food, a well without water, a river without fish—
and many other things which I have no space to mention.

Evidence of the solicitude with which they protected their
treasures is not wanting. The very mode of holding a manuscript
was prescribed, if not by law, at least by general custom. " When
the religious are engaged in reading in cloister or in church,"
says an Order of the General Benedictine Chapter, "they shall
if possible hold the books in their left hands, wrapped in the
sleeve of their tunics, and resting on their knees; their right
hands shall be uncovered with which to hold and turn the leaves
of the aforesaid books[1]." In a manuscript at Monte Cassino[2] is
the practical injunction

> Quisquis quem tetigerit
> Sit illi lota manus ;

and at the same House the possession of handkerchiefs—which
were evidently regarded as effeminate inventions—is specially
excused on the ground that they would be useful—among other
things—"for wrapping round the manuscripts which brethren
handle[3]." Of similar import is the distich at the end of a
fine manuscript formerly in the library of S. Victor :

> Qui servare libris preciosis nescit honorem
> Illius a manibus sit procul iste liber[4].

With these injunctions may be compared a note in a fourteenth century manuscript from the same library :

Whoever pursues his studies in this book, should be careful to
handle the leaves gently and delicately, so as to avoid tearing them
by reason of their thinness ; and let him imitate the example of Jesus
Christ, who, when he had quietly opened the book of Isaiah and read
therein attentively, rolled it up with reverence, and gave it again to the
minister[5] ;

[1] *Medieval Monastic Libraries* : by F. A. Gasquet, p. 15. The passage translated
above occurs in a Custumary of S. Augustine's, Canterbury, MSS. Cotton, Faustina,
c. XII. fol. 196 *b*.

[2] *Cat. Monte Cassino*, II. 299.

[3] Theodmarus Cassinensis to Charlemagne, ap. Hæften, *Disquisitiones Monasticæ*,
fol. 1644, p. 1088.

[4] Delisle, *ut supra*, II. 227.

[5] Delisle, *ut supra*, II. 227. Tu, quicunque studebis in hoc libro, prospice, et
leviter atque dulciter tractes folia, ut cavere possis rupturam propter ipsorum tenui-
tatem ; et imitare doctrinam Jesu Christi, qui cum modeste aperuisset librum Ysaie
et attente legisset, tandem reverenter complicuit ac ministro reddidit. This injunction
occurs, in substance, in the *Philobiblon* of Richard de Bury, ed. Thomas, p. 241.

and the advice of Thomas à Kempis to the youthful students for whose benefit he composed the treatise called *Doctrinale Juvenum* which I have already quoted:

Take thou a book into thine hands as Simeon the Just took the Child Jesus into his arms to carry him and kiss him. And when thou hast finished reading, close the book and give thanks for every word out of the mouth of God; because in the Lord's field thou hast found a hidden treasure[1].

In a similar strain a writer or copyist entreats readers to be careful of his work—work which has cost him an amount of pains that they cannot realise. It is impossible to translate the original exactly, but I hope that I have given the meaning with tolerable clearness:

I beseech you, my friend, when you are reading my book to keep your hands behind its back, for fear you should do mischief to the text by some sudden movement; for a man who knows nothing about writing thinks that it is no concern of his. Whereas to a writer the last line is as sweet as port is to a sailor. Three fingers hold the pen, but the whole body toils. Thanks be to God. I Warembert wrote this book in God's name. Thanks be to God. Amen[2].

Entreaties so gentle and so pathetic as these are seldom met with; but curses—in the same strain probably as those to which the Council of Paris took exception—are extremely common. In fact, in some Houses, a manuscript invariably ended with an imprecation—more or less severe, according to the writer's taste[3]. I will append a few specimens.

This book belongs to S. Maximin at his monastery of Micy, which abbat Peter caused to be written, and with his own labour corrected and punctuated, and on Holy Thursday dedicated to God and S. Maximin on the altar of S. Stephen, with this imprecation that he who should take it away from thence by what device soever, with

---

[1] *Opera Thomæ a Campis*, fol. 1523. Fol. XLVII.

[2] Amice qui legis, retro digitis teneas, ne subito litteras deleas, quia ille homo qui nescit scribere nullum se putat habere laborem; quia sicut navigantibus dulcis est portus, ita scriptori novissimus versus. Calamus tribus digitis continetur, totum corpus laborat. Deo gratias. Ego, in Dei nomine, Vuarembertus scripsi. Deo gratias. From a MS. in the Bibl. Nat. Paris (MS. Lat. 12296) from the Abbey of Corbie: "les caractères dénotent l'époque carlovingienne." Delisle, *ut supra*, II. 121.

[3] On the curse invariably used at S. Victor's, see Delisle, *ut supra*, II. 227 *note*.

the intention of not restoring it, should incur damnation with the traitor Judas, with Annas, Caiaphas, and Pilate. Amen[1].

Should anyone by craft or any device whatever abstract this book from this place [Jumièges] may his soul suffer, in retribution for what he has done, and may his name be erased from the book of the living and not be recorded among the Blessed[2].

A simpler form of imprecation occurs very frequently in manuscripts belonging to S. Alban's:

This book belongs to S. Alban. May whosoever steals it from him or destroys its title be anathema. Amen[3].

A similar form of words occurs at the Cistercian House of Clairvaux, a great school of writing like S. Alban's, but whether it habitually protected its manuscripts in this manner I am unable to say:

May whoever steals or alienates this manuscript, or scratches out its title, be anathema. Amen[4].

A very curious form of curse occurs in one of the manuscripts of Christ Church, Canterbury. The writer repents of his severity in the last sentence.

May whoever destroys this title, or by gift or sale or loan or exchange or theft or by any other device knowingly alienates this book from the aforesaid Christ Church, incur in this life the malediction of Jesus Christ and of the most glorious Virgin His Mother, and of Blessed Thomas, Martyr. Should however it please Christ, who is patron of Christ Church, may his soul be saved in the Day of Judgment[5].

---

[1] Hic est liber Sancti Maximini Miciacensis monasterii, quem Petrus abbas scribere jussit et proprio labore providit atque distinxit, et die cænæ domini super sacrum altare sancti Stephani Deo et sancto Maximino habendum obtulit, sub hujusmodi voto ut quisquis eum inde aliquo ingenio non redditurus abstulerit, cum Juda proditore, Anna et Caiapha atque Pilato damnationem accipiat. Amen. From a Benedictine House at Saint Mesmin, Loiret. Delisle, *ut supra*, III. 384. M. Delisle considers that the words "providit atque distinxit" mean "a été revue et ponctuée."

[2] Quem si quis vel dolo seu quoquo modo isti loco substraxerit anime sue propter quod fecerit detrimentum patiatur, atque de libro viventium deleatur et cum iustis non scribatur. From the Missal of Robert of Jumièges, ed. H. Bradshaw Soc., 8vo. 1896, p. 316.

[3] Hic est liber sancti Albani quem qui ei abstulerit aut titulum deleverit anathema sit. Amen. I owe this quotation to the kindness of my friend Dr James.

[4] *Cat. des MSS. des Departements*, 4to. Vol. I. p. 128 (No. 255).

[5] Quicunque hunc titulum aboleverit vel a prefata ecclesia Christi dono vel vendicione vel accommodacione vel mutacione vel furto vel quocunque alio modo hunc

Lastly, I will quote a specimen in verse, from a breviary now in the library of Gonville and Caius College, Cambridge:

Wher so ever y be come over all
I belonge to the Chapell of gunvylle hall;
He shal be cursed by the grate sentens
That felonsly faryth and berith me thens.
And whether he bere me in pooke or sekke,
For me he shall be hanged by the nekke,
(I am so well beknown of dyverse men)
But I be restored theder agen[1].

On the other hand, the gift of books to a monastery was gratefully recorded and enumerated among the good deeds of their donors. Among the Augustinians such gifts, and the labour expended upon books in general, was the subject of a special service[2].

It is not uncommon to find a monastic library regularly endowed with part of the annual revenue of the House. For instance, at Corbie, the librarian received 10 sous from each of the higher, and 5 sous from each of the inferior officers, together with a certain number of bushels of corn from lands specially set apart for the purpose. This was confirmed by a bull of Pope Alexander III. (1166—1179)[3]. A similar arrangement was made at the library of S. Martin des Champs, Paris, in 1261[4]. At the Benedictine Abbey of Fleury, near Orleans, in 1146, it was agreed in chapter on the proposition of the abbat, that in each year on S. Benedict's winter festival (21 March), he and the priors subordinate to him, together with the officers of the House, should all contribute "to the repair of our books, the preparation of new ones, and the purchase of parchment." The name of each contributor, and the sum that he was to give, are recorded[5]. At the Benedictine Monastery of Ely Bishop Nigel (1133—1174) granted the tithe of certain churches in the diocese "as a perpetual alms to the

librum scienter alienaverit malediccionem Ihesu Christi et gloriosissime Virginis matris ejus et beati Thome martiris habeat ipse in vita presenti. Ita tamen quod si Christo placeat qui est patronus ecclesie Christi eius spiritus salvus in die judicii fiat. Given to me by Dr James, from a MS. in the library of Trinity College, Cambridge.

[1] I have to thank my friend Dr Venn for this quotation. He tells me that it was first pointed out by Dr Swete in *The Caian*, II. p. 127.

[2] See above, p. 71.   [3] Delisle, *ut supra*, II. 124.   [4] *Ibid.* p. 239.

[5] *Ibid.* p. 365. Edwards, *Memoirs of Libraries*, I. 283.

scriptorium of the church of Ely for the purpose of making and repairing the books of the said church[1]." The books referred to were probably, in the first instance, service-books; but the number required of these could hardly have been sufficient to occupy the whole time of the scribes, and the library would doubtless derive benefit from their labours. The *scriptorium* at S. Alban's was also specially endowed.

We must next consider the answer to the following questions: In what part of their Houses did the Monastic Orders bestow their books? and what pieces of furniture did they use? The answer to the first of these questions is a very curious one, when we consider what our climate is, and indeed what the climate of the whole of Europe is, during the winter months. The centre of the monastic life was the cloister. Brethren were not allowed to congregate in any other part of the conventual buildings, except when they went into the frater, or dining-hall, for their meals, or at certain hours in certain seasons into the warming-house (*calefactorium*). In the cloister accordingly they kept their books; and there they wrote and studied, or conducted the schooling of the novices and choir-boys, in winter and in summer alike.

It is obvious that their work must have been at the mercy of the elements during many months of the year, and some important proofs that such was the case can be quoted. Cuthbert, Abbat of Wearmouth and Jarrow in the second half of the eighth century, excuses himself to a correspondent for not having sent him all the works of Bede which he had asked for, on the ground that the intense cold of the previous winter had paralysed the hands of his scribes[2]; Ordericus Vitalis, who wrote in the first half of the twelfth century, closes the fourth book of his Ecclesiastical History with a lament that he must lay aside his work for the winter[3]; and a monk of Ramsey Abbey in Huntingdonshire has

[1] *Supplement to Bentham's Ely*, by Wm Stevenson, 4to. 1817, p. 51. I have to thank my friend the Rev. J. H. Crosby, Minor Canon of Ely Cathedral, for a transcript of Bp Nigel's deed.

[2] *Monumenta Moguntina*, ed. Jaffé, 8vo. Berlin, 1866, in *Bibl. Rer. Germ.* Vol. III. p. 301; quoted in Bede's works, ed. Plummer, p. xx.

[3] See Church's *S. Anselm*, ed. 1885, p. 48. The words are: Nunc hyemali frigore rigens, aliis occupationibus vacabo, praesentemque libellum hic terminare fatigatus decerno. Redeunte vero placidi veris sereno, etc. *Hist. Eccl.* Pars II. lib. IV.

recorded his discomforts in a Latin couplet which seems to imply that in a place so inconvenient as a cloister all seasons were equally destructive of serious work:

> In vento minime pluvia nive sole sedere
> Possumus in claustro nec scribere neque studere[1].

> As we sit here in tempest in rain snow and sun
> Nor writing nor reading in cloister is done.

But, when circumstances were more propitious, plenty of good work that was of permanent value could be done in a cloister. A charming picture has come down to us of the literary activity that prevailed in the Abbey of S. Martin at Tournai at the end of the eleventh century, when Abbat Odo was giving an impulse to the writing of MSS. "When you entered the cloister," says his chronicler, "you could generally see a dozen young monks seated on chairs, and silently writing at desks of careful and artistic design. With their help, he got accurate copies made of all Jerome's commentaries on the Prophets, of the works of Blessed Gregory, and of all the treatises he could find of Augustine, Ambrose, Isidore, and Anselm; so that the like of his library was not to be found in any of the neighbouring churches; and those attached to them used generally to ask for our copies for the correction of their own[2]."

The second question cannot be answered so readily. We must begin by examining, in some detail, the expressions used to denote furniture in the various documents that deal with conventual libraries.

S. Pachomius places his books in a cupboard (*fenestra*); S. Benedict uses only the general term, library (*bibliotheca*), which may mean either a room or a piece of furniture; and the word press (*armarium*), with which we become so familiar afterwards, does not make its appearance till near the end of the eleventh century. Lanfranc does not use it, but as

---

[1] This couplet, written on the fly-leaf of a MS. in the library of the University of Cambridge (IIh. VI. 11), was pointed out to me by my friend F. J. H. Jenkinson, M.A., Librarian.

[2] Herimanni liber de restauratione S. Martini Tornacensis: ap. Pertz, *Mon. Germ.* XIV. 313.

C. L.

I have shewn that he based his statutes, at least to some extent, on the Cluniac Customs, and as they identify the library (*bibliotheca*) with the press (*armarium*), and call the librarian, termed by Lanfranc the keeper of the books, the keeper of the press (*armarius*), we may safely assume that the books to which Lanfranc refers were housed in a similar piece of furniture. Moreover, in Benedictine houses of later date, as for instance at Abingdon and Evesham, the word is constantly employed.

I pointed out in the first chapter that the word press (*armarium*) was used by the Romans to signify both a detached piece of furniture and a recess in a wall into which such a contrivance might be inserted[1]. The same use obtained in medieval times[2], and the passage quoted above from the Augustinian customs[3] shews that the book-press there contemplated was a recess lined with wood and subdivided so as to keep the books separate.

The books to be accommodated in a monastery, even of large size, could not at its origin have been numerous[4], and would easily have been contained in a single receptacle. This, I conceive, was that recess in the wall which is so frequently found between the Chapter-House and the door into the church at the end of the east pane of the cloister. In many monastic ruins this recess is still open, and, by a slight effort of imagination, can be restored to its pristine use. Elsewhere it is filled in, having been abandoned by the monks themselves in favour of a fresh contrivance. The recess I am speaking of was called the common press (*armarium commune*), or common cloister-press (*commune armarium claustri*); and it contained the books appointed for the general use of the community (*communes libri*).

A press of this description (fig. 19) is still to be seen in excellent preservation at the Cistercian monastery of Fossa Nuova in Central Italy, near Terracina, which I visited in

---

[1] See above, p. 37.

[2] See *Dictionnaire du Mobilier*, par Henri Havard, s. v. *Armoire*, and the passages there quoted.   [3] See above, p. 71.

[4] The Cistercian Customs prescribe the possession of nine volumes at least, chiefly service-books, before a house can be founded. *Documents*, p. 253.

the spring of 1900. This house may be dated 1187—1208[1].
The press is in the west wall of the south transept (fig. 21), close
to the door leading to the church. It measures 4 ft. 3 in. wide,
by 3 ft. 6 in. high; and is raised 2 ft. 3 in. above the floor of
the cloister. It is lined with slabs of stone; but the hinges

Fig. 19. Press in the cloister at the Cistercian Abbey of Fossa Nuova.

are not strong enough to have carried doors of any material
heavier than wood; and I conjecture that the shelf also was
of the same material. Stone is plentiful in that part of Italy,
but wood, especially in large pieces, would have to be brought
from a distance. Hence its removal, as soon as the cupboard
was not required for the purpose for which it was constructed.

[1] *Origines Françaises de l'Architecture Gothique en Italie*, par G. Enlart, 8vo.
Paris, 1894, p. 9. This valuable work contains a full and accurate description,
copiously illustrated, of Fossa Nuova and other abbeys in remote parts of Italy.

Two recesses, evidently intended for the same purpose, are
to be seen in the east walk of the cloister of Worcester
Cathedral, formerly a Benedictine monastery. They are between
the Chapter-House and the passage leading to the treasury and
other rooms. Each recess is square-headed, 6 ft. 9 in. high, 2 ft.
6 in. deep, and 11 ft. broad (fig. 20). In front of the recesses is

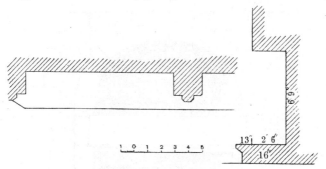

Fig. 20. Groundplan and elevation of the book-recesses in the cloister of
Worcester Cathedral.

a bench-table, 13 in. broad and 16 in. high. This book-press was
in use so late as 1518, when a book bought by the Prior was
"delyvered to yᵉ cloyster awmery[1]."

As books multiplied ampler accommodation for them became
necessary; and, as they were to be read in cloister, it was
obvious that the new presses or cases must either be placed in
the cloister or be easily accessible from it. The time had not
yet come when the collection could be divided, and be placed
partly in the cloister, partly in a separate and sometimes distant
room. This want of book-room was supplied in two ways. In
Benedictine and possibly in Cluniac houses the books were
stored in detached wooden presses, which I shall describe presently; but the Cistercians adopted a different method. At the
beginning of the twelfth century, when that Order was founded,
the need of additional book-space had been fully realised; and,
consequently, in their houses we meet with a special room set
apart for books. But the conservative spirit which governed
monastic usage, and discouraged any deviation from the lines of
the primitive plan, made them keep the press in the wall close
to the door of the church; and, in addition to this, they cut off

---

[1] *The Monastery and Cathedral of Worcester*, by John Noake, Lond., 1866, p. 414.

a piece from the west end of the sacristy, which usually inter-
vened between the south transept and the Chapter-House, and
fitted it up for books. This was done at Fossa Nuova. The
groundplan (fig. 21) shews the press which I have already
figured, and the book-room between the transept and the

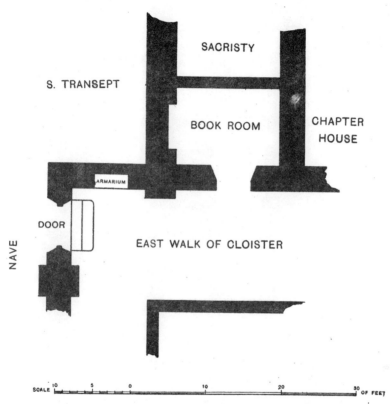

Fig. 21. Groundplan of part of the Abbey of Fossa Nuova.

To shew the book-room and book-press, and their relations to adjoining structures: partly from
M. Enlart's work, partly from my own measurements.

Chapter-House, adjoining the sacristy. It is 14 ft. long by
10 ft. broad, with a recess in its north wall which perhaps once
contained another press.

   There is a similar book-room at Kirkstall Abbey near Leeds,
built about 1150. The plan (fig. 22, A) shews its relation to
the adjoining structures. The *armarium commune* (*ibid.* B) is a

little to the north of the room, as at Fossa Nuova. A room in a similar position, and destined no doubt to the same use, is to be

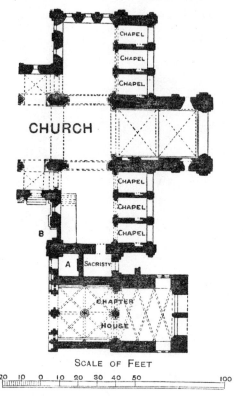

Fig. 22. Groundplan of part of Kirkstall Abbey, Yorkshire.
A, book-room ; B, *armarium commune*.

seen at Beaulieu, Hayles, Jervaulx, Netley, Tintern, Croxden, and Roche.

The catalogue of the books at the Abbey of Meaux in Holderness[1], founded about the middle of the 12th century, has fortunately been preserved ; and it tells us not only what books were kept in one of these rooms, but how they were arranged. After the contents of the presses in the church, which contained chiefly service-books, we come to the "common press in the cloister (*commune almarium claustri*)." On the shelf over the

---

[1] *Chronica monasterii de Melsa.* Rolls Series, Vol. III. App. p. lxxxiii.

door (*in suprema theca*[1] *supra ostium*) were four psalters. The framer of the catalogue then passes to the opposite end of the room, and, beginning with the top shelf (*suprema theca opposita*), enumerates 37 volumes. Next, he deals with the rest of the books, which, he tells us, were in other shelves, marked with the letters of the alphabet (*in aliis thecis distinctis per alphabetum*). If I understand the catalogue correctly, there were eleven of these divisions, each containing an average of about 25 volumes. The total number of volumes in the collection was 316.

Again, the catalogue of the House of White Canons at Titchfield in Hampshire, dated 1400, shews that the books were kept in a small room, on sets of shelves called *columpnæ*, set against the walls. The catalogue begins as follows:

> There are in the Library at Tychefeld four cases to set books on; two of which, namely the first and the second, are on the eastern side. The third is on the south side; and the fourth is on the north side. Each of these has eight shelves [etc.][2].

Nor was this book-closet confined to Cistercian Houses. In the Cluniac Priory at Much Wenlock in Shropshire there is a long narrow room on the west side of the south transept, opening to the cloister by three arches, which could hardly have been put to any other purpose. It is obvious that no study could have gone forward in such places; they must have been intended for security only.

As time went on, and further room for books became necessary, it was provided, at least in some Cistercian Houses, by cutting off two rectangular spaces from the west end of the Chapter-House. There is a good example of this treatment to be seen at Furness Abbey, built 1150—1200. The following description is borrowed from Mr W. H. St John Hope's architectural history of the buildings.

---

[1] The word *theca* signified in classical Latin a case or receptacle in which any object was kept. In medieval Latin it was specially used (*fide* Ducange) for the chest in which the bodies or bones or relics of saints were kept. In this catalogue it is obvious that it may mean either a shelf or a cupboard.

[2] Sunt enim in libraria de Tychefeld quatuor columpnæ pro libris imponendis, unde in orientali fronte due sunt videlicet prima et secunda. In latere vero australi est tercia. Et in latere boreali est quarta. Et earum singule octo habent gradus [etc.].

From the transept southwards the whole of the existing work is of later date, and distinctly advanced character. The ground storey is pierced with five large and elaborate round-headed doorways with good moldings and labels, with a delicate dog-tooth ornament. Three of these next the transept form a group....

The central arch opened, through a vestibule, into the Chapter House. The others open into large square recesses or chambers, with ashlar walls, and rubble barrel-vaults springing from chamfered imposts on each side. In the northern chamber the vault is kept low and segmental, on account of the passage above it of the dorter stair to the church....The southern chamber has a high pointed vault. Neither chamber has had doors, but the northern has holes in the inner jamb, suggestive of a grate of some kind, of uncertain date.

The chambers just described probably contained the library, in wooden presses arranged round the walls[1].

To illustrate this description a portion of Mr Hope's plan of Furness Abbey (fig. 23) is appended. Each room was about 13 ft. square.

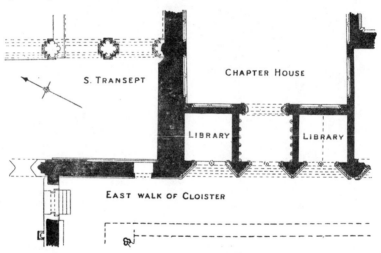

Fig. 23. Groundplan of part of Furness Abbey.

Rooms in a similar position are to be seen at Calder Abbey[2] in Cumberland, a daughter-house to Furness ; and at Fountains

---

[1] *Trans. Cumb. and West. Antiq. and Archæol. Soc.* Vol. XVI. p. 259. I take this opportunity of thanking my friend Mr Hope for allowing me to use his plan of Furness Abbey, and also for pointing out to me the evolution of the Cistercian book-rooms which I have done my best to describe in the text.

[2] *Calder Abbey ; its Ruins and its History.* By A. G. Loftie, M.A.

Fig. 24. Arches in south wall of Church at Beaulieu Abbey, Hampshire,
once possibly used as book-presses.

Abbey there are clear indications that the western angles of the Chapter-House were partitioned off at some period subsequent to its construction, probably for a similar purpose. As the Chapter-House was entered from the cloister through three large round-headed arches, each of the rooms thus formed could be entered directly from the cloister, the central arch being reserved for the Chapter-House itself. The arrangement therefore became exactly similar to that at Furness. Mr Hope thinks that the series of arches in the church wall at Beaulieu in Hampshire, two of which are here shewn (fig. 24), may have been used for a like purpose[1]. There is a similar series of arches at Hayles, a daughter-house to Beaulieu; and in the south cloister of Chester Cathedral there are six recesses of early Norman design, which, if not sepulchral, may once have contained books.

The use of the Chapter-House and its neighbourhood as the place in which books should be kept is one of the most curious features of the Cistercian life. The east walk of the cloister, into which the Chapter-House usually opened, must have been one of the most frequented parts of the House, and yet it seems to have been deliberately chosen not merely for keeping books, but for reading them. At Clairvaux, so late as 1709, the authors of the *Voyage Littéraire* record the following arrangement:

Le grand cloître...est vouté et vitré. Les religieux y doivent garder un perpetuel silence. Dans le côté du chapitre il y a des livres enchaînez sur des pupitres de bois, dans lesquels les religieux peuvent venir faire des lectures lorsqu'ils veulent[2].

A similar arrangement obtained at Citeaux[3].

Having traced the development of the Cistercian book-closet, from a simple recess in the wall to a pair of more or less spacious rooms at the west end of the Chapter-House, I return to my starting-point, and proceed to discuss the arrangement adopted

[1] Mr Hope tells me that he has lately re-examined these recesses, and failed to discover traces of furniture or fittings of any kind within them.

[2] *Voyage Littéraire*, Paris, 1717, Vol. I. p. 101.

[3] *Cat. des Manuscrits des Bibliothèques Publiques de France.* Departements, Tom. V. Catalogue des Manuscrits de Citeaux, No. 635 (p. 405). Parvus liber incathenatus ad analogium cathedre ex opposito capituli.

by the Benedictines. They must have experienced the inconvenience arising from want of space more acutely than the
Cistercians, being more addicted to study and the production of
books. They made no attempt, however, to provide space by
structural changes or additions to their Houses, but were
content with wooden presses in the cloister for their books, and
small wooden studies, called carrells, for the readers and writers.

The uniformity which governed monastic usage was so strict
that the practice of almost any large monastery may be taken
as a type of what was done elsewhere. Hence, when we find a
full record of the way in which books were used in the great
Benedictine House at Durham, we may rest assured that,
mutatis mutandis, we have got a good general idea of the
whole subject. I will therefore begin by quoting a passage
from that valuable work *The Rites of Durham*, a description of
the House drawn up after the Reformation by some one who
had known it well in other days, premising only that it represents the final arrangements adopted by the Order, and takes no
account of the steps that led to them.

In the north syde of the Cloister, from the corner over against the
Church dour to the corner over againste the Dorter dour, was all fynely
glased from the hight to the sole within a litle of the grownd into the
Cloister garth. And in every wyndowe iij Pewes or Carrells, where
every one of the old Monks had his carrell, severall by himselfe, that,
when they had dyned, they dyd resorte to that place of Cloister, and
there studyed upon there books, every one in his carrell, all the after
nonne, unto evensong tyme. This was there exercise every daie.
    All there pewes or carrells was all fynely wainscotted and verie close,
all but the forepart, which had carved wourke that gave light in at ther
carrell doures of wainscott. And in every carrell was a deske to lye
there bookes on. And the carrells was no greater then from one
stanchell of the wyndowe to another.
    And over against the carrells against the church wall did stande
certaine great almeries [or cupbords] of waynscott all full of bookes,
wherein did lye as well the old auncyent written Doctors of the Church
as other prophane authors with dyverse other holie mens wourks, so
that every one dyd studye what Doctor pleased them best, haveinge the
Librarie at all tymes to goe studie in besydes there carrells[1].

At Durham the monastic buildings stood to the south of
the church, and the library-walk of the cloister was that
walk, or alley, or pane, or syde (for all these words are

---

[1] *The Rites of Durham*, ed. Surtees Soc. 1844, p. 70.

used), which had the church to the north of it. The library
was placed there partly for the sake of warmth, partly to secure
greater privacy. At Canterbury and at Gloucester, where the
church was to the south of the conventual buildings, the library-
walk of the cloister was still the walk next to the church, the
other walks, as Mr Hope has pointed out to me, being apparently
kept clear for the Sunday procession.

I propose to explain the system indicated in the above
quotation by reference to a plan of the cloister at Westminster
Abbey, drawn by my friend Mr J. T. Micklethwaite (fig. 25)[1],

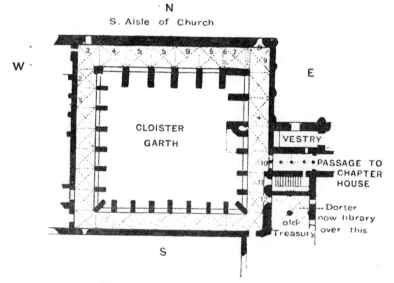

Fig. 25. The cloister, Westminster Abbey.

From Mr Micklethwaite's plan of the buildings.

and by quotations from his notes upon it. At Durham every
vestige of ancient arrangement has been so completely destroyed that it is better to go to another House, where less
mischief has been done, and it happens fortunately that, so far
as the position of the cloister with reference to the church is
concerned, Westminster is the exact counterpart of Durham. I
will consider first the last paragraph of my quotation from the

---

[1] *Notes on the Abbey Buildings of Westminster*, Arch. Journ. XXXIII. pp. 15—49.

Rites of Durham, that namely which deals with the presses for books, there called "almeries or cupbords."

Mr Micklethwaite shews that the two bays at the north end of the west walk of the cloister, and the second bay from the west in the north walk (fig. 25, nos. 1, 2, 4), were appropriated to the novices, by the existence of several sets of nine holes, evidently cut by boys in their idle moods for the playing of some game. Similar holes have been found at Canterbury, Gloucester, and elsewhere. Next he points out that "the nosing of the wall-bench for six feet of the third bay from the west in the north walk, and in the whole of the fourth and fifth bays, and nearly all the sixth, has been cut away flush with the riser, as if some large pieces of furniture had been placed there (*ibid.* nos. 5, 5, 5, 5). These were evidently bookcases." Eastward of these indications of bookcases "the bases of the vaulting-shafts are cut in a way which seems to shew that there was a double screen there (*ibid.* nos. 6, 6), or perhaps there were bookcases arranged so as to form a screen, which is, I think, very likely. Beyond this screen to the right are appearances in the wall [next the cloister-garth] which seem to indicate a blocked-up locker, but they are rather doubtful. And on the left is a large double locker blocked (*ibid.* 7), and the blocking appears to be ancient. This locker is of the date of the wall (Edw. I.), and may have been an additional book-closet provided, because that on the other side of the church-door [to be described presently] had become too small, and [was] blocked up when the larger bookcases were made opposite the carrells[1]."

Lastly, at the risk of some repetition, I will quote a passage from a letter which Mr Micklethwaite was so good as to write to me on this subject, as it brings out some additional points, and states the whole question with great clearness. After describing the position of the bookcases, he proceeds:

There was thus a space, the width of the bench, between the back of the case and the cloister-wall, which would help to keep things dry. Whether the floor was boarded we cannot now tell, but there is evidence that this part of the cloister was cut off from the rest by screens of some sort at both ends, which would make it a long gallery lighted on one side, and with bookcases ranged along the other, not unlike Wren's at

---

[1] *Notes on the Abbey Buildings of Westminster*, Arch. Journ. XXXIII. pp. 21, 22.

Lincoln. The windows must have been glazed; indeed remains of the glazing existed to the end of the 17th century; and there were within my memory marks of fittings along the windows-side which I did not then understand, but which, if they still existed, would I have no doubt tell us something of the *carrells*. A "thorough restoration" has taken away every trace of them.

The "bookcase on the other side of the church door" mentioned above was in the northernmost bay of the east cloister. Mr Micklethwaite says of it:

"Entering the cloister from the church by the east cloister door (*ibid.* no. 8), we find on our left hand a very broad bench against the wall, extending as far as the entrance to the Chapter-House (*ibid.* 10). In the most northern bay the wall-arcade, instead of being brought down by shafts as in the others, is stopped off at the springing by original brackets, as if to allow of some large piece of furniture being placed against the wall. Here, I believe, stood in the thirteenth century the *armarium commune*, or common bookcase (*ibid.* 9). At Durham there is a Norman arched recess in the same place, not mentioned by the writer of the *Rites*, because before his time its use had ceased, books having become more numerous, and being provided for elsewhere[1]."

These notes enable us to imagine what this library was like. It was about 80 feet long by 15 feet broad, extending along four bays of the cloister. It was cut off by a screen at one end, and possibly at the other also; the book-presses stood against the wall, opposite to the windows, which were probably glazed, as we know those at Durham were; and there might have been a wooden floor. Further, the older monks sat in "carrells," as we learn from the custumary of Abbat Ware, who was in office 1258—83. The writer is speaking of the novices, and says that after they have attained a certain degree of proficiency they may sit in cloister, and "be allowed to glance at books taken out of the presses (*armaria*) belonging to the older monks. But they must not be permitted as yet to write or to have carrells[2]."

Whatever may have been the discomfort of this library

---

[1] *Notes on the Abbey Buildings of Westminster*, Arch. Journ. XXXIII. p. 16.
[2] MSS. Mus. Brit. MSS. Cotton, Otho, c. XI. fol. 84.

according to our ideas, there is good reason for believing that
it was in use till 1591, when Dean Williams fitted up part of
the Dorter as a library for the use of the Dean and
Canons[1].

The practice of placing the book-press in the cloister
obtained with equal force in France, for the Benedictines who
wrote the *Voyage Littéraire*, and who would of course be well
acquainted with what was usual in their own Order, remark
with surprise when they visit the ancient abbey of Cruas on
the Rhone, that the press is in the church.

On voit encore dans l'eglise l'armoire où on enfermoit les livres,
contre la coûtume des autres monastères de l'ordre, qui avoient cette
armoire dans le cloître.   On y lit ces vers d'un caractère qui peut avoir
cinq cent ans :

> Pastor jejunat qui libros non coadunat
> Nec panem præbet subjectis quem dare debet[2].

> A shepherd starves whose store of books is low :
> Nor can he on his flock their due bestow.

No example of an English book-press has survived, so far
as I know, but it would be rash to say that none exists ; nor
have I been so fortunate as to find one in France, though I have
taken a great deal of pains to obtain information on the subject.
In default of a press made specially to hold books, I must content
myself with representations of two well-known pieces of furniture
—both preserved in French churches.

The first (fig. 26) stands in the upper sacristy of the Cathedral of Bayeux, over the south transept.   The name usually
given to it, *le Chartrier de Bayeux*, implies that it was made to
hold documents.   M. Viollet-le-Duc does not accept this view,
but considers that it contained reliquaries, with which he probably
would not object to associate other articles of church-plate.

It is of oak, very coarse, rough, and massive.   It is 9 ft.
3 inches high, from floor to top, 17 ft. 2 inches long—(it was
originally 3 ft. longer)—and 3 ft. deep.   There are two rows of
cupboards each 3 ft. 8 inches high, with massive doors that still

---

[1] See a paper by myself in *Camb. Ant. Soc. Proc. and Comm.* IX. pp. 47—56.
[2] *Voyage Littéraire*, ed. 1717.   Part I. 297.

Fig. 26. Part of the ancient press in Bayeux Cathedral, called
Le Chartrier de Bayeux.

From a photograph.

Fig. 27.   Press in the church at Obazine, Central France.
From a photograph.

preserve their original ironwork. The whole piece of furniture has once been painted, indications of which still exist, but the subjects can no longer be made out. M. Viollet-le-Duc[1], who possibly saw the paintings when they were in a better state of preservation than when I examined them in 1896, decides that they once represented the translation of relics.

My second example (fig. 27) is in the church of Obazine in Central France (Département de la Corrèze). It is far simpler and ruder than the press in Bayeux Cathedral; and the style of ornamentation employed indicates a somewhat earlier date; though M. Viollet-le-Duc places the construction of both in the first years of the 13th century. It is 6 ft. 7 in. high, by 7 ft. broad, and 2 ft. 7 in. deep. The material is oak, which still bears a few traces of having once been painted[2].

These pieces of furniture were certainly not made specially for books; but, as they belong to a period when the monastic system was in full, vigorous, life, it is at least probable that they resemble those used by monks to contain their books. I have shewn in the previous chapter that in ancient Rome the press used for books was essentially the same as that used for very different purposes; and I submit that it is unnecessary to suppose that monastic carpenters would invent a special piece of furniture to hold books. They would take the *armarium* that was in daily use, and adapt it to their own purposes.

Before I leave this part of my subject I must mention that there is a third press in the Church of Saint Germain l'Auxerrois, Paris. It stands in a small room over the south end of the west porch, which may once have been a muniment room. It was probably made about a century later than those which I have figured. In arrangement it bears a general resemblance to the example from Bayeux. It consists of six cupboards arranged in two tiers, the lower of which is raised to the level of a bench which extends along the whole length of the piece of furniture, with its ends mortised into those of the cupboards.

---

[1] *Dictionnaire du Mobilier*, s. v. *Armoire*.

[2] Viollet-le-Duc, *ut supra*, p. 4, where full details of the press at Obazine are given. The photograph from which my illustration has been made was specially taken for my use through the kind help of my friend Dr James, who had seen the press in 1899.

The seat of this bench lifts up, so as to form an additional receptacle for books or papers[1].

The curious wooden contrivances called carrells, which are mentioned in the above quotation from the *Rites of Durham*, have of course entirely disappeared. Nothing is said about their height; but in breadth each of them was equal to the distance from the middle of one mullion of a window to the middle of the next; it was made of wainscot, and had a door of open carved work by which it was entered from the cloister. This arrangement was doubtless part of the systematic supervision of brother by brother that was customary in a monastery. Even the aged, though engaged in study, were not to be left to their own devices. I have carefully measured the windows at Durham (fig. 28); and,

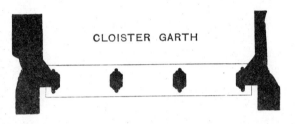

CLOISTER GARTH

Scale |‖‖‖‖‖0   1   2   3   4   5 of Feet

Fig. 28. Groundplan of one of the windows in the cloister of Durham Cathedral.

though they have been a good deal altered, I suppose the mullions are in their original places. If this be so the carrells could not have been more than 2 ft. 9 in. wide, and the occupant would have found but little room to spare. There are eleven windows, so that thirty-three monks could have been accommodated, on the supposition that all were fitted with carrells.

In the south cloister at Gloucester there is a splendid series of twenty stone carrells (fig. 29), built between 1370 and 1412.

[1] Viollet-le-Duc, *ut supra*, p. 14. I have myself examined this press. My friend Mr Hope informs me that there is a press of this character in the nether vestry at S. Peter Mancroft, Norwich, described by him in *Inventories of the parish church of S. Peter Mancroft, Norwich*, Norf. and Norw. Archæol. Soc. XIV. p. 29.

Each carrell is 4 ft. wide, 19 in. deep, and 6 ft. 9 in. high, lighted by a small window of two lights; but as figures do not give a

Fig. 29. Range of carrells in the south cloister at Gloucester Cathedral.
(From Mr Murray's *Handbook to the Western Cathedrals*.)

very vivid idea of size, and as I could not find any one else to do what I wanted, I borrowed a chair from the church and a folio from the library, and sat down to read, as one of the monks might have done six centuries ago (fig. 30). There is no trace of any woodwork appertaining to these carrells; or of any book-press having ever stood near them. The easternmost carrell, however, differs a good deal from the others, and it may have been used as a book-closet. There is a bench-table along the wall of the church opposite to the carrells; but it does not appear to have been cut away to make room for book-presses, as at Westminster. The south alley appears to have been shut off at the east end, and also at the west end, by a screen[1].

This drawing will help us to understand the arrangement of the wooden carrells used at Durham and elsewhere. Each carrell must have closely resembled a modern sentry-box, with this difference, that one side was formed by a light of the window looking into the cloister-garth, opposite to which was the door of entrance. This, I imagine, would be of no great height; and moreover was made of open work, partly that the work of the occupant might be supervised, partly to let as much light as possible pass through into the cloister-library. The seat would be on one side of the carrell and the desk on the other, the latter being so arranged that the light would enter on the reader's left hand.

Carrells seem to have been usual in monasteries from very early times, not to have been introduced at a comparatively late date in order to ensure greater comfort. The earliest passage referring to them is that which I have already quoted[2], shewing that they were in use at Westminster between 1258 and 1283; at Bury S. Edmunds the destruction of the carrells is mentioned among other outrages in a riot in 1327[3]; they occur at Evesham between 1367 and 1379[4]; at Abingdon in 1383—84[5];

---

[1] See Mr Hope's *Notes on the Benedictine Abbey of S. Peter at Gloucester*, in *Records of Gloucester Cathedral*, 1897, p. 23.

[2] See above, p. 93.

[3] *Memorials of S. Edmund's Abbey*, Rolls Series, II. 327. The writer is describing the mischief done by the rioters of 1327 : Deinde claustrum ingressi, cistulas, id est caroles, et armariola fregerunt, et libros et omnia in eis inventa similiter asportaverunt. I owe this quotation to Dr James, *On the Abbey of S. Edmund at Bury*, Camb. Ant. Soc. Octav. Publ. No. XXVIII. p. 158.

[4] *Liber Evesham*, Hen. Bradshaw Soc. 1893, p. 196. Abbat Ombresleye (1367—79) built "paginam illam claustri contiguam ecclesie ubi carolæ fratrum consistunt."

[5] *Accounts of the Obedientiaries of Abingdon Abbey*, ed. Camden Society, 1892, p. 47. "Expense circa sedilia claustri" is the heading of an account for wood bought and for carpenter's work. The sum spent was £2. 15s. 3d.

Fig. 30. A single carrell, Gloucester Cathedral.

and at Christ Church, Canterbury, it is recorded among the good deeds of Prior Sellyng (1472—94), that in the south alley of the cloister "novos Textus quos Carolos ex novo vocamus perdecentes fecit"; words which Professor Willis renders "con-structed there very convenient framed contrivances which are now-a-days called carols[1]." Their use—at any rate in some Houses—is evident from an injunction among the Customs of S. Augustine's, Canterbury, to the effect that the cellarer and others who rarely sit in cloister might not have carrells, nor in fact any brother unless he be able to help the community by copying or illuminating, or at least by adding musical notation[2]. They were in fact devices to provide a certain amount of privacy for literary work in Houses where there was no *Scriptorium* or writing-room. At Durham, according to the author of *Rites*, they were used exclusively for reading.

The above-mentioned Customs of S. Augustine's, written between 1310 and 1344, give a valuable contemporary picture of the organization of one of the more important cloister-libraries. The care of the presses is to be entrusted to the Precentor and his subordinate, called the Succentor. The former is to have a seat in front of the press—which doubtless stood against the wall—and his carrell is to stand at no great distance, on the stone between the piers of the arches next the cloister-garth. The Succentor is to have his seat and his carrell on the bench near the press—by which the bench which commonly ran along the cloister-wall is obviously meant. These arrangements are made "in order that these two officers, or at least one of them, may always be at hand to satisfy brethren who make any demand upon their time[3]." In other words, they were the

---

[1] *Arch. Hist. of the Conventual Buildings of the Monastery of Christ Church, Canterbury.* By R. Willis. 8vo. Lond. 1869, p. 45.

[2] MSS. Mus. Brit. MSS. Cotton, Faustina, c. XII., fol. 149. De karulis in claustro habendis hanc consideracionem habere debent quibus committitur claustri tutela ut videlicet celerarius seu alii fratres qui raro in claustro resident suas karulas in claustro non habeant, set nec aliqui fratres nisi in scribendo vel illuminando aut tantum notando communitati aut et sibimet ipsis proficere sciant.

[3] MSS. Mus. Brit. MSS. Cotton, Faustina, c. XII., fol. 145. ...precentorem et succentorem quibus committitur armariorum custodia. Cantor habebit cathedram suam ante armarium in claustro stantem et carulam suam iuxta desuper lapidem inter columpnas. Succentor vero super scannum iuxta armarium carulam et sedem

librarian and sub-librarian, who were to be always ready to answer questions. It is clear that brethren were not allowed to handle the books as they pleased.

The cloister at Durham, or at least that part of it which was used as a library, was glazed; but whether with white glass or stained glass we are not informed. So obvious a device for increasing both the comfort and the beauty of a much-frequented part of the monastic buildings was doubtless adopted in many other Houses. At Bury S. Edmunds part at least of the cloister had "painted windows representing the sun, moon and stars and the occupations of the months"; at Christ Church, Canterbury, Prior Sellyng (1472—94) "had the south walk of the cloister glazed for the use of the studious brethren"; at Peterborough the windows of the cloister

were all compleat and fair, adorned with glass of excellent painting: In the South Cloyster was the History of the Old Testament: In the East Cloyster of the New: In the North Cloyster the Figures of the successive Kings from King *Peada*: In the West Cloyster was the History from the first foundation of the Monastery of King *Peada*, to the restoring of it by King *Edgar*. Every window had at the bottom the explanation of the History thus in Verse[1].

At Westminster, as recorded above, traces of the insertion of glass have been observed.

In later times, when regular libraries had been built for the monasteries, a special series of portraits occasionally appeared in glass, on a system similar to that worked out in other materials in Roman and post-Roman libraries; and sometimes, in other libraries, subjects are to be met with instead of portraits, to indicate the nature of the works standing near them. But I cannot say whether cloister-glass was ever treated in this way.

suam habebit, ut hii duo vel saltem unus eorum possint semper esse parati ad respondendum fratribus seruicium petentibus.

[1] *History of the Church of Peterburgh.* By Symon Gunton: fol. 1686, p. 103. The author gives the subjects and legends of nine windows. I owe this quotation to the kindness of Mr Hope.

CHAPTER III.

INCREASE OF MONASTIC COLLECTIONS. S. RIQUIER, BOBBIO, DURHAM, CANTERBURY. BOOKS KEPT IN OTHER PLACES THAN THE CLOISTER. EXPEDIENTS FOR HOUSING THEM AT DURHAM, CITEAUX, AND ELSEWHERE. SEPARATE LIBRARIES BUILT IN FIFTEENTH CENTURY AT DURHAM, S. ALBANS, CITEAUX, CLAIRVAUX, ETC. GRADUAL EXTENSION OF LIBRARY AT S. GERMAIN DES PRÈS. LIBRARIES ATTACHED TO CATHEDRALS. LINCOLN, SALISBURY, WELLS, NOYON, ROUEN, ETC.

N the last chapter I attempted to describe the way in which the Monastic Orders provided for the safe keeping of their books, so long as their collections were not larger than could be accommodated in a press or presses in the cloister, or in the small rooms used by the Cistercians for the same purpose. I have now to carry the investigation a step farther, and to shew how books were treated when a separate library was built.

It must not be supposed that an extensive collection of books was regarded as indispensable in all monastic establishments. In many Houses, partly from lack of funds, partly from an indisposition to study, the books were probably limited to those required for the services and for the daily life of the brethren. In other places, on the contrary, where the fashion of book-collecting had been set from very early days, by some abbat or prior more learned or more active than his fellows; and where brethren in consequence had learnt to take a pride in

their books, whether they read them or not, a large collection
was got together at a date when even a royal library could be
contained in a single chest of very modest dimensions. For
instance, when an inventory of the possessions of the Benedictine
House of S. Riquier near Abbeville was made at the request of
Louis le Débonnaire in 831 A.D., it was found that the library
contained 250 volumes ; and a note at the end of the catalogue
informs us that if the different treatises had been entered
separately, the number of entries would have exceeded five
hundred, as many books were frequently bound in a single
volume. The works in this library are roughly sorted under
the headings Divinity, Grammar, History and Geography,
Sermons, Service-books[1]. A similar collection existed at S. Gall
at the same period[2]. In the next century we find nearly seven
hundred manuscripts in a Benedictine monastery at Bobbio in
north Italy[3]; and nearly six hundred in a House belonging to
the same order at Lorsch in Germany[4]. At Durham, also a
Benedictine House, a catalogue made early in the twelfth
century contains three hundred and sixty-six titles[5]; but, as at
S. Riquier, the number of works probably exceeded six or seven
hundred.

These instances, which I have purposely selected from
different parts of Europe, and which could easily have been
increased, are sufficient to indicate the rapidity with which
books could be, and in fact were accumulated, when the taste
for such collections had once been set. Year by year, slowly
yet surely, by purchase, by gift, by bequest, by the zeal of the
staff of writers whom the precentor drilled and kept at work,
the number grew, till in certain Houses it reached dimensions
which must have embarrassed those responsible for its bestowal.
At Christ Church, Canterbury, for instance, the catalogue made
by Henry de Estria, Prior 1285—1331, enumerates about 1850
manuscripts[6].

It must gradually have become impossible to accommodate
such collections as these according to the old method, even

---

[1] *Catalogi Bibliothecarum antiqui ;* ed. G. Bekker, 8vo. 1885, pp. 24—28.
[2] *Ibid.*, pp. 43—53.   [3] *Ibid.*, pp. 64—73.
[4] *Ibid.* p. 82—120.
[5] *Catalogi Veteres Librorum Eccl. Cath. Dunelm.,* ed. Surtees Soc. 1838, pp. 1—10.
[6] See a letter by Dr M. R. James in *The Guardian,* 18 May, 1898.

supposing it was desirable to do so. There were doubtless many duplicates, and manuscripts of value requiring special care. Consequently we find that places other than the cloister were used to keep books in. At Durham, for instance, the catalogues made at the end of the fourteenth century enumerate (1) "the books in the common press at Durham in sundry places in the cloister" (386 volumes)[1]; (2) "the books in the common press at Durham in the Spendment" (408 volumes)[2]; (3) "the inner library at Durham called Spendment" (87 volumes)[3]; (4) "the books for reading in the frater which lie in the press near the entrance to the farmery" (17 volumes)[4]; (5) "the books in the common press of the novices at Durham in the cloister" (23 volumes)[5]. Of the above catalogues the first obviously deals with the contents of the great "almeries of wainscot" which stood in the cloister; the second and third with the books for which no room could be found there, and which in consequence had been transferred to a room on the west side of the cloister, where wages were paid and accounts settled. In the *Rites of Durham* it is termed the treasure-house or chancery. It was divided into two by a grate of iron, behind which sat the officer who made the payments. The books seem to have been kept partly in the outer half of the room, partly within this grate.

At Citeaux, the parent-house of the Cistercian order, a large and wealthy monastery in Burgundy, the books were still more scattered, as appears from the catalogue[6] drawn up by John de Cirey, abbat at the end of the fifteenth century, now preserved, with 312 of the manuscripts enumerated in it, in the public library of Dijon.

This catalogue, written on vellum, in double columns, with initial letters in red and blue alternately, records the titles of

---

[1] *Catalogi Veteres Librorum Eccl. Cath. Dunelm.* Ed. Surtees Soc. 1838, pp. 46—79. This catalogue is dated Easter, 1395.

[2] *Ibid.* pp. 10—34. This catalogue is dated 1391.

[3] *Ibid.* pp. 34—38. Of the same date.

[4] *Ibid.* pp. 80, 81. These volumes are recorded in the first of the above catalogues.

[5] *Ibid.* pp. 81—84. The date is 1395. For a description of the Spendment see *Rites of Durham, ut supra,* p. 71.

[6] Printed in *Catalogue général des manuscrits des Bibliothèques Publiques de France,* V. 339—452.

1200 MSS and printed books; but the number of the latter is not great. It is headed:

Inventory of the books at Citeaux, in the diocese of Chalons, made by us, brother John, abbat of the said House, in the year of our Lord 1480, after we had caused the said books to be set to rights, bound, and covered, at a vast expense, by the labour of two and often three binders, employed continuously during two years[1].

This heading is succeeded by the following statement:

And first of the books now standing (*existencium*) in the library of the dorter, which we have arranged as it is, because the room had been for a long time useless, and formerly served as a tailory and vestry,...but for two years or nearly so nothing or very little had been put there[2].

A bird's-eye view of Citeaux, dated 1674, preserved in the Bibliothèque Nationale, Paris, shews a small building between the Frater and the Dorter, which M. Viollet-le-Duc, who has reproduced[3] part of it, letters "staircase to the dorter." The room in question was probably at the top of this staircase, and the arrangements which I am about to discuss shew beyond all question that the Dorter was at one end of it and the Frater at the other.

There were six bookcases, called benches (*banche*), evidently corresponding to the *sedilia* or "seats" mentioned in many English medieval catalogues. The writer takes the bookcases in order, beginning as follows:

De prima banca inferius versus refectorium (13 vols.).
    In 2ᵃ linea prime banche superius (17 vols.).
In 2ᵃ banca inferius de latere dormitorii (18 vols.).
  „   „   superius   „   „   (14 vols.).
In 2ᵃ banca inferius de latere refectorii (15 vols.).
  „   „   superius   „   „   (18 vols.).

---

[1] Inventarium librorum monasterii Cistercii, Cabilonensis diocesis, factum per nos, fratrem Johannem, abbatem eiusdem loci, anno Domini millesimo cccc octuagesimo, postquam per duos annos continuos labore duorum et sepius trium ligatorum eosdem libros aptari, ligari, et cooperiri, cum magnis sumptibus et expensis fecimus.

[2] Et primo librorum existencium in libraria dormitorii, quam ut est disposuimus, cum locus ipse prius diu fuisset inutilis et dudum arti sutorie et vestiario serviebat, sicut per aliquas annexas armariorumque dispositiones apparebat, sed a 11 annis vel circa nichil aut parum ibi fuerat.

[3] *Dictionnaire raisonné de l'Architecture*, I. 271. He does not give the date, but, when I examined the original in the *Bibliothèque Nationale*, I found it plainly dated 1674. It is a most valuable record, as it shews the monastic buildings, which were greatly altered at the beginning of the last century, in their primitive state.

The third and fifth *banche*, containing respectively 75 volumes and 68 volumes, are described in identical language; but the descriptions of the 4th and 6th differ sufficiently to make quotation necessary:

In quarta banca de latere dormitorii (24 vols.).
    „   „   „   refectorii (16 vols.).
In sexta banca de latere dormitorii (25 vols.).
Libri sequentes sunt in dicta sexta banca de latere dormitorii inferius sub analogio (38 vols.).

It seems to me that the first *banca* was set against the Dorter wall, so that it faced the Frater; and that it consisted of two shelves only, the second of which is spoken of as a line (*linea*)[1]. The second, third, and fifth *banche* were detached pieces of furniture, with two shelves on each side. I cannot explain why the fourth is described in such different language. It is just possible that only one shelf on each side may have been occupied by books when the catalogue was compiled. I conjecture that the sixth stood against the Frater wall, thus facing the Dorter, and that it consisted of a shelf, with a desk below it, and a second shelf of books below that again.

Besides these cases there were other receptacles for books called cupboards (*armaria*) and also some chests. These are noted in the following terms:

Secuntur libri existentes in armariis librarie.
In primo armario de latere versus refectorium (36 vols.).
In secundo armario (53 vols.).
In tertio armario (24 vols.).
Sequuntur libri existentes in cofro seu archa juxta gradus ascensus ad vestiarium in libraria (46 vols.).
In quadam cista juxta analogium de latere refectorii (9 vols.).

The total of the MSS. stored in this room amounts to 509. In addition to these the catalogue next enumerates "Books of the choir, church, and cloister (53 vols.); Books taken out of the library for the daily use of the convent (29 vols.); Books chained on desks (*super analogiis*) before the Chapter-House (5 vols.); on the second desk (5 vols.); on the third desk (4 vols.); on the fifth desk (4 vols.); Books taken out of the library partly to be

---

[1] With this use of the word *linea* may be compared the word *rayon*, now usually used in France for a shelf, especially a book-shelf.

placed in the cloister, partly to be divided among the brethren (27 vols.); Books on the small desks in the cloister (5 vols.); Books to be read publicly in convent or to be divided among the brethren for private reading (99 vols.)." These different collections of MSS., added together, make a total of 740 volumes, which seem to have been scattered over the House, wherever a spare corner could be found for them.

The inconvenience of such an arrangement, or want of arrangement, is obvious; and it must have caused much friction in the House. We can imagine the officer in charge of the finances resenting the intrusion of his brother of the library with an asperity not wholly in accordance with fraternal charity. And yet, so strong is the tendency of human nature to put up with whatever exists, rather than be at the trouble of changing it, no effectual steps in the way of remedy were taken until the fifteenth century. In that century, however, we find that in most of the large monasteries a special room was constructed to hold books. Reading went forward, as heretofore, in the cloister, and I conceive that the books stored in the new library were mainly intended for loan or for reference. As at Durham, the monks could go there when they chose.

These conventual libraries were usually built over some existing building, or over the cloister. Sometimes, especially in France, the library appears as an additional storey added to any building with walls strong enough to bear it; sometimes again as a detached building. I will cite a few examples of libraries in these different positions.

At Christ Church, Canterbury, a library, about 60 ft. long by 22 ft. broad, was built by Archbishop Chichele between 1414 and 1443, over the Prior's Chapel[1], and William Sellyng (Prior 1472—1494) "adorned [it] with beautiful wainscot, and also furnished it with certain volumes chiefly for the use of those addicted to study, whom he zealously and generously encouraged and patronised[2]."

---

[1] Godwin, *De Præsulibus Angliæ*, ed. Richardson, I. 126.

[2] *Anglia Sacra*, I. 145. Librariam etiam supra Capellam Prioris situatam perpulcrâ cælaturâ adornavit, quam etiam nonnullis libris instaurari fecit, ad usum maxime literarum studiis deditorum, quos miro studio et benevolentia nutrivit et fovit.

At Durham Prior Wessyngton, about 1446, either built or thoroughly repaired and refitted a room over the old sacristy, between the Chapter-House and the south Transept, or, as the *Rites* say, "betwixt the Chapter House and the Te Deum wyndowe, being well replenished with ould written Docters and other histories and ecclesiasticall writers[1]." Wessyngton's work must have been extensive and thorough, for it cost, including the repairs of the books, £90. 16s. 0d.[2]—at least £1100 or £1200 at the present value of money. The position of this library will be understood from the illustration (fig. 31). The room is 44 ft. 10 in. long, by 18 ft. wide, with a window at each end, 13 ft. wide, of five lights, and a very rough roof of oak, resting on plain stone corbels.

At Gloucester the library is in a similar position, but the date of its construction is uncertain. It has been described as follows by Mr Hope:

Fig. 31. Library at Durham, built by Prior Wessyngton about 1446.

The library is an interesting room of fourteenth century date, retaining much of its original open roof. The north side has eleven windows, each of two square-headed lights and perfectly plain... [There are no windows on the south side.] The large end windows are late perpendicular, each of seven lights with a transom. There are other alterations, such as the beautiful wooden corbels from

[1] *Rites of Durham*, p. 26.

[2] Item structura ij fenestrarum in Libraria tam in opere lapideo, ferrario et vitriario, ac in reparacione tecti descorum et ij ostiorum, necnon reparacione librorum se extendit ad iiij^{xx}x^l. xvj^s. et ultra. *Hist. Dunelm. Scriptores tres.* Ed. Surtees Soc. p. cclxxiii.

which the roof springs, which are probably contemporary with the work
of the cloister when the western stair to the library was built, and the
room altered.

At Winchester a precisely similar position was selected
between the Chapter-House and the south transept, above a
passage leading from the cloister to the ground at the south-
east end of the church.

At the Benedictine House of S. Albans the library was
begun in 1452 by John Whethamstede, Prior, and completed
in the following year at the cost of £150[1]—a sum which
represents about £2000 at the present day—but the position
has not been recorded.

At Worcester, also Benedictine, it seems probable that the
library occupied from very early times the long, narrow room
over the south aisle of the nave to which it was restored in 1866.
This room, which extends from the transept to the west end of
the church, is 130 ft. 7 in. long, 19 ft. 6 in. wide, and 8 ft. 6 in.
high on the south side. It is lighted by twelve windows, eleven
of which are of two lights each, and that nearest to the transept
of three lights. The room is approached by a circular stone
staircase at the south-west angle of the cathedral, access to
which is from the outside only[2].

At Bury S. Edmund's abbat William Curteys (1429—45)
built a library, on an unknown site: but his work is worth
commemorating, as another instance of the great fifteenth
century movement in monasteries for providing special rooms
to contain books.

At S. Victor, Paris, an Augustinian House, the library was
built between 1501 and 1508, I believe over the sacristy; at
Grönendaal, near Brussels, also Augustinian, it was built over
the whole length of the north cloister (a distance of 175 feet), so
that its windows faced the south.

The Franciscan House in London, commonly called Christ's
Hospital, had a noble library, founded 21 October, 1421, by Sir
Richard Whittington, mercer and Lord Mayor of London. By

---

[1] *Regist. Abbatiæ Johannis Whethamstede Abbatis monasterii sancti Albani iterum
susceptæ :* ed. H. T. Riley, Rolls Ser. Vol. I. p. 423.

[2] *Hist. and Ant. of Worcester.* By V. Green, 4to. Lond. 1796. Vol. I. p. 79.
The measurements in the text were taken by myself in 1895.

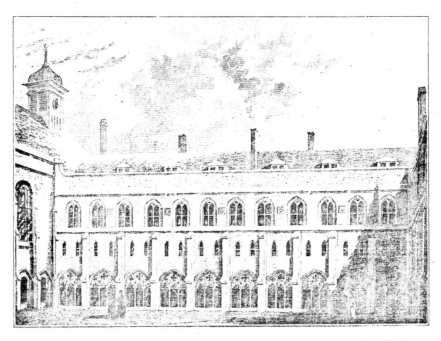

Fig. 32. Library of the Grey Friars House, London, commonly called
Christ's Hospital.

From Trollope's History.

Christmas Day in the following year the building was roofed in; and before three years were over it was floored, plastered, glazed, furnished with desks and wainscot, and stocked with books. The cost was £556. 16s. 8d.; of which £400 was paid by Whittington, and the rest by Thomas Wynchelsey, one of the brethren, and his friends[1]. It extended over the whole of one alley of the cloister (fig. 32). Stow tells us that it was 129 ft. long, by 31 ft. broad[2]; and, according to the letters patent of Henry VIII., dated 13 January, 1547, by which the site was conveyed to the City of London, it contained "28 Desks and 28 Double Settles of Wainscot[3]."

I have recounted the expedients to which the monks of Citeaux were reduced when their books had become too numerous for the cloister. I will now describe their permanent library. This is shewn in the bird's-eye view dated 1674 to which I have already referred, and also in a second similar view, dated 1718, preserved in the archives of the town of Dijon[4], where I had the good fortune to discover it in 1894. It is accompanied by a plan of the whole monastery, and also by a special plan[5] of the library (fig. 35). The buildings had by this time been a good deal altered, and partly rebuilt in the classical style of the late renaissance; but in these changes the library had been respected. I reproduce (fig. 33) the portion of the view containing it and the adjoining structures, together with the corresponding ground-plan (fig. 34).

The authors of the *Voyage Littéraire*, Fathers Martène and Durand, who visited Citeaux in 1710, thus describe this library:

[1] *Monumenta Franciscana*, ed. J. S. Brewer, Rolls Ser. Vol. I. p. 319, from a document called "Prima fundatio fratrum minorum Londoniæ," MSS. Cotton, Vitellius, F. xii.

[2] Stow's *Survey*, ed. Strype, fol. Lond. 1720, Book 3, p. 130.

[3] *History of Christ's Hospital*, by Rev. W. Trollope, 4to. Lond. 1834, App. p. xxiii. The view of the library (fig. 32) is borrowed from this work.

[4] I have to thank M. Joseph Garnier, Archiviste du Département, for his great kindness, not only in allowing me to examine these precious relics, but in having them conveyed to a photographer, and personally superintending a reproduction of them for my use.

[5] This plan is not dated, but, from internal evidence, it forms part of the set to which the bird's-eye view and the general ground-plan belong. They were taken when "des projets," as the heading calls them, were being discussed. One of these was an increase of the library by the addition of a long gallery at the east end at right angles to the original construction.

Citeaux sent sa grande maison et son chef d'ordre. Tout y est grand, beau et magnifique, mais d'une magnificence qui ne blesse point la simplicité religieuse....

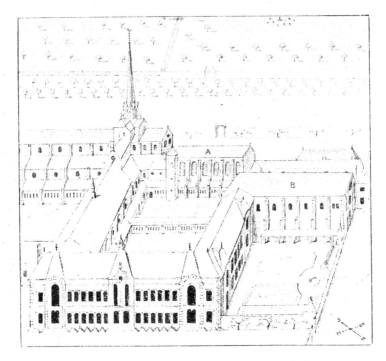

Fig. 33. Bird's-eye view of part of the Monastery of Citeaux.

From a drawing dated 1718. A, library; B, farmery.

Les trois cloîtres sont proportionnez au reste des bâtimens. Dans l'un de ces cloîtres on voit de petites cellules comme à Clervaux, qu'on appelle les écritoires, parce que les anciens moines y écrivoient des livres. La bibliothèque est au dessus ; le vaisseau est grand, voûté, et bien percé. Il y a bon fonds de livres imprimez sur toutes sortes de matières, et sept ou huit cent manuscrits, dont la plupart sont des ouvrages des pères de l'église[1].

The ground-plan (fig. 34) shews the writing-rooms or *scriptoria*, apparently six in number, eastward of the church ; and the bird's-eye view (fig. 33) the library built over them. Unfortunately we know nothing of the date of its construction. It occupied the greater part of the north side of a cloister called

---

[1] *Voyage Littéraire de deux Religieux Benedictins*, 4to. Paris, 1717, I. 198, 221.

"petit cloître" or Farmery Cloister, from the large building on the

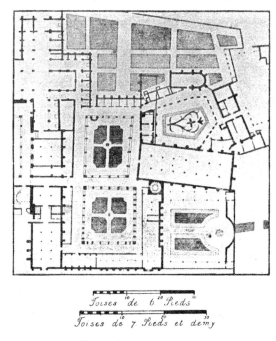

Fig. 34. Ground-plan of part of the Monastery of Citeaux.
From a plan dated 1718.

east side originally built as a Farmery (fig. 33, B). It was approached by a newel-stair at its south-west corner (fig. 35). This

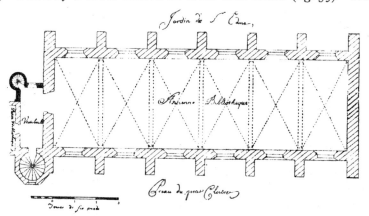

Fig. 35. Ground-plan of the Library at Citeaux.

stair gave access to a vestibule, in which, on the west, was a door leading into a room called small library (*petite bibliothèque*), apparently built over one of the chapels at the east end of the church (fig. 34). The destination of this room is not known. The library proper was about 83 feet long by 25 feet broad[1], vaulted, and lighted by six windows in the north and south walls. There was probably an east window also, but as explained above, it was intended, when this plan was drawn, to build a new gallery for books at this end of the older structure.

I proceed next to the library at Clairvaux, a House which may be called the eldest daughter of Citeaux, having been founded by S. Bernard in 1115. This library was built in a position precisely similar to that at Citeaux, namely, eastward of the church, on the north side of the second cloister, over the *Scriptoria*. Begun in 1495, it was completed in 1503; and was evidently regarded as a work of singular beauty, over which the House ought to rejoice, for the building of it is commemorated in the following stanzas written on the first leaf of a catalogue made between 1496 and 1509, and now preserved in the library at Troyes[2]:

La construction de cette librairie.

Jadis se fist cette construction
Par bons ouvriers subtilz et plains de sens
L'an qu'on disoit de l'incarnation
Nonante cinq avec mil quatre cens.

Et tant y fut besongnié de courage
En pierre, en bois, et autre fourniture
Qu'après peu d'ans achevé fut louvrage
Murs et piliers et voulte et couverture.

Puis en après l'an mil v^e et trois
Y furent mis les livres des docteurs:
Le doux Jésus qui pendit en la croix
Doint paradis aux dévotz fondateurs.

Amen.

We fortunately possess a minute description of Clairvaux, written, soon after the completion of the new library, by the secretary to the Queen of Sicily, who came there 13 July, 1517,

---

[1] I have taken 1 *toise* = 6·39 feet.

[2] I have to thank M. Léon Dorez, of the Bibliothèque Nationale, Paris, for kindly lending me his transcript of this catalogue, and for continual help in all my researches.

and was taken, apparently, through every part of the monastery[1]. The account of the library is as follows:

Et de ce même costé [dudit cloistre] sont xiiii estudes où les religieulx escripvent et estudient, lesquelles sont très belles, et au dessus d'icelles estudes est la neufve librairerie, à laquelle l'on va par une vis large et haulte estant audict cloistre, laquelle librairie contient de longeur lxiii passées, et de largeur xvii passées.

En icelle y a quarante huic banctz, et en chacun banc quatre poulpitres fournys de livres de touttes sciences, et principallement en théologie, dont la pluspart desdicts livres sont en parchemin et escript à la main, richement historiez et enluminez.

L'édiffice de ladicte librairie est magnificque et massonnée, et bien esclairé de deux costez de belles grandes fenestres, bien vitrés, ayant regard sur ledict cloistre et cimitière des Abbez. La couverture est de plomb et semblablement de ladite église et cloistre, et tous les pilliers bouttans d'iceulx édiffices couverts de plomb.

Le devant d'icelle librairie est moult richement orné et entaillé par le bas de collunnes d'estranges façons, et par le hault de riches feuillaiges, pinacles et tabernacles, garnis de grandes ymaiges, qui décorent et embelissent ledict édifice. La vis, par laquelle on y monte, est à six pans, larges pour y monter trois hommes de front, et couronné à l'entour de cleres voyes de massonerie. Ladicte librairerie est toute pavée de petits carreaulx à diverses figures.

It will be interesting to place by the side of this description a second, written nearly two hundred years later, by the authors of the *Voyage Littéraire*, who visited Clairvaux in the spring of 1709:

Le grand cloître...est voûté et vitré. Les religieux y doivent garder un perpétuel silence. Dans le côté du chapitre il y a des livres enchaînez sur des pupitres de bois, dans lesquels les religieux peuvent venir faire des lectures lorsqu'ils veulent....

Du grand cloître on entre dans le cloître du colloque, ainsi appellé, parce qu'il est permis aux religieux d'y parler. Il y a dans ce cloître douze ou quinze petites cellules tout d'un rang, où les religieux écrivoient autrefois des livres: c'est pourquoy on les appelle encore aujourd'hui les écritoires. Au-dessus de ces cellules est la bibliothèque, dont le vaisseau est grand, voûté, bien percé, et rempli d'un grand nombre de manuscrits, attachez avec des chaînes sur des pupitres, mais il y a peu de livres imprimez[2].

The plan of the substruction of this new library, as shewn on

---

[1] Printed in Didron, *Annales Archéologiques*, 1845, III. 228. The article is entitled: *Un grand monastère au* XVIme *siècle.* I owe this reference to my friend Mr W. H. St John Hope, Assistant Secretary to the Society of Antiquaries.

[2] *Voy. Litt.* I. 101, 102.

the ground-plan of Clairvaux given by Viollet Le Duc[1], is exactly the same as that of Citeaux (fig. 33) but on a larger scale. The library itself, as there, was approached by a newel stair at its south-west corner. This stair was hexagonal, and of a diameter sufficient to allow three men to ascend at the same time. The library was of great extent—being about 206 feet long by 56 feet broad—if the dimensions given in the above account be correct, and if I am right in supposing a pace (*passée*) to be equivalent to a modern *mètre*; vaulted, and well lighted. The Queen's secretary seems to have been specially struck by the beauty, the size, and the decoration of the windows. The floor was paved with encaustic tiles.

It will be interesting to note how, in some Houses, the library slowly expanded itself, occupying, one after another, every coign of vantage-ground. An excellent example of this growth is to be found in the abbey of Saint Germain des Près, Paris; and fortunately there are several views, taken at different periods before the Revolution, on which the gradual extension of the library can be readily traced. I append a portion of two of these. The first (fig. 36), dated 1687, shews the library over the south walk of the cloister, where it was placed in 1555. It must not, however, be supposed that no library existed before this. On the contrary, the House seems to have had one from the first foundation, and so early as the thirteenth century it could be consulted by strangers, and books borrowed from it. The second view (fig. 37), dated 1724, shews a still further extension of the library. It has now invaded the west side of the cloister, which has received an upper storey; and even the external appearance of the venerable Frater, which was respected when nearly all the rest of the buildings were rebuilt in a classical style, has been sacrificed to a similar gallery. The united lengths of these three rooms must have been little short of 384 feet. This library was at the disposal of all scholars who desired to use it. When the Revolution came it contained more than 49,000 printed books, and 7000 manuscripts[2].

---

[1] *Dictionnaire de l'Architecture*, I. 267.

[2] For the history of this library see Bouillart's work cited at the foot of Fig. 37; and Franklin, *Anciennes Bibliothèques de Paris*, Vol. I. pp. 107—134.

Fig. 36. Part of the Abbey of S. Germain des Près, Paris.
From a print dated 1687; reproduced in *Les Anciennes Bibliothèques de Paris,*
par Alf. Franklin, Vol. 1. p. 126.

1 Porta major monasterii. 4 Sacrarium. 8 Bibliotheca.
2 Atrium ecclesie. 5 Claustrum parvum B. M. 9 Dormitoria R. Patrum Congregationis.
3 Regalis basilica. 7 Dormitorium. 10 Aulæ Hospitum. 12 Refectorium.

Fig. 37. Part of the Abbey of S. Germain des Près, Paris.

From a print in *Histoire de l'Abbaye Royale de Saint Germain des Prez*, par Dom Jacques Bouillart, fol. Paris, 1724, lettered "l'Abbaye...telle qu'elle est présentement."

A. Porte Extérieure.	H. Grand Cloître.
B. Maisons de l'enclos.	I. Bibliothèque.
C. Parvis de l'Eglise.	K. Dortoir.
D. L'Eglise.	L. Réfectoire.
F. Sacristie.	M. Cuisine.
G. Petit Cloître.	Z. Dortoir des Hôtes.

I now pass to Cathedrals, which vied with monasteries in the possession of a library; and, as might be expected, the two sets of buildings throw light on each other. I regret that it has now become impossible to discover the site or the extent of such a library as that of York, which was well stocked with books so early as the middle of the eighth century; or of that of Notre Dame de Paris, which was a centre of instruction as well as of learning; but some good examples of capitular libraries can be found in other places; and, like those of the monasteries, they were for the most part built in the fifteenth century. I will begin with the library of Lincoln Cathedral, part of which is still in existence[1].

The Cathedral of Lincoln was founded at the close of the eleventh century, and in the middle of the twelfth we find the books belonging to it kept in a press (*armarium*). We learn this from the heading of a list[2] of them when placed in the charge of Hamo, Chancellor 1150—1182, written on the first page of a copy of the Vulgate, the first volume in the collection:

Quando Hamoni cancellario cancellaria data fuit et librorum cura commissa, hos in armario invenit libros et sub custodia sua recepit, scilicet :

Bibliothecam in duobus voluminibus [etc.].

The list which follows enumerates 42 volumes, together with a map of the world. To this small collection there were added in Hamo's time, either by his own gift or by that of other benefactors, 31 volumes more; so that before his death the press contained 73 volumes, probably a large collection for that period. Besides these, there were service-books in the charge of the bursar (*thesaurarius*), and song-books in that of the precentor. The three collections were probably kept in the church.

The first indication of a separate room to contain books is afforded by the gift of a volume by Philip Repyndon, Bishop 1405—1419, in which year he resigned. It is given after his resignation, "to the new library to be built within the Church of Lincoln." Again, Thomas Duffield, formerly Chancellor, who died in 1426, bequeathed another book "to the new library of the aforesaid church." The erection of the new library may therefore be placed between 1419 and 1426.

A catalogue, now in the muniment room at Lincoln, which, on internal evidence, may be dated about 1450, enumerates 107

---

[1] For the historical information contained in this narrative, which originally appeared as a paper in the *Camb. Ant. Soc. Proc. and Comm.* IX. 37 for 18 February, 1895, I am indebted to an article in *The Builder*, 2 April, 1892, pp. 259—263, by my friend the late Rev. E. Venables, Canon and Precentor of Lincoln.

[2] This list has been printed in the Appendix to *Giraldus Cambrensis* (Rolls Series), VII. 165—171.

works, of which 77 (more or less) have been identified as still in the library. The heading, which I will translate, refers to a chaining of the books which had recently taken place, possibly after the construction of the cases which I shall describe in a subsequent chapter.

It is to be noted that in this indenture are enumerated all the books in the library of the church of blessed Mary of Lincoln which have lately been secured with locks and chains; of which indenture one part is stitched into the end of the black book of the aforesaid church, and the other part remains in...[1].

The library—a timber structure—was placed over the northern half of the east walk of the cloister. At present only three bays at the north end remain; but there were originally two bays more, at the south end, between the existing structure and the Chapter-House. These were destroyed in 1789, when the following Chapter Order was made (7 May):

That the old Library adjoining to the Chapter House shall be taken down, and the part of the Cloysters under it new leaded and the walls compleated, and the Stair case therto removed, and a new Stair Case made, agreable to a plan and estimate of the Expence thereof.

I will now briefly describe the room, with the assistance of the plan (fig. 38)[2], and the view of the interior (fig. 39).

The walls are 9 ft. 8 in. high, from the floor to the top of the wall-plate. They are divided into bays, each 7 ft. 9 in. wide, by vertical shafts, from which, at a height of 5 ft. 9 in. from the ground, spring the braces which support the tiebeams of the roof. These are massive beams of oak, slightly arched, and molded on their under-surface. Their position is indicated by dotted lines on the plan (fig. 38). The whole roof is a splendid specimen of fifteenth century work, enriched with carving in the finest style of execution. There is a bold ornament in the centre of each tiebeam; and at the foot of the central joist in each bay, which is wider than the rest, and molded, while the others are

---

[1] Memorandum quod in ista indentura continentur omnes libri existentes in libraria ecclesie beate Marie Lincoln de novo sub seruris cathenati, cuius quidem indenture una pars consuitur in fine nigri libri dicte ecclesie et altera pars remanet in... The rest of the line is illegible. I have to thank the Rev. A. R. Maddison for kindly lending me his transcript of this valuable MS.

[2] For this plan I have to thank my friend T. D. Atkinson, Esq., of Cambridge, architect.

Fig. 39. Interior of the Old Library, Lincoln Cathedral.

The open door leads into Dean Honywood's Library, described in Chapter VIII.

plain, there is an angel, projecting horizontally from the wall. The purlin, again, is molded, and where it intersects the central joist a subject is carved: an angel playing on a musical

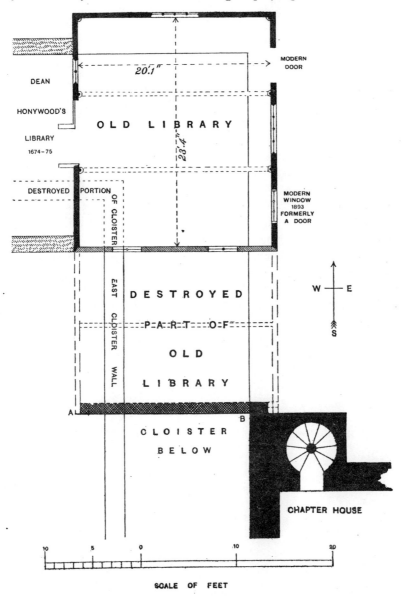

Fig. 38. Plan of the Old Library, Lincoln Cathedral.

instrument—a bird—a rose—a grotesque figure—and the like. Below the wall-plate is a cornice, 12 in. deep, ornamented with a row of quatrefoils above a row of battlements. Beneath these there is a groove, which seems to indicate that the walls were once panelled or plastered.

It is probable that there was originally a row of equidistant windows in the east and west walls, one to each bay on each side; but of these, if they ever existed, no trace remains. There must also have been a window at the north end, and probably one at the south end also. The present windows are plainly modern. The room is known to have suffered from a fire, which tradition assigns to 1609; and probably the original windows were changed during the repairs rendered necessary at that time.

It is not easy to decide how this library was approached. It has been suggested that the stone newel stair at the north-west corner of the Chapter-House, was used for this purpose; but, if that be the case, how are we to explain the words in the above order "the Stair Case thereto removed"; and an item which occurs in the Cathedral Accounts for 1789, "taking down the old stairs, strings, and banisters, 14s."? It appeared to me, when examining the building, that there had been originally a door on the east side, now replaced by a window, as shewn on

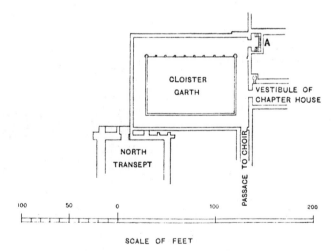

SCALE OF FEET

Fig. 40. Plan of the Cloister, etc., Lincoln Cathedral.

the plan (fig. 38). Possibly the staircase destroyed in 1789 led to this door, which was conveniently situated in the centre of a bay. The staircase built in 1789 is the one still existing at the north-east corner of the old library (fig. 40, A).

At Salisbury Bishop Osmund (1078—99) is stated to have "got together a quantity of books, for he himself did not disdain either to write books or to bind them after they had been written"[1]; but the library, as elsewhere, was a work of the fifteenth century. The foundation is very clearly recorded in an act of the Chapter, dated 15 January, 1444—45. The members present decide that as it is desirable, "for divers reasons, to have certain schools suitable for lectures, together with a library for the safe keeping of books and the convenience of those who wish to study therein—which library up to the present time they have been without—such schools and library shall be built as soon as possible over one side of the cloister of the church, at the cost of William [Ayscough] now Bishop of Salisbury, the Dean, and the Canons of the aforesaid church[2].' Accordingly, a building was erected, extending over the whole length of the east cloister, conveniently approached by the staircase at the south-west corner of the south transept, which originally led only to the roof. This library was curtailed to its present dimensions, and otherwise altered, in consequence of a Chapter Order dated 25 November, 1758, part of which I proceed to quote:

That the southern part of the library be taken down as far as the partitions within which the manuscripts are placed, the whole being found much too heavy to be properly supported by the Cloysters, which were never designed originally to bear so great a weight.

That the roof of the northern part of the library (where the Theological lecture antiently used to be given by the Chancellor of the Church) be taken down; the walls lowered, and a new and lighter roof be placed in its room; and that the same be fitted up in a neat and convenient manner for the reception of the present books and any others which shall hereafter be added to them.

[1] William of Malmesbury, *Gesta Pontificum*, Rolls Ser. p. 183.

[2] Ex eo quod visum est eis vtile et necessarium diuersis causis eos moventibus habere quasdam scolas competentes pro lecturis suis vna cum libraria ad conseruacionem librorum et vtilitatem inibi studere volencium qua hactenus caruerunt statuerunt... quod super vna parte claustri eiusdem ecclesie huiusmodi scole edificentur...cum libraria [etc.]. Chapter Act Book. I have to thank A. R. Malden, Esq., Chapter Clerk, for his kind assistance.

The appearance of the library, as the execution of the above order left it, will be understood from the view (fig. 41), taken from the roof of an adjoining alley of the cloister. Internally the room is 66 feet long, 20 feet wide, and 12 ft. 9 in. high. It has a flat plaster ceiling, part of the "new and lighter roof" imposed on the lowered walls in 1758. The fittings are wholly modern.

The library attached to S. Paul's Cathedral, London, by which I mean the medieval cathedral commonly called Old S. Paul's, was in a similar position. Its history is succinctly recorded by Dugdale. After describing the cemetery called Pardon Church Hawgh, with the cloister that surrounded it, he proceeds:

The Library.

Over the East quadrant of the before mentioned Cloyster, was a fair *Library* built, at the costs of *Walter Shiryngton*, Chancelour of the Duchy of Lancaster in King Henry the 6th's time: But in the year MDXLIX. 10. *Apr.* both Chapell, Cloyster, and Monuments, excepting onely that side where the *Library* was, were pulled down to the ground, by the appointment of *Edward* Duke of Somerset, then Lord Protector to King *Edward* 6. and the materialls carried into the Strand, towards the building of that stately fabrick called Somerset-House, which he then erected; the ground where they stood being afterwards converted into a Garden, for the Pettie Canons[1].

Nothing is known of the dimensions or arrangement of the above room; but, as it was over a cloister, it must have been long and narrow, like that which

---

[1] Dugdale, *History of S. Paul's Cathedral*, fol. 1658, p. 132.

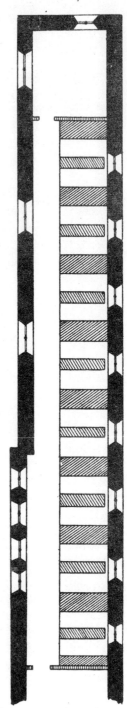

Fig. 42. Plan of the Library in Wells Cathedral.

Fig. 41. Exterior of the Library at Salisbury Cathedral, looking north-east.

still exists in a similar position at Wells Cathedral, which I will briefly mention next.

The Chapter Library at Wells Cathedral occupies the south end of a long, narrow room over the east pane of the cloister, approached by a spiral staircase from the south transept. This room is about 162 feet long by 12 feet wide; the portion assigned to the library is about 106 feet long (fig. 42). The roof was originally divided into 13 spaces by oak principals, very slightly arched, resting on stone corbels. There were two windows on each side to each space. In the part fitted up as a library the principals have been plastered over to imitate stone, and the joists between them concealed by a ceiling. There is a tradition that this room was fitted up as a library in 1472. The present fittings, which I shall have occasion to mention in a subsequent chapter, were put up when the library was refitted and stocked with books after the Restoration[1].

These four examples—at Lincoln, Salisbury, S. Paul's, and Wells—are typical of Cathedral libraries built over a cloister. I will next notice some that were detached.

The library of Lichfield Cathedral[2] stood on the north side

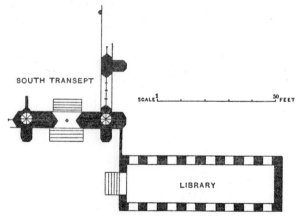

Fig. 43. Plan of the Library at Lichfield Cathedral.

From *History and Antiquities of Staffordshire*, by Stebbing Shaw, fol. Lond. 1798, Vol. II. p. 244.

[1] I have fully described this library and its fittings in *Camb. Ant. Soc. Proc. and Comm.* 1891. Vol. VIII., pp. 6—10.

[2] My account of the library at Lichfield is derived from the *History and Antiquities of the Church and City of Lichfield*, by Rev. Th. Harwood, 4to. Gloucester, 1806, p. 180; and the Chapter Act Book, which I was allowed to examine through the kindness of my friend the Very Rev. H. M. Luckock, D.D., Dean.

of the cathedral, west of the north door, at some little distance from the church (fig. 43). It was begun in 1489, when Thomas Heywood, dean, " gave £40 towards building a library of brick," and completed in 1493. It was about 60 feet long by 15 feet wide, approached by a flight of stairs. As the Chapter Order (9 December, 1757) which authorised its destruction speaks of the "Library, Chapter Clerk's House, and Cloisters," I suspect that it stood on a colonnade, after the manner of the beautiful structure at Noyon, a cathedral town in eastern France, at no great distance from Amiens.

This library—which I have carefully examined on two occasions—was built in pursuance of the following Order of the Chapter, 16 November, 1506.

Le 16. iour de Nouembre audit an, l'affaire de la Librairie se remet sus. Le sieur Doyen offre cent francs pour cet œuure. Et le 20. iour de Nouembre, ouy le Maistre de Fabrique et Commissaires à ce deputez, fut arrestée le long de l'allée qui meine de l'Eglise à la porte Corbaut ; et à cet effect sera tiré le bois à ce necessaire de nos forests, et se fera ladite Librairie suiuant le pourtrait ou patron exhibé au Chapitre le sixiesme iour de Mars 1506. Le Bailly de Chapitre donne cent sols pour ce bastiment, à condition qu'il en aura une clef[1].

This library (fig. 44) is, so far as I know, an unique specimen of a library built wholly of wood, supported on wooden pillars with stone bases, so that it is raised about 10 feet above the stone floor on which they rest, probably for the sake of dryness. There is a legend that a market used to be held there ; but at present the spaces between the pillars have been filled in on the south side. The one here represented (fig. 45) stands on the north side, in a small yard between the library and the cathedral.

The site selected for the building is on the south side of the choir of the cathedral, with its longest axis north and south. It measures 72 feet in length by 17 feet in width between walls, but was originally longer, a piece having been cut off at the south end, where the entrance now is, and where the library is now terminated by a stone wall of classical character. Tradition places the entrance at the opposite end,

---

[1] Levasseur, *Annales de L'Eglise Cathédrale de Noyon*, 4to. Paris, 1633, p. 1111. A marginal note tells us that the gift of the Bailly de Chapitre was accepted 14 June, 1507.

Fig. 44. Chapter-Library at Noyon, France.

by means of an external staircase ; an arrangement which would
have been more convenient for the members of the Chapter, as
they could have approached it through their vestry, which is
on the south side of the choir.   There are now nine windows

Fig. 45.   A single pillar of the cloister beneath the Chapter Library at Noyon.

on the east side—originally there were at least ten ; but none
on the west side, and it is doubtful if there ever were any, as
they would be rendered useless by the proximity of other
structures.   The fittings are modern and without interest.

At Bayeux also the Chapter-library is a detached building
—of stone, in two floors, about 40 feet long by 26 feet wide,
but I have not been able to discover the date at which it was
built; and at York a detached library was built 1421—22 at
the south-west corner of the south transept.   This building, in
two floors, the upper of which appears to have held the books,
is still in existence.

The Cathedral library at Troyes, built by Bishop Louis Raguier between 1477 and 1479, to replace an older structure, was in an unusual position, and arranged in an unusual manner. It abutted against the south-east angle of the south transept, from which it could be entered. It was nearly square, being 30 feet long by 24 feet broad; and the vault was supported on a central pillar, from which radiated the six desks which

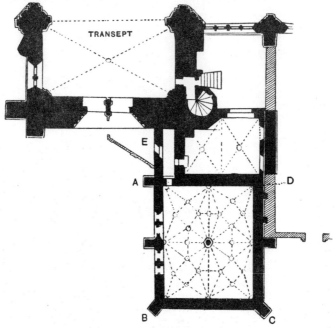

Fig. 46.   Plan of the Library at the south-east angle of the south transept of the Cathedral at Troyes.

A, B, C, D, Library; E, Entrance from vestibule in front of south transept door.   The room on the east side of this passage was used to keep records in.

contained the books (fig. 46). It was called *La Theologale*, because lectures on theology were given in it, as in the library at Salisbury. The desks were taken down in 1706, and the whole structure swept away in 1841—42, by the Departmental Architect, in the course of "a thorough restoration[1]."

At this point I cannot refrain from mentioning a somewhat anomalous library-foundation at Worcester, due to the zeal of

[1] *Voyage archéologique...dans le Département de l'Aube.*   A. F. Arnaud.   4to. Troyes 1837, pp. 161—163.

Bishop Carpenter (1444—76), though both structure and foundation have been long since swept away[1]. In 1464 he built and endowed a library in connexion with the charnel-house or chapel of S. Thomas, martyr, a detached building on the north side of the cathedral. The deed in which this foundation is recorded contains so many interesting particulars that I will state briefly the most important points insisted upon[2].

The Bishop begins by stating that by ancient arrangement the sacrist of the cathedral, assisted by a chaplain, is bound to celebrate mass daily in the charnel-house or chapel aforesaid, to keep it in repair, and to supply it with ornaments and vestments. For this purpose an annual endowment of 15 marks has been provided. He then describes his own foundation.

In accordance with the intention of his predecessors, and actuated by a desire to increase the knowledge of our holy faith, he has built a library in the aforesaid charnel-house, and caused certain books to be chained therein. Further, lest these volumes should be left uncared for, and so be damaged or abstracted, he has caused a dwelling-house for a master or keeper of the said books to be erected at the end of the said library; and he has conferred on the said keeper a new stipend, in addition to the old stipend of 15 marks.

This keeper must be a graduate in theology, and a good preacher. He is to live in the said chantry, and say mass daily in the chapel thereof. He is to take care of all the books in the library, which he is to open on every week-day for two hours before None, and for two hours after None, to all who wish to enter for the purpose of study. He is to explain hard and doubtful passages of scripture when asked to do so, and once in every week to deliver a public lecture in the library. Moreover on Holy Thursday he is to preach in the cathedral, or at the cross in the burial-ground.

Further, in order to prevent any book being alienated, or carried away, or stolen from the library, a tripartite list of all the books is to be made, wherein the true value of each is to be

---

[1] For the library belonging to the monastery see p. 108.

[2] The deed is copied in *MSS. Prattinton* (Soc. Ant. Lond.), Vol. VIII. p. 379. For this reference I have to thank the Rev. J. K. Floyer, M.A., librarian of Worcester Cathedral. See his *Thousand Years of a Cathedral Library* in the *Reliquary* for Jan. 1901, p. 7.

set down. One of these lists is to be retained by the Bishop, another by the sacrist, and a third by the keeper. Whenever a book is bequeathed or given to the library it is to be at once set down in this list together with its true value.

On the Friday after the feast of Relics (27 January) in each year, the sacrist and the keeper are carefully to compare the books with the list; and should any book have disappeared from the library through the carelessness of the keeper, he is to replace it or the value of it within one month, under a penalty of forty shillings, whereof twenty shillings is to be paid to the Bishop, and twenty shillings to the sacrist. When the aforesaid month has fully expired, the sacrist is to set apart out of his own salary a sum sufficient to pay the above fine, and to purchase and chain in the library as soon as possible another book of the same value and material.

The keeper is to receive from the sacrist an annual salary of ten pounds, and four yards of woollen cloth to make him a gown and hood.

The sacrist is to keep the chapel, library, books, and chains, together with the house built for the use of the keeper, in good repair; and he is, moreover, to find and maintain the vestments and lights required for the chapel. All these duties he is to swear on the Holy Gospels that he will faithfully perform.

My enumeration of Cathedral libraries would be sadly incomplete if I did not say a few words about the splendid structure which is attached to the Cathedral of Rouen[1]. The Chapter possessed a respectable collection of books at so early a date as 1120; this grew, and, 29 July, 1424, it was decided to build "a study or library (*quoddam studium seu vnam librariam*)," which was completed in 1428. Fifty years afterwards—in 1477— it was decided that the library should be extended. The first thought of the Chapter was that it should be built of wood, and the purchase of good stout timber (*bona et grossa ligna*)

---

[1] My principal authority for the history of the Chapter Library is the Minute-Book of the Dean and Chapter of Rouen Cathedral, now preserved in the Archives de la Ville at Rouen, where I had the pleasure of studying it in September, 1896. A summary of it is given in *Inventaire-Sommaire des Archives Départementales* (Seine Inférieure), 4to. Paris, 1874, Vol. II. I have also consulted *Recherches sur les Bibliothèques...de Rouen*, 8vo., 1853.

is ordered.   This plan, however, was evidently abandoned almost as soon as it was formed, for two years afterwards (20 April 1479) "the library lately erected" is mentioned. These words can only refer to the existing structure which is built wholly of stone.   A week later (28 April) William Pontis, master-mason, was asked to prepare a design for a staircase up to the library.   This he supplied on the following day.   In June of the same year the Chapter had a serious difference of opinion with him on the ground that he had altered the design and exceeded the estimate.   They came, however, to the wise conclusion that he should go on with the work and be requested to finish it with all dispatch.

In the following spring (20 March 1480) it was decided to prolong the library as far as the street; and in 1481 (18 September) to build the beautiful stone gate surmounted by a screen in open-work through which the court is now entered. This was completed by the end of 1482.   The whole structure had therefore occupied about five years in building.

The library, together with a building of older date next to the Cathedral which serves as a sort of vestibule to it, occupies the west side of what is still called, from the booksellers' shops which used to stand there, *La Cour des Libraires*.   The whole building measures 105 ft. in length, by 25 ft. in breadth.   The library proper is lighted by six windows in the east wall, and by two windows in the north wall.   The masonry of the wall under these windows and the two lancets by which it is pierced indicate that advantage had been taken of an earlier building to form the substructure of the library.   The west wall must always have been blank.   Access to the library was obtained directly from the transept by means of the beautiful stone staircase in two flights which Pontis built in 1479.   This staircase leads up to a door marked BIBLIOTHECA which opens into the vestibule above mentioned.   In 1788 a room was built over the library to contain the archives of the church, and the staircase was then ingeniously prolonged so as to reach the new second-floor.

Unfortunately the minutes of the Chapter tell us nothing about the original fittings of this room[1].   In 1718 the books

---

[1] The Canons held a long debate, 28 May, 1479, "de ambonibus seu lutrinis in nova libraria fiendis et collocandis"; but finally decided to use the furniture of the old library for the present.

C. L.   9

were kept in cupboards protected by wire-work, over which were
the portraits of benefactors to the library[1].

At present the archives have disappeared; the few books
that remain have replaced them in the upper storey, and the
library is used as a second vestry. The illustration (fig. 47)
shews the interior of the *Cour des Libraires*, with the beautiful gate of entrance from the street. The library occupies the
first floor. Beneath are the arches under which the shops used
to be arranged; and above is the library of 1788.

---

[1] *Voyage Liturgique de la France*, par Le Sieur de Moléon, 1718, p. 268. I have
to thank Dr James for this quotation.

Fig. 47. Interior of the *Cour des Libraires*, Rouen, shewing the gate of entrance from the street, and the Library.

CHAPTER IV.

THE FITTINGS OF MONASTIC LIBRARIES AND OF COLLEGIATE
LIBRARIES PROBABLY IDENTICAL. ANALYSIS OF SOME
LIBRARY-STATUTES. MONASTIC INFLUENCE AT THE
UNIVERSITIES. NUMBER OF BOOKS OWNED BY COLLEGES.
THE COLLEGIATE LIBRARY. BISHOP COBHAM'S LIBRARY
AT OXFORD. LIBRARY AT QUEENS' COLLEGE, CAMBRIDGE.
AT ZUTPHEN. THE LECTERN SYSTEM. CHAINING OF
BOOKS. FURTHER EXAMPLES AND ILLUSTRATIONS.

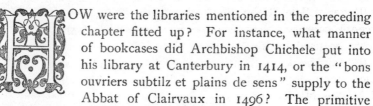OW were the libraries mentioned in the preceding
chapter fitted up? For instance, what manner
of bookcases did Archbishop Chichele put into
his library at Canterbury in 1414, or the "bons
ouvriers subtilz et plains de sens" supply to the
Abbat of Clairvaux in 1496? The primitive
book-presses have long ago been broken up; and the medieval
devices that succeeded them have had no better fate. This
dearth of material need not, however, discourage us. We have,
I think, the means of discovering with tolerable certainty what
monastic fittings must have been, by comparing the bookcases
which still exist in a more or less perfect form in the libraries
of Oxford and Cambridge with such monastic catalogues as give
particulars of arrangement and not merely lists of books.

The collegiate system was in no sense monastic, indeed it
was to a certain extent established to counteract monastic
influence; but it is absurd to suppose that the younger communities would borrow nothing from the elder—especially
when we reflect that the monastic system, as inaugurated by

S. Benedict, had completed at least seven centuries of successful existence before Walter de Merton was moved to found a
college, and that many of the subsequent founders of colleges
were more or less closely connected with monasteries. Further,
as we have seen that study was specially enjoined upon monks
by S. Benedict, it is precisely in the direction of study that we
might expect to find features common to the two sets of communities. And, in fact, an examination of the statutes affecting
the library in the codes imposed upon some of the earlier
colleges at Oxford and Cambridge, leads us irresistibly to the
conclusion that they were derived from monastic Customs,
using the word in its technical sense, and monastic practice.
The resemblances are too striking to be accidental.

I shall therefore, in the next place, review, as briefly as I
can, the statutes of some of the above colleges, taking them in
chronological order[1]; and I shall translate some passages from
them.

But first let me mention that the principle of lending books
to students under a pledge was accepted by the University of
Oxford many years before colleges were founded. It is recorded
that Roger L'Isle, Dean of York, in the early part of the
thirteenth century, "bestowed several exemplars of the holy
Bible to be used by the Scholars of Oxford under a pledge";
that the said books, with others, were "locked up in chests, or
chained upon desks in S. Mary's Chancel and Church to be
used by the Masters upon leave first obtained"; that certain
officers were appointed to keep the keys of these chests, and to
receive the pledges from those that borrowed the books; and
that the books were so kept "till the library over the Congregation House was built, and then being taken out, were set
up in pews or studies digested according to Faculties, chained,
and had a keeper appointed over them[2]."

---

[1] The Statutes of the Colleges of Oxford and Cambridge bearing on the care of
books have been thoroughly analysed by Professor Willis in his essay on "The
Library," *Arch. Hist.* III. pp. 387—471, which I edited and completed. I have
therefore not thought it necessary to acknowledge each quotation separately, but I
wish it to be understood that this section of my present book is to a great extent
borrowed from him.

[2] Wood, *History and Antiquities of the University of Oxford*, ed. Gutch, 4to.
Oxford, 1796, Vol. II. Part 2, p. 910.

In the statutes of Merton College, Oxford, 1274, the teacher of grammar (*grammaticus*) is to be supplied with a sufficient number of books out of the funds of the House, but no other mention of books occurs therein[1]. The explanatory ordinances, however, given in 1276 by Robert Kilwardby (Archbishop of Canterbury 1273—79), direct that the books of the community are to be kept under three locks, and to be assigned by the warden and sub-warden to the use of the Fellows under sufficient pledge[2]. In the second statutes of University College (1292), it is provided, "that no Fellow shall alienate, sell, pawn, hire, lett, or grant, any House, Rent, Money, Book, or other Thing, without the Consent of all the Fellows"; and further, with special reference to the Library:

Every Book of the House, now given, or hereafter to be given, shall have a high value set upon it when it is borrowed, in order that he that has it may be more fearful lest he lose it; and let it be lent by an Indenture, whereof one part is to be kept in the common Chest, and the other with him that has the Book: And let no Book, belonging to the House, be lent out of the College, without a Pawn better (than the Book), and this with the Consent of all the Fellows.

Let there be put one Book of every Sort that the House has, in some common and secure Place; that the Fellows, and others with the Consent of a Fellow, may for the Future have the Benefit of it.

Every Opponent in Theology, or Reader of the Sentences, or a Regent that commonly reads (*regens et legens communiter*), when he wants it, shall have any necessary Book, that the House has, lent to him Gratis; and when he has done with it, let him restore it to that Fellow, who had formerly made choice of it[3].

The statutes of Oriel College, dated 1329, lay down the following rules for the management of books:

The common books (*communes libri*) of the House are to be brought out and inspected once a year, on the feast of the Commemoration of Souls [2 November], in presence of the Provost or his deputy, and of the Scholars [Fellows].

Every one of them in turn, in order of seniority, may select a single book which either treats of the science to which he is devoting himself,

---

[1] *Commiss. Docts.* (Oxford), Vol. I. Statutes of Merton College, Cap. 2, p. 24.

[2] *Sketch of the Life of Walter de Merton*, by Edmund [Hobhouse], Bishop of Nelson, New Zealand, 8vo. Oxford, 1859, p. 39.

[3] *Annals of University College*, by Wm. Smith, 8vo. 1728, pp. 37—39. I have compared Mr Smith's version with the Statute as printed by Anstey, *Munimenta Academica*, I. 58, 59, and have made a few corrections.

or which he requires for his use. This he may keep, if he please, until the same festival in the succeeding year, when a similar selection of books is to take place, and so on, from year to year.

If there should happen to be more books than persons, those that remain are to be selected in the same manner[1].

The last clause plainly shews how small the number of the books must have been when the statute was written. Their safety was subsequently secured by an ordinance of the Provost and Scholars, which, by decree of the Visitor, dated 13 May, 1441, received the authority of a statute. The high value set upon the books is shewn by the extreme stringency of the penalties imposed for wilful loss or failure of restitution. After describing the annual assemblage of the Provost and Fellows, as directed in the former statute, the new enactment proceeds as follows:

Any person who absents himself on that day, so that the books selected by him are neither produced nor restored; or who, being present, refuses to produce or to restore them; or who refuses to pay the full value, if, without any fraud or deception on his part, it should happen that any one of them be missing; is to be deprived of all right of selecting books for that year; and any person who wittingly defers the aforesaid production or restitution till Christmas next ensuing, shall, *ipso facto*, cease to be a Fellow.

Further, any scholar who has pawned or alienated, contrary to the common consent of the college, any book or object of value (*jocale*) belonging to the college; or who has even suggested, helped, or favoured, such pawning or alienation, shall, *ipso facto*, cease to be a member of the Society[2].

The statutes of Peterhouse, Cambridge, dated 1344, class the books of the Society with the charters and the muniments, and prescribe the following rules for their safe custody:

In order that the books which are the common property of the House (*communes libri*), the charters, and the muniments, may be kept in safe custody, we appoint and ordain that an indenture be drawn up of the whole of them in the presence of at least the major part of the scholars, expressing what the books are, and to what faculty they belong; of which indenture one part is to be deposited with the Master, the other with the Deans, as a record of the transaction.

The aforesaid books, charters, and muniments are to be placed in one or more common chests, each having two locks, one key of which shall for greater security be deposited with the Master, the other with the Senior Dean, who shall cause the books to be distributed to those

---

[1] *Commiss. Docts.* (Oxford), Vol. I. Statutes of Oriel College, p. 14.
[2] *Ibid.* p. 22.

scholars who have need of them, in the manner which has been more fully set forth in the section which treats of the office of the Deans[1].

The section referred to prescribes that the Deans

are to distribute them [the books] to the scholars in such manner as shall appear to them expedient; and further, they shall, if they think proper, make each scholar take an oath that he will not alienate any book so borrowed, but will take all possible care of it, and restore it to the Master and Dean, at the expiration of the appointed time[2].

In 1473 Dr John Warkworth became Master. He was evidently a lover of books, for he gave to the Library fifty-five volumes, which he protected, after the fashion of an earlier age, by invoking a curse upon him who should alienate them. Moreover, during his Mastership, in 1480, the College enacted or adopted a special statute headed, *De libris Collegii*, which may be thus translated:

In the name of God, Amen. As books are the most precious treasure of scholars, concerning which there ought to be the most diligent care and forethought, lest, as heretofore, they fall to decay or be lost, it is hereby appointed, settled, and ordained, by the Master and Fellows of the House or College of S. Peter in Cambridge, that no book which has been chained in the library there shall be taken away from, or removed out of, the library, except by special assent and consent of the Master and all the resident Fellows of the aforesaid College—it being understood that by resident Fellows a majority of the whole Society is meant.

Provided always that no book which has been given to the library on condition of being kept perpetually chained therein shall, by virtue of this statute, be on any pretence removed from it, except only when it needs repair.

Provided also that every book in the library which is to be selected and distributed shall have a certain value set upon it by the Master and the two Deans, and that indentures shall be drawn up recording the same.

Once in every two years, in the Michaelmas Term, a fresh selection and distribution shall be held of every book which is not chained in the Library—the precise day to be fixed by the Master and the Senior Dean.

No book so selected and distributed shall pass the night out of College, except by permission of the Master and the President and the other Dean who is not President; provided always that the said book be not kept out of the College for six months in succession.

---

[1] *Commiss. Docts.* (Cambridge), II. 38. De omnibus libris Domus, Munimentis, et Chartis custodiendis.

[2] *Ibid.* p. 17. De Duobus Decanis et eorum officio.

If it should happen that a given book be not brought in and produced on the aforesaid day of fresh selection and distribution, then the person who is responsible for it shall pay to the Master, or in his absence to the Senior Dean, the full value of the said absent book, under pain of being put out of commons until it be restored.

Every Fellow who is not present on the aforesaid day shall appoint a deputy, who shall be prepared to bring in any books which may have been lent to him, on the day when a fresh distribution is to take place, under pain of being put out of commons[1].

The statutes given in 1350 to Trinity Hall, Cambridge, by the Founder William Bateman (Bishop of Norwich 1344—56), contain rules which are more stringent than those already quoted, and were evidently written in contemplation of a more considerable collection of volumes. A list of the books which he himself presented to Trinity Hall is appended to his statutes, and a special chapter (*De libris collegii*) is allotted to the Library. This may be translated as follows:

On the days appointed for the general audit of accounts [in the Michaelmas and Easter Terms] all the books which have been received, or shall be received in future, either from our own liberality, or from the pious largess of others, are to be laid out separately before the Master and all the resident Fellows in such manner that each volume may be clearly seen; by which arrangement it will become evident twice in each year whether any book has been lost or taken away.

No book belonging to the aforesaid College may ever at any time be sold, given away, exchanged, or alienated, under any excuse or pretext; nor may it be lent to anybody except a member of the College; nor may it be entrusted in quires, for the purpose of making a copy, to any member of the College, or to any stranger, either within the precincts of the Hall or beyond them; nor may it be carried by the Master, or any one else, out of the Town of Cambridge, or out of the aforesaid Hall or Hostel, either whole or in quires, except to the Schools; provided always that no book pass the night out of College, unless it be necessary to bind it or to repair it; and when this happens, it is to be brought back to College as soon as possible after the completion of the binding or the repair.

Moreover, all the books of the College are to be kept in some safe room, to be assigned for the College Library, so that all the Scholars of the College may have common access to them. We give leave, however, that the poor scholars of the college may have the loan of books containing the texts of Canon and Civil Law for their private use for a certain time, to be fixed at the discretion of the Master and the three Senior Fellows, provided they be not taken out of College; but the books of the Doctors of Civil and Canon Law are to remain continuously in the

[1] *Commiss. Docts.* (Cambridge), II. 44. Statutum de libris Collegii.

said Library Chamber, fastened with iron chains for the common use of the Fellows[1].

It is evident that this statute was regarded as a full and satisfactory expression of what was required, for it is repeated, with additions or omissions to suit the taste of the respective founders, in the statutes of New College (1400), All Souls' (1443), Magdalen (1479), Corpus Christi (1517), Brasenose (1521), Cardinal College (1527) and S. John's College (1555), at Oxford; and in those of King's College, Cambridge.

Among these changes a few are sufficiently important to require special notice. At New College William of Wykeham allows students in civil law and canon law to keep two text-books "for their own special use during the whole time they devote themselves to those faculties in our College, provided they do not possess such books of their own"; the "remaining text-books, should any be left over, and also the glosses or commentaries of the Doctors of civil and canon law, may be lent to the persons belonging to those faculties by the method of annual selection, as in the other faculties"; the "books which remain unassigned after the Fellows have made their selection are to be fastened with iron chains, and remain in the Common Library for the use of the Fellows[2]"; the wishes of donors, whether expressed by will or during their lifetime, are to be respected; and, lastly, the safety of the Library is to be secured by three locks, two large, and one small, of the kind called "a clickett." The keys of the two former are to be kept by the Senior Dean and the Bursar respectively; of the clickett each Fellow is to have a separate key. At night the door is to be carefully locked with all three keys[3].

At All Souls' College, the founder, Henry Chichele (Archbishop of Canterbury 1414—43), makes the books to be chained the subjects of definite choice. The principle of an annual selection is maintained, except for "those books which, in obedience to the will of the donors, or the injunction of the Warden, the Vice-Warden, and the Deans, are to be chained

---

[1] *Commiss. Docts.* (Cambridge), II. 432. De libris Collegii.

[2] The words are "in libraria communi...ad sociorum communem usum continue remanere."

[3] *Commiss. Docts.* (Oxford), Vol. I. Statutes of New College, p. 97. De libris collegii conservandis et non alienandis.

for the common use of the Fellows and Scholars." Further, the preparation of a catalogue is specially enjoined. Every book is to be entered in a register by the first word of the second leaf, and every book given to the Library is to bear the name of the donor on the second leaf, or in some other convenient position. The books are to be inspected once in every year, after which the distribution, as provided for by Bateman and Wykeham, is to take place. Each Fellow who borrows a book is to have a small indenture drawn up containing the title according to the first word of the second leaf, and an acknowledgment that he has received it. These small indentures are to be left in charge of the Warden, or, in his absence, of the Vice-Warden[1].

In the statutes of Magdalen College, the founder, William Waynflete (Bishop of Winchester 1447—87), maintains the provisions of Wykeham and Chichele, but introduces an injunction of his own, to the effect that every Fellow or Scholar who uses the Library is to shut the book he has consulted before he leaves and also the windows ; and the last to use the Library at night is to go through the whole room and see that all the windows are shut and not to leave the door open—under a severe penalty[2].

At Corpus Christi College, the founder, Richard Fox (Bishop of Winchester 1501—28), insists upon safeguards against the indiscriminate chaining of books:

No book is to be brought into the Library or chained there, unless it be of suitable value and utility, or unless the will of the donor have so directed ; and none is to be taken out of it, unless it so happen that there be there already a considerable number on the same subject, or that another copy in better condition and of greater value, to take its place, have been presented by some benefactor.

By this means those books which are of greater value, or which contain material of greater utility to students in each Faculty, will be stored up in the Library ; while those which are not fit for the Library, or of which a sufficient number of copies already exist in it, may be distributed to the Fellows of the College, according to the system of indentures between the borrower and the President, or in his absence the Vice-President, or one of the Deans[3].

---

[1] *Commiss. Docts.* (Oxford), Vol. I. Statutes of All Souls' College, p. 54. De custodia bonorum ad capellam pertinentium.

[2] *Ibid.* Vol. II. Statutes of Magdalen College, p. 60. De custodia librorum, ornamentorum, jocalium, et aliorum bonorum collegii.

[3] *Ibid.* Statutes of Corpus Christi College, p. 89. De custodia bonorum Collegii.

The Bishop was evidently afraid that the Library should be overcrowded, for he even allows books to be sold, in the event of their becoming so numerous as to be no longer of use to the Fellows for the purpose of being borrowed.

Lastly I will translate the following College Order or Statute which was in force at Pembroke College, Cambridge. Unfortunately it is without date, but from internal evidence may take rank with some of the earliest enactments already quoted.

Let there be in the aforesaid House a Keeper of the Books, who shall take under his charge all the books belonging to the community, and once in each year, namely on the feast of the Translation of S. Thomas the Martyr [7 July], or at the latest within the eight days immediately following, let him render to the community an account of the same, by exhibiting each book in order to the Master and Fellows.

The inspection having been made, after the Fellows have deliberated, let him distribute them to each Fellow in proportion to his requirements. And let the said Keeper have ready large pieces of board (*tabulas magnas*), covered with wax and parchment, that the titles of the books may be written on the parchment, and the names of the Fellows who hold them on the wax beside it. When they have brought their books back, their names shall be erased, and their responsibility for the books shall come to an end, the keeper remaining liable. So shall he never be in ignorance about any book or its borrower.

No book is to be taken away or lent out of the House on any pretext whatever, except upon some occasion which may appear justifiable to the major part of the community; and then, if any book be lent, let a proper pledge be taken for it which shall be honourably exhibited to the Keeper[1].

Let us consider, in the next place, what points of library-management have been brought into the most prominent relief by the above analysis of College statutes. We find that the "Common Books" of the House—by which phrase the books intended for the common use of the inmates are meant—are placed on the same footing as the charters, muniments, and valuables (*jocalia*). They are to be kept in a chest or chests secured by two or three locks requiring the presence of the same number of officials to open them. These volumes may not be borrowed indiscriminately, but each Scholar (Fellow)

---

[1] This passage is quoted in a short account of Pembroke College Library, drawn up by Matthew Wren, D.D., while Fellow, as the preface to a volume dated 1617, in which he recorded the names of those who had presented books to the Library. The words at the end of the statute are: "sub cautione idonea custodi librorum exposita sine fraude."

may choose the book he wants, and write a formal acknowledgment that he has received it, and that he is bound to restore
it or pay the value of it, under a severe penalty. Once a year
the whole collection is to be audited in the presence of the
Master of the College and all the Fellows, when a fresh
distribution is to be made. The books not so borrowed are to
be put in "some common and secure place"; an arrangement
which was subsequently developed into a selection of books
required for reference, and the chaining of them in "the Library
Chamber for the common use of the Fellows."

The Register of Merton College, Oxford, contains many
interesting entries which shew that these directions respecting
the choice and loan of books were faithfully observed. I will
translate a few of them[1]:

On the twenty-fourth day of October [1483] choice was made of
the books on philosophy by the Fellows studying philosophy.
On the eleventh day of November [1483], in the Warden's lodging,
choice was made of the books on theology by the Fellows studying
theology[2].
On the eighteenth day of March [1497] choice of books on logic
was held in the Common Hall[3].

The next entry is particularly valuable, as it proves that all
the books on a given subject, no matter how numerous, were
occasionally distributed :

On the twenty-sixth day of the same month [August, 1500] choice
was made of the books on philosophy. It was found that there were in
all 349 books, which were then distributed among the Fellows studying
philosophy[4].

In 1498 (14 December) the Warden wished to borrow a

---

[1] The history of Merton College has been most admirably written, in Mr Robinson's
series of College histories, by my friend Bernard W. Henderson, M.A., Fellow and
Librarian. His researches have thrown a new light on the library, and especially on
the date of the fittings. My most cordial thanks are due to him, to the Warden and
to the Bursar, for their kindness in allowing me access to the library, and also to all
the documents referring to it.

[2] *Reg. Vet.* fol. 7 b. Vicesimo quarto die Octobris celebrata erat eleccio librorum
philosophie inter philosophicos collegii socios.

Undecimo die mensis Novembris celebrata erat eleccio librorum theologie in domo
custodis inter Theologos collegii socios.

[3] *Ibid.* fol. 110. 18°. die eiusdem mensis [Marcii] fuit eleccio librorum logicalium
in Alta Aula.

[4] *Ibid.* fol. 125 b.

book from the library, whereupon a record of the following formalities was drawn up[1]:

On the same day a book of College Orders (on the second leaf *ter posita*) was taken out of the library with the consent of all the Fellows. And leave was given to the Warden, in the presence of the four senior Fellows, to make use of it for a season. As a caution for this book the aforesaid Warden deposited a certain other book, viz. S. Jerome's commentary on Matthew and the Epistles of Paul (on the second leaf *sunt*). This book lay in our possession as caution for the other book of College Orders[2]; but, because this book was an insufficient caution, there was deposited with it as a supplementary caution another book, namely: Jerome on Isaiah, Jeremiah, and Ezekiel.

The Warden kept the book for a year, at the expiration of which we find the following entry[3]:

On the last day but one of the same month [1499] the Warden returned to the Vice-Warden the book of College Orders (on the second leaf *ter posita*) which he had had out of the library for his own use for a season on depositing a sufficient caution.
Whereupon the Vice-Warden returned to him his cautions, namely, the commentary of S. Jerome on Matthew (second leaf *sunt*), and another, namely, S. Jerome's exposition of Isaiah, Jeremiah, and Ezekiel (second leaf, *Audi cela*).

Lastly, I will quote a record of the solemn reception of a gift to the library:

On the same day [2 August, 1493] a handsome book was given to the College through John Godehew, Bachelor, by two venerable men, Robert Aubrey and Robert Feyld, to be chained in the common library of the House for the perpetual use of those studying in it. It is Hugh of Vienne on the Apocalypse, on the second leaf *quod possessio eius*. Let us therefore pray for them[4].

These provisions savour of the cloister. The "common books" represent the "common press (*armarium commune*)" with which we are so familiar there; the double or triple locks with which the book-chests are secured recall the rules for safeguarding the said press; the annual audit and distribution of books is directed in Lanfranc's statutes for English Benedictines; the borrowing under a pledge, or at least after an entry made

---

[1] *Reg. Vet.* fol. 118.

[2] The words are: "qui quidem liber jacuit pro caucione alterius libri decretorum collegii."

[3] *Ibid.* fol. 121.

[4] *Ibid.* fol. 100 b.

by the Librarian on his roll of the name of the book and the
name of the brother who borrowed it, was universal in monasteries; and the setting apart of certain books in a separate
room to which access was readily permitted became a necessity
in the larger and more literary Houses. Lastly, the commemoration of donors of books is specially enjoined by the
Augustinians[1].

This close similarity between monastic and secular rules
need not surprise us. I have shewn in the preceding chapter
how faithfully the Benedictine rules for study were obeyed by
all the Monastic Orders; and I know not from what other
source directions for library-management could have been
obtained. Besides, in some cases the authors of the rules which
I have been considering must themselves have had experience
of monastic libraries. Walter de Merton is said to have been
educated in an Augustinian Priory at Merton; Hugh de
Balsham, founder of Peterhouse, was Bishop of Ely; William
Bateman, whose library-statute was so widely applied, had been
educated in the Benedictine Priory at Norwich, and his brother
was an abbat; Henry Chichele was Archbishop of Canterbury, where, as I have shewn, a very extensive collection of
books had been got together, to contain which worthily he
himself built a library.

Secondly, monastic influence was brought directly to bear
on both Universities through student-monks; and at Oxford,
which was specially selected as the University for monastic
colleges, the Benedictines founded Gloucester House, now
Worcester College, so early as 1283. This college had a library,
on the south side of the chapel, which was built and stocked
with books at the sole charge of John Whethamstede, Abbat
of S. Albans[2]—whose work in connexion with the library of
that House has been already recorded[3]. Durham College,
maintained by the Benedictines of Durham, was supplied with
books from the mother-house, lists of which have been preserved[4]; and subsequently a library was built there to contain

---

[1] See above, p. 71.
[2] Dugdale, *Mon. Angl.* IV. 403—406.
[3] See above, p. 108.
[4] *Cat. Vet. Libr. Eccl. Cath. Dunelm.* ed. Surtees Soc. pp. 39—41.

the collection bequeathed in 1345 by Richard de Bury (Bishop of Durham 1333—45)[1]. Lastly, Leland tells us that at Canterbury College in the same University the whole furniture of the library (*tota bibliothecæ supellex*) was transferred from the House of Christ Church, Canterbury[2]. It is, I submit, quite inconceivable that the fittings supplied to these libraries could have been different from those commonly used in the monasteries of S. Albans, Durham, and Canterbury.

Further, it should be noted that the erection of a library proper was an afterthought in many of the older colleges, as it had been in the monasteries. For instance, at Merton College, Oxford, founded 1264, the library was not begun till 1377; at University College, founded 1280, in 1440; at Balliol College, founded 1282, in 1431; at Oriel College, founded 1324, in 1444; at Pembroke College, Cambridge, founded 1347, in 1452. William of Wykeham, who founded New College, Oxford, in 1380, was the first to include a library in his quadrangle; and, after the example had been set by him, the plan of every subsequent college includes a library of sufficient dimensions to last till the Reformation, if not till the present day.

The above dates, covering as they do at least two-thirds of the fifteenth century, shew that the collegiate libraries were being built at the same time as the monastic. This coincidence of date, taken in conjunction with the coincidences in enactment which I have already pointed out, seems to me to supply an additional argument in support of my theory that the internal fittings of collegiate and monastic libraries would be identical. Besides, no forms are so persistent as those of pieces of furniture. A workman, once instructed to make a thing in a particular way, carries out his instructions to the letter, and transmits them to his descendants.

Before we consider what these fittings were, I will briefly deal with some other questions affecting collegiate libraries, as, for instance, their size, position, and general arrangement. And first, as regards the number of books to be accommodated.

It happens, unfortunately, that very few catalogues have been

---

[1] Wood, *History etc.*, Vol. II. p. 910.

[2] Leland, *Comm. de Script. Brit.* ch. 131. I owe this important quotation to the kindness of Dr James.

preserved of the libraries referred to in the above statutes; but, if we may estimate the extent of the remainder from those of which we have some account, we shall see that the number of volumes contained in a collegiate library must have been extremely small. For instance, the catalogue[1] appended to Bishop Bateman's statutes, dated 1350, enumerates eighty-four volumes, classed under the following subjects, in two divisions[2], viz. those presented to the College for the immediate use of the Fellows (*A*); and those reserved for the Bishop's own use during his life (*B*):

	A	*B*
Books on Civil Law	7	3
Books on Canon Law	19	13
Books on Theology	3	25
Books for the Chapel	7	7
	36	48

At King's Hall, in 1394, eighty-seven volumes only are enumerated[3]; and even in the University Library not more than 122 volumes were recorded in 1424[4]. They were distributed as follows:

[Books on General Theology][5]	54
Books on Scholastic Theology (*Theologia disputata*) .	15
Books on Moral Philosophy	5
Books on Natural Philosophy	12
Books on Medicine (*medicinalis philosophia*) . .	5
Books on Logic	1
Books on Poetry	0
Libri sophisticales	1
Books on Grammar	6
Books on History (*Libri cronicales*)	0
Books on Canon Law	23
Total	122

[1] Printed in the *Camb. Antiq. Soc. Comm.*, Vol. II. p. 73.

[2] The headings of the two lists are as follows: "Libri per nos de presenti dicto nostro Collegio dati et in dicto Collegio ex nunc ad Sociorum communem usum perpetuo remansuri."

"Libri vero de presenti per nos dicto collegio dati, quorum usum nobis pro vitæ nostræ tempore quamdiu nobis placuerit duximus reservandum, immediate inferius describuntur."

[3] *Arch. Hist.* Vol. II. p. 442. History of Trinity College.

[4] *Collected Papers of Henry Bradshaw*, 8vo. Camb., 1889, pp. 19—34.

[5] No heading to the first division of the list is given in the catalogue.

The catalogue of the Library of Queens' College, dated 1472, enumerates one hundred and ninety-nine volumes[1]; the second catalogue of the University Library, dated 1473, three hundred and thirty volumes[2]; an early catalogue of the library of S. Catharine's Hall, one hundred and four volumes, of which eighty-five were given by the Founder[3]; and a catalogue of the old library of King's College, dated 1453, one hundred and seventy-four volumes. In these catalogues the books are not directly classed under heads, but arranged roughly, according to subject, in their respective cases[4].

At Peterhouse in 1418 we find a somewhat larger collection, namely, three hundred and eighty volumes, divided among seventeen subjects. The general heading of the catalogue[5] states that it contains "all the books belonging to the house of S. Peter in Cambridge, both those which are chained in the library, those which are divided among the Fellows, and those of which some are intended to be sold, while certain others are laid up in chests within the aforesaid house." This language shews that by the time the catalogue was made the collection had been divided into books for the use of the Fellows (*libri distribuendi*) and books chained in the library (*libri cathenati in libraria*); in other words, into a lending library and a library of reference. We are not told how this division had been made, or at what time; but it is evident that by 1418 it had become permanent, and no longer depended on the tastes or studies of the Fellows. There was one set of books for them to select from, and another for them to refer to; but the two were quite distinct[6].

In the next place I will analyse the catalogue in order to shew what subjects were represented, and how many volumes

[1] *Camb. Ant. Soc. Comm.*, Vol. II. p. 165.

[2] *Ibid.* Vol. II. p. 258.

[3] *Camb. Ant. Soc. Quarto Publ.*, No. 1. This catalogue represents the state of the library at the end of the fifteenth century, for it contains the books given by Richard Nelson, who founded a Fellowship in 1503, and probably gave his books at the same time, "sub ea condicione quod semper remanerent cum tribus sociis."

[4] From my additions to the essay on "The Library," by Professor Willis, p. 404.

[5] This catalogue, written at the beginning of the old parchment Register of the College, has been printed by Dr James in his *Catalogue of the MSS. in the Library of Peterhouse.* 8vo. Camb., 1899, pp. 3—26.

[6] From my additions to the essay on "The Library," by Professor Willis, p. 402.

there were in each. And first of the contents of the library of reference:

Libri theologie cathenati	61
Isti sunt libri Naturalis Philosophie cathenati in librario	26
Libri Metaphisice	3
„ Moralis Philosophie	5
„ Astronomie	13
„ Alkenemie	1
„ Arsmetrice	1
„ Musice	1
„ Geometrie	1
„ Rethorice	1
„ Logice	5
„ Gramatice	6
„ Poetrie cathenati	4
„ De Cronicis cathenati	4
„ Medicine cathenati	15
„ Iuris Ciuilis cathenati	9
„ Iuris Canonici cathenati	18
Ex dono ducis exonie	1
„ M. Joh. Sauage	2
Libros subscriptos donavit Mag. Edm. Kyrketon .	7
„ contulit M. W. Lichfeld	2
Ex dono M. W. Redyct	4
Libros subscriptos contulit M. Joh. Fayre . .	3
„ contulit M. Will. More	13
„ „ M. John Ledes	14
	220

The books that were to be divided among the Fellows are classed as follows:

Libri theologie assignati sociis	63
„ Philosophie Naturalis Metaphisice et Moralis diuisi inter socios	19
„ Logice diuisi inter socios	15
„ Poetrie et Gramatice assignati sociis . .	13
„ Medicine	3
„ Iuris Ciuilis diusi inter socios . . .	20
„ „ Canonici diuidendi inter socios . .	19
„ empti ad usum…sociorum collegii cum pecuniis eiusdem collegii	8
	160

In framing these tables I have included among the *Libri cathenati* those specially presented to the College, 46 in number; but I have not attempted to sort them according to subject. I have also assumed that any book or books representing a given class, if not represented in the lending library, as Astronomy, Arithmetic, Music, etc., would be chained for reference. The number of this class, 220, if added to the 160 of the other class, gives the required total, 380.

In addition to these tables it will be interesting to construct a third, containing the subject and number of the books represented in both collections:

	Chained	Lent
Theology	61	63
Natural Philosophy	26	
Metaphysics	3	19
Moral Philosophy	5	
Logic	5	15
Grammar	6	
Poetry	4	13
Medicine	15	3
Civil Law	9	20
Canon Law	18	19
	152	152

The subjects of the books included in this latter table represent, in a very clear and interesting way, the studies pursued at Peterhouse in the 14th and 15th centuries. It is prescribed by the statutes, dated 1344, that the scholars are to study Arts, Aristotelian Philosophy, or Theology; but that they are to apply themselves to the course in Arts until, in the judgment of the Master and Fellows, or at least of the larger and wiser portion of that body, they are sufficiently instructed to proceed to the study of Theology[1]. Two may study Civil Law or Canon Law, but no more at the same time; and one may study Medicine[2]. For both these lines of study special leave is required.

The course of Arts comprised Grammar, Logic, Aristotle, Arithmetic, Music, Geometry, and Astronomy. In the first of these, including Poetry, the lending library contained more volumes than the reference library; in Logic it had three times

---

[1] *Commiss. Docts.* (Cambridge), Vol. I. p. 21. Stat. 24.   [2] *Ibid.* p. 22.

as many; in Philosophy (Aristotle and his commentators) it was well supplied; but, on the other hand, Music, Geometry and Astronomy were wholly wanting. Theology is represented by 63 volumes as against 61 in the reference library; Civil Law by 20 volumes against 9 in the reference library; and Canon Law by 19 against 18. In Medicine, however, there were only 3 against 15. By a curious coincidence the number of volumes in the two collections dealing with the subjects represented in both is the same. The subject most in request, as might have been expected, was Theology. Next to this come Civil Law and Canon Law. Medicine was evidently unpopular. I have no explanation to offer for the curious fact that Arithmetic, Music, Geometry, and Rhetoric are represented by only a single volume apiece in the library of reference[1].

These examples, which there is no reason to regard as exceptional, are sufficient to shew that an ordinary chamber would be large enough to contain all the volumes possessed by a college, even after some of the more generally useful books of reference had been chained to desks for the resort of students.

It has been already shewn that what Professor Willis calls "a real library—that is to say, a room expressly contrived for the purpose of containing books[2]"—was not introduced into the plan of colleges for more than a century after their first foundation. He points out that such rooms can be at once recognised by their equidistant windows, which do not, as a rule, differ from those of the ordinary chambers, except that they are separated by much smaller intervals. Examples of this arrangement are still to be seen at S. John's College, Jesus College, and Queens' College, Cambridge; but perhaps the most characteristic specimen of all is that which was built over the Hall at Pembroke College in the same University, by Laurence Booth (Master 1450—1480), the aspect of which has been preserved in Loggan's print, here reproduced (fig. 48)[3].

The upper chamber (solarium) which Thomas Cobham (Bishop of Worcester 1317—27) began to build over the old

[1] This analysis of the catalogue of Peterhouse Library is borrowed from the Introduct'on which I had the pleasure of contributing to my friend Dr James' Catalogue.

[2] Arch. Hist., The Library, p. 404.   [3] Arch. Hist., vol. i., p. 138.

Fig. 48. Pembroke College, Cambridge, reduced from Loggan's print, taken about 1688.

A, Chapel; B, Library; C, Hall; D, Master's Lodge; E, Kitchen; F, Master's Garden; G, Fellows' Garden.

Congregation House on the north side of S. Mary's Church, Oxford, about 1320, for the reception of the books which he intended to present to the University, is the earliest of these

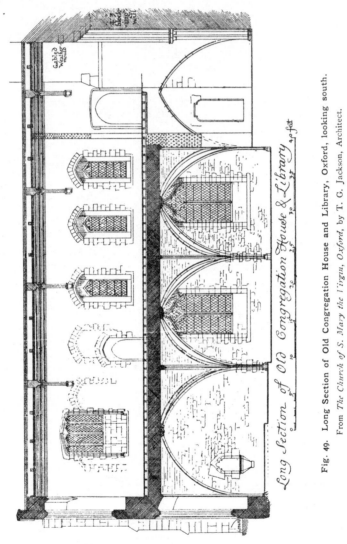

Fig. 49. Long Section of Old Congregation House and Library, Oxford, looking south.

From *The Church of S. Mary the Virgin, Oxford*, by T. G. Jackson, Architect.

libraries in existence. It still retains on the south side part of a range of equidistant single-light windows of the simplest character, which, as just stated, mark the destination of the

apartment. This room is about forty-five feet long by eighteen
feet broad, and, in its original state, had probably seven single-
light windows on each side, and a window of two lights
at the east end[1] (fig. 49). A long controversy between the
University and Oriel College rendered the benefaction useless
for more than forty years; and it was not until 1367 that the
University passed a statute directing that Bishop Cobham's
books are to be chained, in proper order; and that the Scholars
who wish to use them are to have free access to them at convenient hours (*temporibus opportunis*). Lastly, certain volumes,
of greater value, are to be sold, to the value of forty pounds,
or more, if a larger sum can be obtained for them, for the
purpose of purchasing an annual rent-charge of sixty shillings,
to be paid to a chaplain, who is to pray for the soul of the
aforesaid Thomas Cobham, and other benefactors; and who is
to take charge of the books given by him and them, and of
all other books heretofore given, or hereafter to be given,
to the University[2]. The passing of this statute may probably
be regarded as the first institution of the office of University
Librarian. Notwithstanding this statute, however, the University did not obtain peaceful possession of their library until 1410,
when the controversy was finally extinguished by the good
offices of their Chancellor, Richard Courtenay[3].

As a type of a collegiate library I will select the old library
of Queens' College, Cambridge. This room, on the first floor of
the north side of the quadrangle, forms part of the buildings
erected in 1448. It is 44 ft. long by 20 ft. wide (fig. 50), and is
lighted by eleven windows, each of two lights, six of which are
in the south wall and five in the north wall. The windows in
the south wall have lost their cusps, but they are retained in
those in the north wall—and the library has in all points
suffered less from modern interference than almost any other
with which I am acquainted. The bookcases have been altered

---

[1] I have to thank my friend Mr T. G. Jackson, architect, for kindly lending me this
section of Bishop Cobham's Library. For his history of the building, see his *Church
of St Mary the Virgin, Oxford,* 4to. 1897, pp. 90—106. With regard to the number
of windows he notes (p. 102): There would have been eight, two to a bay, were it not
that the tower buttresses occupy half the western bay.

[2] Anstey, *Mun. Acad.* I. 227.

Jackson, *ut supra,* p. 98.

and patched more than once, in order to provide additional shelf-room; but at the bottom of the more modern super-

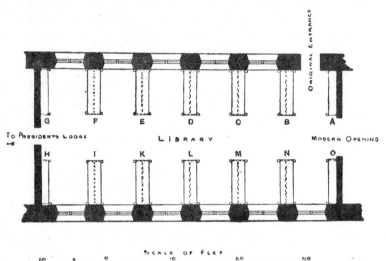

Fig. 50. Ground-plan of the Library at Queens' College, Cambridge.

structure part at least of the original medieval desk may be detected. If this fragment be carefully examined it will be found that there is on the inside of each end of the bookcase a groove which evidently once supported a desk 6 ft. 6 in. long, and of a height convenient for a seated reader to use[1] (fig. 51). The books lay on their sides on this desk, to which they were chained in a way that I shall explain directly, and a bench for the reader was placed between each pair of desks. In the plan (fig. 50) I have added the half-desk which once stood against the west wall; and I have lettered all the desks according to the catalogue made in 1472 by Andrew Docket, the first President.

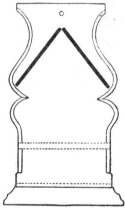

Fig. 51. Elevation of book-desk in Library of Queens' College, Cambridge[2].

[1] The total height of this desk-end is 66 in.; from the ground to the beginning of the groove 31 in.; each slit is 19 in. long.

[2] For scale see fig. 62, p. 163.

It should be carefully noted, when studying this plan, that the distance between each pair of windows is not more than 2 feet, and that the end of the desk covers the whole of this space. If this fact be borne in mind when examining libraries that are now fitted up in a different way, it becomes possible to detect what the original method was.

I propose to name this system of fittings the lectern-system; and I shall shew, as we proceed, that it was adopted, with various modifications, in England, France, Holland, Germany and Italy.

Fortunately, one example of such fittings still exists, at Zutphen in Holland, which I visited in April, 1894. Shortly afterwards I wrote the following description of what is probably a unique survival of an ancient fashion[1].

The library in which these fittings occur is attached to the church of SS. Peter and Walburga, the principal church of the town. A library of some kind is said to have existed there from very early times[2]; but the place where the books were kept is not known. In 1555 a suggestion was made that it would be well to get together a really good collection of books for the use of the public. The first stone of the present building was laid in 1561, and it was completed in 1563. The author of the *Theatrum Urbium Belgicæ,* John Blaeu, whose work was completed in 1649, describes it as "the public library poorly furnished with books, but being daily increased by the liberality of the Senate and Deputies[3]."

The room is built against the south choir-aisle of the church, out of which a door opens into it. In consequence of this position the shape is irregular, for the church is apsidal, and the choir-aisle is continued round part of the apse. It is about 60 feet long, by 26 feet broad at the west end. In the centre are four octagonal columns on square bases, supporting a plain quadripartite vault. The room is thus divided longitudinally into two aisles, with a small irregular space at the east end.

The diagrammatic ground-plan, here subjoined (fig. 52), will

---

[1] *Camb. Ant. Soc. Proc. and Comm.* Vol. VIII. pp. 379—388, 7 May, 1894.

[2] The existing Library is still called the New Library.

[3] *Novum ac Magnum Theatrum Urbium Belgicæ,* fol. Amsterdam, 1649, s. v. Zutphania. For these historical facts I have to thank my friend Mr Gimberg, *Archivarius* at Zutphen.

help to make this description clear. It makes no pretensions to accuracy, having been drawn from notes only[1].

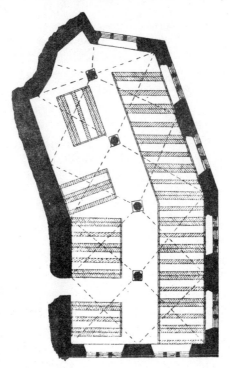

Fig. 52. Ground-plan of the Library at Zutphen.

There are two windows, each of three lights, at the west end of the room, and four similar windows on the south side, one to each bay. There is a fifth window, now blocked, at the south-east corner. Some of these windows contain fragments of richly coloured stained glass—among which the figure of a large green parrot is conspicuous; but whether these fragments were brought from the church, or are part of the glass originally supplied to the library, there is no evidence to shew. Most of these windows are partially blocked, having been damaged, it is said, in one of the numerous sieges from which Zutphen has suffered. The position of the church, close to the fortifications, as Blaeu's bird's-eye view shews, makes this story

[1] I have to thank Mr T. D. Atkinson, architect, for drawing this plan.

Fig. 53. General view of the north side of the Library attached to the church of S. Walburga at Zutphen.

probable. The floor is paved with red tiles. The general appearance of the room will be understood from the view of the north aisle reduced from a photograph (fig. 53)[1].

There are eighteen bookcases, or desks; namely, ten on the south side of the room, and eight on the north side (fig. 52). The material is oak; the workmanship very rude and rough. I will describe those on the south side first. Each is 9 feet long by 5 feet $5\frac{1}{4}$ inches high, measured from the floor to the top of the finial on the end; and the lower edge of the desk on which the books lie is 2 feet $6\frac{1}{4}$ inches above the floor; but the

Fig. 54. Desk and reader on the south side of the Library at Zutphen.
From a photograph.

general plan, and the relative dimensions of the different parts, will be best understood from the photograph of a single desk at which a reader is seated (fig. 54), and from the elevation of one of the ends (fig. 55, A), beside which I have placed the elevation

[1] I have again to thank Mr Gimberg for this photograph. It was a work of no small difficulty owing to the imperfect light.

of one of the desks at Queens' College (B). The photograph
shews that in fixing the height of the desk above the ground

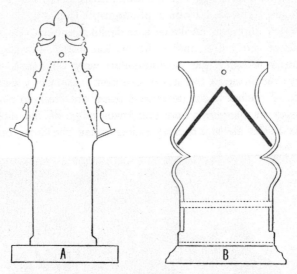

Fig. 55.   Elevation of (A) one of the bookcases in the Library at Zutphen : (B) one of
those in the Library at Queens' College, Cambridge[1].

the convenience of readers has been carefully considered. The
iron bar that carries the chains is locked into the ornamental
upright, passes through a staple in the middle of the desk, and
into the upright at the opposite end, which is left plain. This
bar is half an inch in diameter, and one inch above the level
of the top of the desk. It is prevented from bending by passing
through a staple fixed in the centre of the desk. A piece
of ornamental iron-work is fixed to the upright. It is made
to represent a lock, but is in reality a mere plate of metal,
and the tongue, which looks as
though it were intended to move,
is only an ornament, and is pierced
by the keyhole. The lock is sunk
in the thickness of the wood, behind this plate, and the bar, which
terminates in a knob, is provided
with two nicks, into which the bolts

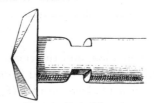

Fig. 56.   End of iron bar,
Zutphen.

[1] For scale see fig. 62, p. 163.

of the lock are shot when the key is turned (fig. 56). Between each pair of desks there is a seat for the reader.

The desks on the north side of the room differ slightly

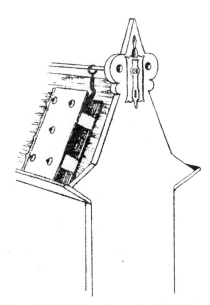

Fig. 57. End of one of the desks on the north side of the Library, Zutphen.

from those on the south side. They are rather larger, the ends are of a different shape and devoid of ornament (fig. 57), and there is a wider interval between the bar and the top of the desk. It seems to me probable that the more highly ornamented desks are those which were put in when the room was first fitted up, and that the others were added from time to time as new books had to be accommodated.

The books are attached to the desk by the following process. A chain was taken about 12 inches long, more or less, consisting of long narrow links of hammered iron. These links exactly resemble, both in shape and size, those of a chain which may still be seen in the library of the Grammar School at Guildford, Surrey[1]. This chain, of which a piece is

---

[1] I have described this library in *Camb. Ant. Soc. Proc. and Comm.* Vol. VIII. pp. 11—18.

here figured (fig. 58), was probably made in 1586, or only 23
years after the building of the library
at Zutphen. It terminates, like those
at Zutphen (fig. 59), in a swivel (to
prevent entanglement), attached to
the ring which is strung upon the bar.
The attachment of the chain to the
book was effected by means of a piece
of metal bent round so as to form a
loop through which the last link of
the chain was passed. The ends of
the loop, flattened out, were attached
by nail or rivet to the edge of the
stout wooden board which formed the
side of the book. This mode of attachment will be best seen in the
volume which I figure next (fig. 60)
—a collection of sermons printed at
Nuremberg in 1487. It is believed to
have once belonged to a Dominican
House at Bamberg, in the library of
which it was chained[1].

The iron loop in this specimen
(fig. 60) is fastened to what I call the
right-hand board of the book; by
which I mean the board which is to
the right hand of a reader when the
book lies open before him; but the
selection of the right-hand or the left-
hand board depended on individual
taste. Further the mode of attachment is never the same in two examples. The iron and rivets are often
clumsy, and do considerable damage
to the leaves, by forcing them out of
shape and staining them with rust.

In this method of chaining no provision is made for removing any book

Fig. 58. Piece of chain, shewing
the ring attached to the bar,
the swivel, and one of the
links, actual size. Guildford.

[1] This book is now in the University Library, Cambridge.

from the desk when not wanted, and placing it on a shelf
beneath the desk, as was
done in some Italian mo-
difications of the system.
Each volume must lie on
the desk, attached by its
chain, like a Bible on a
church-lectern. The smallest
number of volumes on any
desk at Zutphen is six; the
largest, eleven; the total,
316. Most of those on the
south side of the room were
printed during the first half

Fig. 59. Piece of the iron bar, with chain,
Zutphen.

of the sixteenth century; those on the north side are much
later, some as late as 1630. I did not see any manuscripts.

Fig. 60. Chained book, from a Dominican House at Bamberg, South Germany.

If we now reconsider the indications preserved at Queens'
College, it will, I feel sure, be recognised that the desks at

Zutphen explain them, and enable us to realise the aspect of what I conceive to have been the most ancient method of fitting up a collegiate or a monastic library. When such a room first became necessary in a monastery, and furniture suitable for it was debated, a lectern would surely suggest itself, as being used in the numerous daily services, and proving itself singularly convenient for the support of books while they were being read.

Another example of such fittings was once to be seen at Pembroke College, Cambridge, in the library above the hall (fig. 48). In Dr Matthew Wren's account of that library already quoted there is a passage which may be translated as follows :

> I would have you know that in the year 1617 the Library was completely altered and made to assume an entirely new appearance. This alteration was rendered necessary by the serious damage which, to our great sorrow, we found the books had suffered—a damage which was increasing daily—partly from the sloping form of the desks, partly from the inconvenient weight of the chains (*tum ex declivi pluteorum fabricâ, tum ex ineptâ mole catenarum*)[1].

These desks were copied at S. John's College in the same University. A contract dated 20 June, 1516, provides that the contractor

> shall make all the Desks in the Library wythin the said college of good and substanciall and abyll Tymber of Oke mete and convenient for the same Library, aftir and accordyng to the Library within... Pembroke Hall[2].

The Library here referred to was on the first floor to the south of the Great Gate of the college. It is now divided into chambers, but its original extent can be readily made out by its range of equidistant windows. The wall-spaces dividing these are $28\frac{1}{2}$ inches wide, practically the same as those at Queens' College.

At Peterhouse also a similar arrangement seems to have subsisted when the catalogue of 1418 was made. The very first book, a Bible, is said to stand " in the sixth lectern on the

---

[1] *Arch. Hist.*, The Library, III. 429.   It is obvious that these heavy chains must have been attached to the lower edge of one of the boards, and that the bar must have been below the desk and not above it.   See above, p. 139.

[2] *Arch. Hist.* II. 244.

west side (*lectrino 6° ex parte occidentali*)." The word *lectrinum* is unusual, but it emphasizes the form of the desk more clearly than any other.

Fig. 61. Single desk in the old Library, Lincoln Cathedral.

A splendid example of this type of case is to be seen at Lincoln (fig. 61), where three "stalls" or desks, belonging to the

C. L. 11

old library already described[1], are still preserved. Each is about 7 ft. long, 3 ft. broad, and 4 ft. 4 in. high to the top of the sloping portion. At each end, and in the centre, is a massive molded standard, 7 ft. 2 in. high, terminating in a boldly carved finial; and these three standards are connected together by a band of open-work, of a design similar to that of the cornice of the library. Half way between this band and the top of the desk is the bar to carry the chains, now of wood, but formerly of course of iron; and below this again is a shelf 18 in. wide, projecting slightly beyond the sloping portion of the desk. The edge of the desk is protected by a ledge, as usual, and under it is a second shelf extending the whole width of the piece of furniture. What was the use of these shelves? As the bar is above the desk, not below it, the books must have reposed, as a general rule, upon the desk, instead of being laid on their sides on the shelf below it when not wanted by a reader. The chains would not have been long enough to allow of any other arrangement. I think, therefore, that the lower shelf must have been a constructional contrivance, to assist in keeping the standards in their places. The narrow upper shelf, on the other hand, was probably intended for the convenience of the reader. He might place on it, temporarily, any book that he was not using, and which got in his way while he was reading one of those beside it; or, if he was making extracts, he might set his inkstand upon it.

These desks evidently stood in the old library against the shafts of the roof, for one of the ends has been hollowed out in each to receive the shaft; and the finial, which is left plain on that side, is bent over slightly, to admit it under the brace (fig. 39).

As I have now described three varieties of the lectern-system, I will place before my readers, side by side, elevations of each of the three (fig. 62) drawn to the same scale. It will be seen that they resemble each other exactly in essentials. The differences observable are accidental, and may be referred to individual taste.

That this form of desk was recognised on the continent as

---

[1] See above, pp. 117—121.

typical of library-fittings is proved by its appearance in a French
translation of the first book of the *Consolation of Philosophy* of

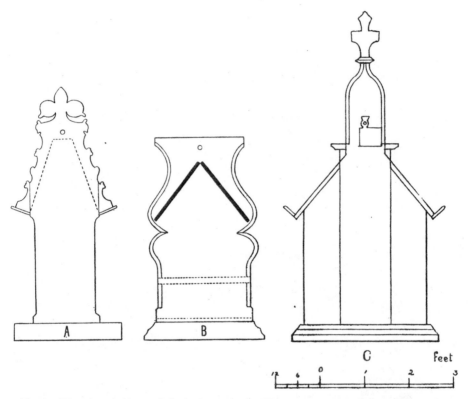

Fig. 62. Elevation of (A) one of the bookcases in the Library at Zutphen; (B) one of those in the
Library at Queens' College, Cambridge; (C) one of those in the Library of Lincoln Cathedral.

Boethius, which I had the good fortune to find in the British
Museum[1] (fig. 63). This manuscript was written in Flanders
towards the end of the fifteenth century. In such a work the
library shewn requires what I may term generalised fittings.
An eccentric peculiarity would have been quite inadmissible.

In the Stadtbibliothek of Nuremberg some of the oldest
works on jurisprudence still preserve their chains. Each has

---

[1] MSS. Harl. 4335. The picture hanging on the wall represents Philosophy
offering her consolation to a sick man.

a short chain about 12 in. long fixed on the upper edge of the left-hand board. The title is written on the middle of the upper edge of the right-hand board. It is obvious that these volumes must have lain on a desk with their titles uppermost[1].

Fig. 63. Interior of a Library.

From a MS. of a French translation of the first book of the *Consolation of Philosophy* by Boethius: written in Flanders towards the end of the fifteenth century.

It is probable that similar fittings were used in the library of the Sorbonne, Paris, which was first established in 1289, with books chained for the common convenience of the Fellows (*in communem sociorum utilitatem*)[2]. This library was divided into

[1] For this information I have to thank my friend, Bernard W. Henderson, M.A., Fellow of Merton College, Oxford.

[2] Delisle, *Cabinet des manuscrits*, II. 186, *note*.

Fig. 64. Library of the Collège de Navarre, Paris, now destroyed.

two separate collections, which formed, so to speak, two distinct libraries. The first, called the great library, or the common library, contained the books most frequently studied. They were chained, and could only be taken out under the most exceptional circumstances. A statute, dated 1321, the provisions of which recall the collegiate statutes summarised above, directed that the best book the society possessed on each subject should be thus chained. The second division of the library, called the small library, contained duplicates, books rarely consulted, and generally all those of which the loan was authorised under certain conditions[1]. The following description of this library has been given by Claude Hémeré (Librarian 1638—43) in his MS. history. This I proceed to translate:

The old library was contained under one roof. It was firmly and solidly built, and was 120 feet long by 36 feet broad...Each side was pierced with 19 windows of equal size, that plenty of daylight both from the east and the west (for this was the direction of the room) might fall upon the desks, and fill the whole length and breadth of the library. There were 28 desks, marked with the letters of the alphabet, five feet high, and so arranged that they were separated by a moderate interval. They were loaded with books, all of which were chained, that no sacrilegious hand might [carry them off. These chains were attached to the right-hand board of every book] so that they might be readily thrown aside, and reading not be interfered with. Moreover the volumes could be opened and shut without difficulty. A reader who sat down in the space between two desks, as they rose to a height of five feet as I said above, neither saw nor disturbed any one else who might be reading or writing in another place by talking or by any other interruption, unless the other student wished it, or paid attention to any question that might be put to him. It was required, by the ancient rules of the library, that reading, writing, and handling of books should go forward in complete silence[2].

This description indicates desks similar to those of Zutphen. Even the height is the same.

A library which vividly recalls the above account, with 19 windows on one side and probably the same number on the other, was built in 1506 for the Collège de Navarre, Paris, now the École Polytechnique[3]. My illustration (fig. 64) is from a

---

[1] This account is, in the main, a translation of that given by M. Delisle, _ut supra_.

[2] Bibl. Nat. Par. MSS. Lat. 5493. For the history of this library see Delisle, _ut supra_, pp. 142—208; Franklin, _Anciennes Bibliothèques de Paris_, 1. pp. 221—317.

[3] Franklin, _ut supra_, vol. 1. p. 399.

photograph taken shortly before its destruction in 1867. I
have calculated that it was about 108 ft. long by 30 ft. wide.

The library of the Collège d'Autun, Paris, was similarly
arranged. An inventory taken 29 July, 1462, records: "dix
bancs doubles, à se seoir d'une part et d'autre, et ung poupitre;
esquelz bancs et poupitre ont esté trouvez enchaisnez les livres
qui s'ensuyvent, qui sont intitulez sur la couverture d'iceulx[1]."
The catalogue enumerates 174 volumes, or rather more than 17
for each "banc" or lectern. The expression *bancs doubles* is
interesting, as it seems to imply that there were at that time
libraries in which *bancs simples* were used; that is to say,
lecterns with only one sloping surface instead of two.

A study of the catalogue drawn up in 1513 for the
Augustinian House of S. Victor, Paris, by Claude de Grandrue,
one of the monks, shews that the same system must have
been in use there. Further, his catalogue is an excellent
specimen of the pains taken in a large monastery to describe
the books accurately, and to provide ready access to them. A
brief prefatory note informs us that the desks are arranged in
three rows, and marked with a triple series of letters. The first
row is marked A, B, C, etc.; the second AA, BB, etc.; the third
AAA, BBB, etc. To each of these letters are appended the
numbers 1, 2, 3, 4 and so on, to shew the position of the required
volume. For instance—to take one at random—*Abælardi con-
fessio* is marked P. 13: that is, it is the thirteenth book on the
desk in the first row marked P. When the catalogue proper—
in which each manuscript is carefully described—was finished,
the author increased its usefulness by the composition of an
alphabetical index[2].

How, I shall be asked, can the form of the bookcase or desk
(*pulpitum*) be inferred from this catalogue? I reply: In the
first place, because there are no shelf-marks. The librarian
notes the letter of the desk, and the place of each book on it,
but nothing more. Secondly, because the number of manuscripts
accommodated on each desk is so small. There are 50 desks,

---

[1] Franklin, *Bibliothèques de Paris*, II. 70.
[2] Delisle, *ut supra*, II. 228—231; Franklin, *ut supra*, I. 135—185. The catalogue
of Claude de Grandrue is in the Bibliothèque Nationale, fonds latin, No. 14767; the
alphabetical index in the Bibliothèque Mazarine, No. 1358.

and 988 manuscripts—or, an average of little more than 19 to each. At Zutphen the average is exactly 18. This piece of evidence, however, is so important that I will give it in detail. The following table, compiled by myself from the catalogue, gives the letters used to mark the desks, and the number of manuscripts on each.

A	13	AA	13	AAA	15
B	21	BB	16	BBB	16
C	13	CC	19	CCC	17
D	18	DD	18	DDD	19
E	17	EE	21	EEE	17
F	20	FF	17	FFF	29
G	18	GG	18	GGG	24
H	16	HH	17	HHH	29
I	16	II	23	III	25
K	17	KK	21	KKK	29
L	22	LL	21	LLL	23
M	21	MM	20	MMM	26
N	18	NN	20		———
O	14	OO	13		269
P	19	PP	23		
Q	22	QQ	27		
R	14	RR	26		
S	14	SS	28		
T	21	TT	24		
	———		———		
	334		385		

These totals give a general total of 988 manuscripts, which, divided by 50, makes the average number for each desk, as stated above, 19·76.

Further, my theory is supported by the positive evidence of a description of this library (unfortunately without date) quoted by M. Delisle: " Les livres estoient couchez et enchaisnez, sur de longs pupitres, et une allée entre deux[1]." It is obvious that the English system of placing each lectern between a pair of windows could not have been maintained here.

At Queens' College, Cambridge, the catalogue, dated 1472, enumerates 192 volumes, divided over 10 desks and 4 half-desks, each called a step (*gradus*). There were (avoiding fractions) 8 books on each half-desk, and 15 on each complete desk; so

---

[1] Delisle, p. 228, *note.*

that by comparing the plan (fig. 50) and elevation of a desk (fig. 51) with the views of the library at Zutphen, a good idea of a college library in the fifteenth century can be obtained.

Before I leave the lectern-system, I will describe two eccentric specimens of it. The first is still to be seen at Trinity Hall, Cambridge; the second once existed at the University of Leyden.

The library of Trinity Hall is thoroughly medieval in plan, being a long narrow room on the first floor of the north side of the second court, 65 feet long by 20 feet wide, with eight equidistant windows in each side-wall, and a window of four lights in the western gable. It was built about 1600, but the fittings are even later, having been added between 1626 and

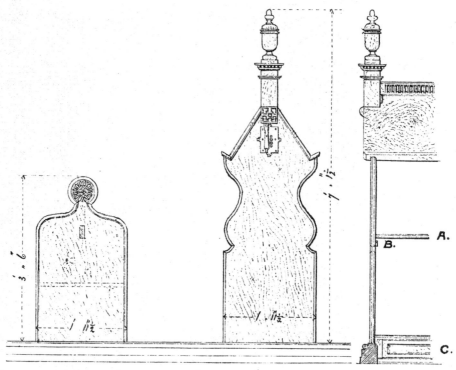

SCALE ½ INCH TO 1 FOOT.

Fig. 66. Elevation of a book-desk and seat in the Library of Trinity Hall, Cambridge.

Fig. 65. General view of the Library at Trinity Hall, Cambridge.

Fig. 68. A French Library of 1480.

From MS. 164 in the Fitzwilliam Museum, Cambridge.

1645 during the mastership of Thomas Eden, LL.D. They are therefore a deliberate return to ancient forms at a time when a different type had been adopted elsewhere.

There are five desks and six seats on each side of the room, placed, as usual, at right angles to the side-walls, in the interspaces of the windows, and in front of the windows, respectively. Their arrangement, and the details of their construction, will be understood from the general view (fig. 65), and from the elevation (fig. 66).

These lecterns are of oak, 6 feet 7 inches long, and 7 feet high, measured to the top of the ornamental finial. There is a sloping desk at the top, beneath which is a single shelf (fig. 66, A). The bar for the chains passes under the desk, through the two vertical ends of the case. At the end farthest from the wall, the hasp of the lock is hinged to the bar and secured by two keys (fig. 67). Beneath the shelf there is at either end a slip of wood (fig. 66, B), which indicates that there was once a moveable desk which could be pulled out when required. The reader could therefore consult his convenience, and work either sitting or standing (fig. 65). For both these positions the heights are very suitable, and at the bottom of

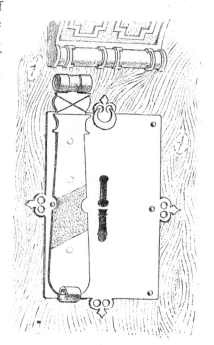

Fig. 67. Lock at end of book-desk,
Trinity Hall.

the case was a plinth (fig. 66, C), on which he could set his feet. The seats between each pair of desks were of course put up at the same time as the desks themselves. They shew an advance in comfort, being divided into two, so as to allow support to the reader's back.

Similar desks occur in a beautiful miniature (fig. 68) from

a manuscript (now in the Fitzwilliam Museum, Cambridge[1]) written in France about 1480. They appear to be solid— possibly fitted with cupboards for books under the sloping portion. No seats are shewn, and, as a reader is standing between them consulting a book, it may be concluded that they could only be used by students in that position.

Lastly, I reproduce (fig. 69) a print by Jan Cornelis Woudanus, shewing the library of the University of Leyden in 1610[2]. The bookcases were evidently contrived with the view of getting the largest number possible into the room. Each contained a single row of books, chained to a bar in front of the shelf; and, also for the purpose of saving the space usually occupied by a seat, readers were obliged to consult them standing. There are eleven bookcases on each side of the room, each containing from 40 to 48 volumes. At the end of the room are two cupboards, probably for manuscripts; and to the right of the spectator is a third press, marked *Legatum Josephi Scaligeri.* He died in January, 1609. Further, as an illustration of the usual appliances for study found in libraries at this period, and often mentioned in catalogues and account-books, I would draw attention to the globes and maps.

I present these bookcases at this point of my researches with some diffidence, for they can hardly be said to represent the lectern-system. On the other hand, they do not exactly represent any other; and I therefore submit that they may be looked at here, as transitional specimens, bridging over the interval between the desks we have lately been considering, and those which we shall have to consider in the next chapter.

---

[1] The MS. (No. 164) is by Frère Jehan de Castel.

[2] This reproduction is from a copy of the print now in the Fitzwilliam Museum, Cambridge. It also occurs on a reduced scale in *Les Arts au Moyen Age et à l'Époque de la Renaissance* par Paul Lacroix, 4°. Paris, 1869, p. 492; and in *Illustrium Hollandiae et Westfrisiae Ordinum etc.* 4°. Lugd. Bat., 1614.

BIBLIOTHECA LUGDUNO-BATAVÆ CUM PULPITIS ET ARCIS VERA IXNOGRAPHIA.

Fig. 69.   The interior of the Library of the University of Leyden.

CHAPTER V.

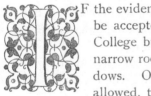F the evidence brought forward in the last chapter
be accepted, the Library which a Monastery or
College built in the fifteenth century was a long
narrow room lighted by rows of equidistant windows. Occasionally, if neighbouring buildings
allowed, there was a window at the end of the
room also. The fittings were lecterns of wood. On these the
books were laid, each volume being fastened by a chain to a
bar usually placed over the desk, but occasionally, in all
probability, in front of it or beneath it. The readers sat on
benches immoveably fixed opposite to each window. It is
obvious that reading was convenient enough so long as the
students were few, but if they were numerous and the books
chained too closely together much annoyance must have been
caused. When the University of Oxford petitioned Humphrey
Duke of Gloucester in 1444 to help them to build a new library,
they specially dwelt upon the obstacles to study arising from
the overcrowded condition of the old room. "Should any
student," they said, "be poring over a single volume, as often

happens, he keeps three or four others away on account of the books being chained so closely together[1]."

Further, the lectern-system was so wasteful in the matter of space, that, as books accumulated, some other piece of furniture had to be devised to contain them. The desk could not be dispensed with so long as books were chained; and it therefore occurred to an ingenious carpenter that the required conditions would be fulfilled if the two halves of the desk were separated, not by a few inches, but by a considerable interval, or broad shelf, with one or more shelves fixed above it. Thus a case was arrived at containing four shelves at least, two to each side of the case, which could be made as long as the width of the library permitted. I propose to call this system "the stall-system," from the word *staulum* (sometimes written *stalla*, *stallus*, or *stallum*), which is frequently applied to a case for books in a medieval library.

There are at least five fine examples of this system at Oxford —none, I am sorry to say, at Cambridge. There was a set at Clare College, supplied to the old Library about 1627, but they have since been altered by the removal of the desks. Those at Oxford are at Corpus Christi College (1517), S. John's College (1596), Sir Thomas Bodley's library (1598), Merton College (1623), Jesus College (1677—79), Magdalen College (of uncertain date).

As a type of this system I shall take the library of Corpus Christi College, founded in 1516 by Richard Fox, Bishop of Winchester. The library was ready for the fittings by the end of March in the following year, as we learn from a building account preserved by Hearne:

8 Henry VIII. This boke made from the xvth day off March unto the xxxti day off the same Moneth [30 March, 1517].

Md. couenauntyd and agreid wyth Comell Clerke, for the makyng off the dextis in the liberary, to the summe off xvi, after the maner and forme as they be in Magdaleyn college, except the popie heedes off the seites, thes to be workmanly wrowght and clenly, and he to have all maner off stooff foond hym, and to have for the makyng off on dexte xs the sum off the hole viii. li.[2]

---

[1] Macray, *Annals of the Bodleian Library*, p. 7. The words used are : Jam enim si quis, ut fit, uni libro inhæreat, aliis studere volentibus ad tres vel quatuor pro vicinitate colligationis præcludit accessum.

[2] Hearne's *Glastonbury*, ed. 1722, p. 286.

Fig. 70. Bookcases and seat in the Library at Corpus Christi College, Oxford.

From a photograph taken in 1894.

The arrangement and appearance of these most interesting cases will be understood from the general view (fig. 70) and from the elevation (fig. 71), but I shall proceed to describe them with some minuteness.

The library occupies the first floor of the south side of the quadrangle opposite to the entrance. It is 79 feet 6 inches long, by 21 feet broad, with ten equidistant windows, about 3 feet 6 inches apart, on each side. At the west end there is an inner library, occupying the angle between the south and west sides of the quadrangle. On each side there are nine bookcases, each 8 ft. 6 in. high, 2 ft. wide, and 7 ft. 6 in. long, divided by partitions into three compartments.

I have carefully studied these cases on several occasions, and it seems to me that the only alterations introduced since the

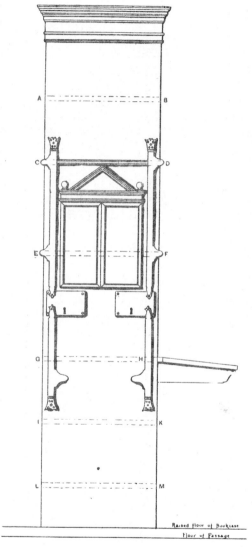

Fig. 71.   Elevation of one bookcase in the Library of Corpus Christi College, Oxford.

original construction are : (1) the addition of about two feet to the upper portion of the case in order to provide additional shelf-room ; (2) a slight change in the arrangements of the desk for the reader ; and (3) the addition of the catalogue frame, which by its style is evidently Jacobean, to the end next the central alley. Originally each case had two shelves only, one on the level of the desk (fig. 71, G, H), and the second about half-way between it and the original top of the case (*ibid.* E, F). Before chaining fell into disuse the cases were heightened so as to provide an additional shelf (*ibid.* C, D). At present the number has been further increased by the addition of a fourth shelf above the desk (*ibid.* A, B), and two below it (*ibid.* I, K, L, M). The desks have been altered by a change in the position of the bracket, and by the suppression of the slit through which the chains usually passed, as I shall explain below.

The system of chaining used for the lectern-system required modification and extension to suit this new arrangement of shelves. At Corpus Christi College most of the iron-work remains (fig. 70); but it is necessary to go elsewhere to find chained books actually in use. Of such chaining I know no better example than the Chapter Library in Hereford Cathedral, from a study of which I will describe the system, and shew that it is the same as that employed at Corpus Christi College and elsewhere.

The Chapter Library at Hereford was originally over the west cloister, and there is evidence that it was being fitted up in 1394, when Walter de Rammesbury, B.D., gave £10 for the desks[1]. The original building has long since been destroyed, and the books were transferred from one place to another until the present beautiful structure was built on the old site in 1897.

Throughout these changes some very ancient bookcases have been preserved. They have been taken to pieces and altered several times, but are probably, in the main, those put up in 1394. Above all, one of them possesses, in thorough working order, the system of chaining, parts of which are to be met with on the cases at Oxford which we have been considering. Of

---

[1] *Fasti Herefordenses*, by Rev. F. T. Havergal. 4°, 1869, p. 181. A Chapter-order dated 16 February, 1589, directed the removal of the books to the Lady Chapel, and the erection of a school on the ground where the Library had once stood.

Fig. 73. Part of a bookcase in the Chapter Library, Hereford.

the accompanying illustrations the first (fig. 72) gives a general
view of the most complete case, that which now contains the

Fig. 72.   Bookcase in the Chapter Library, Hereford Cathedral.
From a sketch taken in 1876.

manuscripts, and the second (fig. 73) shews one compartment
of the same case with the books, chains, desk etc.   This case is
9 ft. 8 in. long, 2 ft. 2 in. wide and 8 ft. high, exclusive of the
cornice.   The material is unplaned oak, very rough ; the ends
are 2—3 in. thick, made of three planks fastened together with
strong wooden pegs.   The desk has been a good deal altered,
and is now inconveniently low, but, as the books were chained, it
is evident that there must always have been desks on each case,
and moreover the hook which held them up is still to be seen in
several places.   The frames to
contain the catalogue, which
closely resemble those at Oxford, are known to have been
added in the 17th century by
Thomas Thornton, D.D., Canon
Residentiary.

   As the books were to stand
upright on a shelf, not to lie on
their sides on a desk, it was
necessary to attach the chain in
a different manner.   A narrow

Fig. 74.   Part of a single volume, shewing
the clasp, the ring for the chain, and the
mode of attaching it : Hereford.

strip of flat brass was passed round the left-hand board (fig. 74)
and riveted to it, in such a
manner as to leave a loop
in front of the edge of the
board, wide enough to admit
an iron ring, an inch and
a quarter in diameter, to
which one end of the chain
was fastened. The book is
placed on the shelf with the
fore-edge turned outwards,
and the other end of the
chain is fastened to a second
ring, rather larger than the
former, which plays along
an iron bar (fig. 75). For
the two upper shelves these
bars, which are $\frac{1}{2}$ in. in
diameter, are supported in
front of the shelf, at such a

Fig. 75. A single volume, standing on
the shelf, with the chain attached
to the iron bar: Hereford.

distance from it as to allow of easy play for the rings (fig. 73).
Each bar extends only from partition to partition, so that three
bars are needed for each
shelf. For the lowest shelf
there are also three bars,
set two inches behind the
edge of the shelf, so as to
keep the rings and chains
out of the way of the desk.
The bars for the upper
shelves rest in iron sockets
screwed to the woodwork
at the juncture of the horizontal shelves with the vertical divisions and ends respectively. The socket fixed
to the end of the bookcase
which was intended to stand

Fig. 76. Iron bar and socket, closed to prevent
removal of the bar: Hereford.

against the wall is closed by an iron plate (fig. 76), so that the bar cannot pass beyond it. At the opposite end, that which would usually face the alley between the two rows of bookcases, the bars are secured by lock and key in the following manner. A piece of flat iron is nailed to the end of the bookcase, just above the level of the uppermost shelf (fig. 77). Attached to this by a hinge is a hasp, or band of iron, two inches wide, and rather longer than the interval between the two shelves. Opposite to each shelf this iron band expands into a semicircular plate, to which a cap is riveted for the reception of the head of the socket in which the bar rests (fig. 77); and just below the middle shelf it drops into a lock and is secured by a key (fig. 73). A second hasp, similarly constructed, secures the lowest of the three bars; but, as that bar is behind, and not in front of, the shelf to which it belongs, the arrangements described above are reversed. One lock and key serves for the ironwork belonging to the three shelves.

Fig. 77. Iron bar, with part of the iron plate or hasp which is secured by the lock and keeps the bar in place: Hereford.

The chains are made of links of hammered iron as shewn in the sketch (fig. 78) which represents a piece of one of the actual size. There is usually a swivel in the centre, probably to prevent twisting. They vary somewhat in length, and in the length of the links, according to the shelf on which the books to which they belong are ranged, it being obviously necessary to provide for the convenient placing of a book on the desk when a reader wished to consult it. The most usual dimensions are 3 ft. 4 in., 3 ft. 6 in., 4 ft. 3 in.

The removal of any of the volumes, or the addition of a new one, must have been a tedious and inconvenient operation. The bar would have to be withdrawn, and all the rings set free. Moreover, if this change had to be effected in one of the compartments remote from the end of the case which carried

the lock, the bar belonging to each of the other compartments
would have to be withdrawn before the
required volume could be reached.

If the views (figs. 70, 71) of the bookcases at Corpus Christi College, Oxford,
be attentively examined, it will be seen
that the ironwork exactly resembles that
at Hereford. We find similar sockets to
contain the bars at the junction of the
horizontal shelves and vertical uprights,
and a similar system of iron hasps to
prevent the bars from being withdrawn.

The desk for the reader would of
course vary according to individual taste.
As a general rule it was attached to the
ends of the case by strong hinges, so that
it could be turned up and got out of the
way when any alteration in the ironwork
had to be carried out. Iron hooks to
hold it up were not unfrequently provided. One of these, from the Bodleian
Library, is here figured (fig. 79). It was
also usual to provide a slit in this desk,
about 2 in. wide, as close as possible to
the shelf, for the chain attached to the
book in use to pass through. This is
well shewn in the view of a single bookcase in Merton College, Oxford (fig. 83).

I will next describe the library of
Merton College, Oxford. There is still
considerable doubt respecting the date of
some of the bookcases, but the appear-

Fig. 78. Piece of chain, shewing the swivel : Hereford.
Actual size.

ance of the library is so venerable, so unlike any similar room
with which I am acquainted, that it must always command
admiration, and deserve study[1].

[1] For the historical facts in the following account I am indebted to Mr Henderson's History, to the merits of which I have already drawn attention. I have also
made copious extracts from the College account-books. Further, I have carefully
studied the library on several occasions, and have had the benefit of the professional
assistance of my friend Mr T. D. Atkinson, Architect.

Fig. 80. Exterior of the Library at Merton College, Oxford, as seen from 'Mob Quadrangle.'

From a photograph by H. W. Taunt, 1899.

The library occupies the whole of the first floor of the south side of "Mob Quadrangle" and the greater part of the same floor of the west side (fig. 80). It is entered through a doorway in the south-western angle of the court, whence a staircase leads up to the vestibule (fig. 81). This room is separated from the two divisions of the library by lofty oak screens, elaborately carved and ornamented in the style of the early renaissance.

Fig. 79. Hook to hold up the desk.
Bodleian Library, Oxford.

The two rooms into which the library is divided have a uniform width of 20 ft. 6 in. The west room, called by tradition Old Library, is 38 ft. 6 in. long (A, B, fig. 81); the south room, or New Library, is 56 ft. 6 in. long (C, D, fig. 81).

The west room is lighted by seven equidistant lancet windows in each of the west and east walls, and by two dormer windows of peculiar design on the side of the roof next to the court. The south room is similarly lighted by ten lancets in each of the north and south walls, and on the side next to the court by two dormer windows like those in the west room. This room moreover has an open space at the east end, about 10 ft. long, lighted by a window of two lights in each of the north and south walls respectively, and by an oriel of five lights in the east wall. In both rooms there is a waggon-roof of five cants boarded, and divided into panels by molded ribs with little bosses at the intersections (fig. 82).

The blank wall at the north end of the west room is panelled with oak of an elaborate and beautiful design for a height of about 12 ft. (fig. 82). The space above this is decorated with panels of plaster-work. The large square central panel contains the arms of the college ; the circular panel to the west those of John Whitgift (Archbishop of Canterbury 1583—1604); and the similar panel to the east those of Sir Henry Savile (Warden 1585—1621).

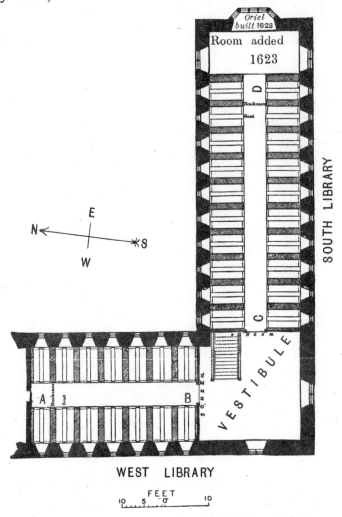

Fig. 81. Ground-plan of the Library at Merton College, Oxford.

The east end of the south room is similarly treated, but the oak panelling is less elaborate. In the plaster-work above it the arms of the college are flanked on the north by those of George Abbot (Archbishop of Canterbury 1611—1633) and on the south by those of Sir Nathaniel Brent (Warden 1621—1651).

Fig. 82. Interior of the west Library at Merton College, Oxford.

From a photograph by H. W. Taunt, 1899.

Fig. 83. Bookcase in the west Library of Merton College, Oxford.

From a photograph by H. W. Taunt, 1899.

Both rooms are floored with rough oak planking On this are laid four sleepers, each about 5 in. square, parallel with the side-walls. The two central sleepers have their outside edge roughly chamfered. Into these the bookcases and the seats are morticed. The central alley, 5 ft. wide, is in both rooms paved with encaustic tiles.

In the west room there are twelve complete cases and four half-cases; in the south room there are twenty complete cases and two half-cases (fig. 81); in both rooms arranged in the usual manner with respect to the walls and windows.

In order to present as vivid an idea as possible of these beautiful cases, I reproduce here a photograph of a single compartment from the west library, with a seated reader at work (fig. 83). The case is made to look rather higher than it really is, but this distortion can be easily corrected by comparing the height of the standard with that of the seated figure.

In the west room each case (figs. 82, 83) is 7 ft. 5 in. long, 1 ft. 5 in. wide and 6 ft. high from the top of the sleeper to the top of the cornice. The material is oak. The ends are nearly 2 in. thick, and next the wall are shaped roughly with an adze. Each case is separated into two divisions by a central partition; and originally there was a desk 1 ft. 3 in. wide on each side of the case. These desks were immoveable, and nailed to rough brackets. There were two shelves only to each case: one just above the level of the desk, and a second about half-way between it and the cornice (fig. 84).

The system of ironwork by which the books were secured can be easily recovered by studying the scars on the ends of the cases next the central alley. At the lower end of the standard, two feet from the ground, was an iron bar which carried the chains of all the books which stood on the shelf just above the level of the desk, without reference to the side from which they were to be consulted. This bar was secured by a separate hasp and lock. The bars for the upper shelf, one on each side of the case, were obviously secured by a system similar to that described above at Hereford and Corpus Christi College. The whole system has been indicated on the elevation (fig. 84), which should be compared with the reproduction of one of the cases in the west room (fig. 83). Originally no books stood below the desk. The comfort of readers was considered by the insertion of a bar of wood to rest the feet on, between the seat and the bookcase (fig. 84).

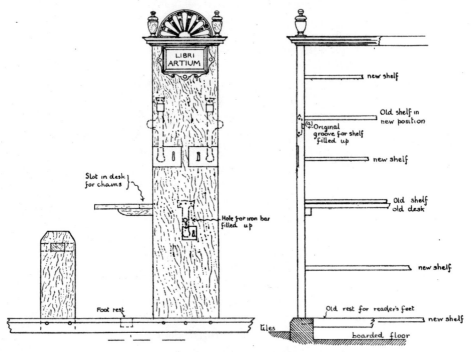

Fig. 84.   Elevation of a bookcase and seat in the West Library at Merton College, Oxford.

Measured and drawn by T. D. Atkinson, Architect.

In the south room the cases are on the same general plan as in the west room; but the system of chaining appears to have been slightly different, and to have approximated more closely to what I may call the Hereford type.

In both rooms each case has a picturesque enrichment at the end of the standard above the cornice, and a small oblong frame just below it to contain the general title of the books within the case. The west room is devoted to LIBRI ARTIUM, with the exception of the three cases and the half-case at the north end of the east side, which are marked CODICES MSS. These are protected by latticed doors of wood. In the south room the cases on the south side are all lettered L. THEOLOGIAE; on the north side the first three are lettered L. MEDICINAE; the next L. MEDIC. IURISPP. and the last five L. IURIS PRVDENTIÆ. In this room the last cases at the east end on each side have latticed doors like those on the corresponding cases in the west room.

The building of this library is recorded in four separate account-rolls extending from the beginning of the first year of Richard II. to the third year of the same king, that is from 1377 to 1379. From these documents it appears that the building cost £462. 1s. 11½d.

From this first construction to the beginning of the sixteenth century—a space of 125 years—the accounts furnish us with no information; but, from what we learn afterwards, it would appear that the internal walls were unplastered, that the roof-timbers were unprotected, and that the only light was admitted through the narrow lancet windows.

In 1502—3 the panel-work (*celatura*) on the roof of the west library was put up at a cost of £27. 6s. 0d. The account contains also a charge for painting the bosses (*nodi*) at the intersection of the moldings that separate the panels. Mr Henderson points out that these ornaments prove the existing ceiling to be that put up in 1503; for among them are the Tudor Rose, the dolphin of Fitzjames (Warden 1483—1507), and the Royal Arms used from Henry IV. to Elizabeth, but altered by James I.

After this another long interval occurs during which no work done to the library is recorded; but in 1623 the south room was taken in hand, and the changes introduced into it were so extensive that it is referred to in the accounts as New Library (*Nova Bibliotheca*), a name which it still retains.

In the first place the room at the east end (fig. 81) was thrown into it, and the oriel window constructed, together with the two large dormers on the side next the court (fig. 80). These works, by which light was so largely increased, prove how gloomy the library must have been before they were undertaken. Next, after important repairs to the walls and floor, and the construction of the decorative plaster-work at the east end, the old bookcases were sold, and Benet the joiner supplied twenty new cases and one half-case. The only old case remaining is, by tradition, the half-case against the screen on the north side as one enters from the vestibule.

It is therefore certain that the cases and seats in the south room date from 1623. It is unfortunately equally certain that we know nothing about the date of those in the west room; and we are therefore unable to say whether the cases in the south room were copied from them in 1623, or whether the reverse process took place at some unknown date. If we adopt the pleasing theory that in the west room we have very early cases, constructed possibly when the library was built, we must still admit that these relics of a remote past have been altered at some subsequent period, so as to be brought into conformity with the cases in the south room; for the cornices and the frames for the titles are precisely similar in the two rooms.

The difference between the two sets of cases in the method of chaining, to which attention has been already drawn, may bear on the question of date. As time went on chaining would be modified in the direction of simplicity; and to replace a single central bar by two lateral ones is a step towards this, for under such conditions the addition or removal of a book would entail less displacement. Further, it must be recognised that these cases, whether extremely ancient or comparatively modern, differ in many particulars from those to be met with elsewhere. They are lighter, narrower and more elegant. Again, when the ground-plan of the library is considered (fig. 81) it will be seen that their ends occupy nearly the whole space between a pair of windows. In other examples of the stall-system this is not the case.

The only explanation I have to offer for the whole difficulty is the following. The library was constructed for the lectern-system, with wall-spaces not more than 2 ft. wide, and was so fitted up. When books had become numerous the western library was taken in hand, and the lecterns altered into stalls, the single central bar being retained. At the same time, in all probability, the dormers were inserted. It is remarkable that these changes should not be recorded in the accounts, but possibly they were carried out as the result of a special benefaction[1]. In 1623 the stalls which had been placed in the west room, having been found convenient, were copied for the south room.

I will in the next place briefly notice the distinctive points of the other examples of the stall-system in Oxford.

At S. John Baptist's College the library was built in 1596, and we may presume was fitted up soon afterwards, as Wood records numerous donations of books in the years immediately succeeding, and the appointment of a keeper to take charge of them in 1603[2]. This library, on the first floor of the south side of the second quadrangle, is 112 feet long by 26 feet wide, with eight windows of two lights in each wall. The bookcases, of which there are eight on each side between the windows, with a half-case against the west wall, are rather larger than those at Corpus Christi College, being 10 feet high, and 2 feet 6 inches wide. They have a classical cornice and terminal pediment. The titles of the subjects are painted at the tops of the stalls as at Merton College. A few traces of chaining are still to be detected. The desks have not been altered. Each is in two divisions, as at Corpus, separated by a central bracket, and it has the slit to admit the chains. The long iron hinges are evidently original. The seats resemble those at Corpus.

The bookcases at Trinity College, set up in 1618, and those at Jesus College, made probably in 1679, call for no special remark.

Between 1598 and 1600 Sir Thomas Bodley refitted the library over the Divinity School. This noble room is 86 feet long by 32 feet wide. These dimensions contrast forcibly with those of the long narrow rooms to which we have been accustomed; and it is probably on account of the great width that the 10 windows on each side have two lights apiece. At right angles to these walls, which face north and south, there are nine bookcases on a side with a half-case at each end. Here again we find so close a resemblance to the cases at Corpus

---

[1] In the bursar's accounts for 1605, among other charges for the library, is the following entry: "pro pari cardinum ad sedem in bibliotheca 12ᵈ." If I am right in thinking that this refers to the desks for the readers in the west library it proves that the existing cases had been set up before 1605.

[2] Wood, *Colleges and Halls*, p. 551.

Christi College, that a particular description is unnecessary. It should be noted, however, that, as at S. John's College, they had been made of a greater height (8 feet 4 inches) in the first instance, so as to accommodate two shelves above that on the level of the desk. These shelves are proved to be original by the existence, at the juncture of the shelves with the upright divisions, of the plates of iron which originally carried the sockets for the bar. The rest of the ironwork has been removed, and it is difficult to detect traces of its former existence, because modern shelves have been set against the ends of the cases. The hole for the lowest bar, however, remains in the same relative position . as at Corpus Christi College; and, as the ironwork for supporting the bars is identical with what still remains there, it seems safe to conclude that no new principle was introduced. The desks are modern, but the large and ornamental brackets which support them are original, and the iron hooks (fig. 79) still remain by which they were prevented from falling when turned up. The position of these hooks shews that each desk was 19 inches broad. There were originally seats between each pair of cases, as may be seen in Loggan's view of the interior of the library, where their ends are distinctly shewn.

A special feature of this room is the beautiful open roof, practically that which Sir Thomas Bodley put up in 1599. The principals and tie-beams are ornamented with arabesques, while the flat surface between them is divided into square compartments on which are painted the arms of the University. On the bosses that intervene between these compartments are the arms of Bodley himself.

I mentioned at the beginning of this chapter that the stall-system had been represented in the library at Clare College, Cambridge. The old library was a long narrow room over the old chapel, and we know on the authority of William Cole[1] that it was "fitted up with wainscote Classes on both sides." These "classes" had been put up shortly before 1627, when the Duke of Buckingham, then Chancellor of the University, was taken to see them. When this library was pulled down in 1763 they were removed to the new library which had been fitted up

---

[1] Add. MSS. Mus. Brit. 5803, MSS. Cole, II. 9.

20 years previously, and ranged round the room in front of the modern shelves. They are splendid specimens of carpentry-work, and bear so close a resemblance to the cases in the library of S. John's College, that it may be assumed that they were copied from them[1]. When the removal took place they were a good deal altered, and a few years ago some fragments which had not been utilised were found in a lumber-closet. One of the standards (fig. 85), with its brackets, shews that the cases were once fitted with desks, the removal of which was ingeniously concealed by the insertion of slips of wood in the style of the older work[2]. I have not been able to discover any traces of chaining, but as there are a number of seats in the library, very like those in Corpus Christi College, Oxford, it is more than probable that chains were once employed.

Fig. 85. Stall-end in the Library of Clare College, Cambridge.

The stall-system was not only popular in Oxford itself, but was adopted as a standard for bookcases, and reproduced elsewhere.

The first example I will cite is at Westminster Abbey[3], where part of the dorter was fitted up as a library during the years 1623 and 1624 by John Williams, Bishop of Lincoln and afterwards Archbishop of York, who was dean of Westminster from 1620 to his death in 1650. In the flowery rhetoric of his biographer Bishop Hacket:

With the same Generosity and strong propension of mind to enlarge the Boundaries of Learning, he converted a wast Room, scituate in the

---

[1] *Arch. Hist.* III. 453.

[2] I have described these fragments in *Camb. Ant. Soc. Proc.*, Vol. VIII. p. 18.

[3] See my paper in *Camb. Ant. Soc. Proc. and Comm.*, Vol. IX. p. 37.

East side of the Cloysters, into *Plato's* Portico, into a goodly Library;
model'd it into decent shape, furnished it with Desks and Chains,
accoutred it with all Utensils, and stored it with a vast Number of
Learned Volumes[1].

This library—which has not been materially altered since
1625—occupies the north end of what was once the dorter. It
is 60 feet long, by 33 feet 4 inches broad. There are twelve
bookcases—evidently the "desks" recorded by Williams' biographer. Each is 10 feet 10 inches long, 2 feet broad, and
8 feet 3 inches high, divided by plain uprights into three
compartments. There are three shelves, below which is a desk
for the reader, resting on brackets, and provided with the usual
slit for the chains to pass through. These desks are hinged.
The cases are quite plain, with the exception of a molded
cornice; above which, on the end of each, is some scroll-work.
There is also a small frame to contain the catalogue. It is
probable that there were originally seats for readers between
each pair of cases. I cannot discover any certain evidence of
chaining, and yet "chains" are distinctly enumerated among
the dean's benefactions. There are faint scars at the intersection of some of the shelves and uprights which may be
screwholes—but I cannot feel certain on the point.

I have already given the plan of the cathedral library at
Wells (fig. 42). After the Restoration this building was re-fitted
during the episcopate of Robert Creighton (Bishop 1670—1672),
with the help of donations from the celebrated Dr Richard
Busby, and Dr Ralph Bathurst, who was dean from 1670 to
1704. It is important to remember that Bathurst was also
master of Trinity College, Oxford, an office which he retained
until his death. As he is described in the MS. List of Benefactors preserved in the library as having taken a foremost part
in fitting it up (*in Bibliothecâ hac instaurandâ* ἐργοδιώκτης),
the selection of the bookcases may with much probability be
ascribed to him. His own college has still bookcases which
once must have been excellent specimens of the stall-system.

There are eight bookcases at Wells, of plain unpainted deal,
projecting from the west wall between the windows (fig. 42).

---

[1] *Scrinia reserata:* a Memorial...of John Williams, D.D....By John Hacket. Fol.
Lond. 1693, pp. 46, 47.

Fig. 87. Bookcases in the Library of Durham Cathedral.

From a photograph.

They are 8 ft. 6 in. long, 8 ft. 1 in. high and 3 ft. broad.
Seven of them have desks on both sides, but the last—that
placed against the partition at the south end, which screens off
a small room for a study—has a desk on one side only.   There
is no shelf below the desk, but two above it. ·They are fitted
with the usual apparatus for chaining.   Between each pair of
bookcases, in front of the·window, is a seat for the reader.
These cases resemble so closely those at Corpus Christi College,
Oxford, that the source from which they were derived cannot
be doubtful.

Was this library ever chained?   A Walton's Polyglot, 1657,
had evidently been pre-
pared for chaining, and
in a novel fashion, the
plate to carry the chain
being attached to the
left-hand board close to
the back of the volume
(fig. 86)—so that it was
evidently set on the shelf
in the ordinary way, and
not with the fore-edge
turned to the spectator,
as is usual in chained
libraries.   But with this
exception I could not

Fig. 86.   Ring for attachment of chain, Wells.

discover indications of the attachment of a plate on any of the
volumes.   If I am right in concluding that the books in this
library were never chained, the cases are a curious instance of
the maintenance of fashion.   Dean Bathurst ordered a bookcase,
and it was supplied to him with all its fittings complete, whether
they were to be used or not.

My last example is from Durham Cathedral, where John
Sudbury, dean from 1661 to 1684, fitted up the ancient Frater
as a library.   The room is about 115 feet long by 30 feet wide,
with nine windows in each side-wall.   Their sills are ten feet
from the ground.

The cases (fig. 87) are evidently the work of a carpenter
who was thoroughly conversant with the stall-system.   They

had originally two shelves only above the desk, the entablature, now visible on the ends only, being carried along the sides. The shelf below the desk is also modern. These cases are ten feet apart, and between each pair, instead of a reader's seat, is a dwarf bookcase terminating in a desk. Attached to it on each side is a seat conveniently placed for a reader to use the desk on the side of the principal case.

I have shewn that the stall-system made its appearance at Oxford early in the sixteenth century, but I have not been able to discover who introduced it. My own impression is that it was monastic in its origin; and I can prove that it fits at least two monastic libraries exactly. This theory will also explain the prevalence of such cases at Oxford, and their almost total absence from Cambridge, where monastic influence was never exercised to the same extent.

I will begin with Canterbury, where, as I mentioned above[1], the library was over the Prior's Chapel. The construction of this chapel is described as follows by Professor Willis:

Roger de S. Elphege, Prior from 1258 to 1263, completed a chapel between the Dormitory and Infirmary....The style of its substructure shews that it was begun by his predecessor....[It] is placed on the south side of the Infirmary cloister, between the Lavatory tower and Infirmary. Its floor was on the level of the upper gallery, and was sustained by an open vaulted ambulatory below. This replaced the portion of the original south alley [of the cloister] which occupied... that position....But, as this new substructure was more than twice as broad as the old one, the chapel was obtruded into the small cloister-garth, so as to cover part of the façade of the Infirmary Hall, diminish the already limited area, and destroy the symmetry of its form[2].

Above this chapel Archbishop Chichele built the library which Prior Sellyng fitted up. It stood east and west, and of course must have been of the same size as the chapel beneath it, namely, according to Professor Willis, 62 feet long on the north side, 59 feet long on the south side, and 22 feet broad. The door was probably at the south-west corner, at the head of a staircase which originally led only to the chapel beneath it.

[1] See above, p. 106.

[2] *Arch. Hist. of...Monastery of Chr. Ch. Cant.* 8vo. 1869, p. 65. This chapel was pulled down at the end of the 17th century and the present library, called the Howley library, built in its place.

From these measurements I have constructed a plan of the room (fig. 88), and of the bookcases which I am about to describe. The windows are of course imaginary, but, I submit, justified by the uniform practice of medieval libraries.

I am able to reconstruct this library because I have had the good fortune to come across a very curious document[1] which gives sufficient data for the purpose. It is contained in a MS. volume, now the property of the Dean and Chapter of Canterbury, composed of several quires of paper stitched into a parchment cover. They once belonged to, and were probably written by, Brother William Ingram, who was *custos martirii* in 1503 ; and in June 1511 was promoted to the office of Pitancer. The accounts and memoranda in the book are of a very miscellaneous character. The part which concerns the library consists of a note of the books which were repaired in 1508. This is headed :

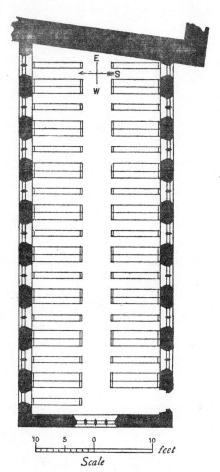

Fig. 88. Conjectural plan of the Library over the Prior's Chapel at Christ Church, Canterbury.

Repairs done to the books contained in the library over the chapel of our lord the Prior, namely, in new byndyng and bordyng with covers and claspyng and chenyng, together with sundry books of the gift of the

---

[1] I have to thank my friend Mr W. H. St John Hope, Assistant Secretary of the Society of Antiquaries, for first drawing my attention to it; and the Dean and Chapter of Canterbury for leave to use it.

aforesaid Prior, namely, in the year of our Lord 1508, and the year of the reign of King Henry VII., 23[1].

The writer goes round the room, beginning at the west end. He proceeds along the north side, and returns along the south side, to the point whence he started, enumerating on his way the bookcases and their shelves, the volumes removed, and, occasionally, a note of the repairs required. For my present purpose I will content myself with his account of a single bookcase, the first on the list. The writer begins thus: " From the upper shelf on the east side in the first seat (*de superiori textu*[2] *ex orienti parte in prima* (sic) *sedile*)." Three volumes are enumerated. " From the lower shelf (*de inferiori textu*)," two volumes. " From the upper shelf on the other side of the same seat (*de superiori textu ex altera parte eiusdem sedilis*)," seven volumes. " From the lower shelf (*de inferiori textu*)," five volumes. In this way eight seats, i.e. bookcases, are gone through on this side of the room. The writer next turns his attention to the south side, and goes through eight more seats, beginning with: " From the east side of the upper shelf on the south side (*de textu superiori ex parte australi incipiendo. In parte orientali*)." The examination was evidently thorough, and, as the same number of seats is enumerated for each side of the room, we may, I think, safely conclude that all were examined, and that the whole number in the library was sixteen.

The passages I have quoted shew that each of these book-cases had an upper and lower shelf on each side, on which the books stood, so as to be conveniently consulted by readers on each side; the books were chained; and, in consequence, there must have been a desk, presumably below the shelves on each side; and a seat for the reader. I have embodied these require-ments in the accompanying sketch or diagram (fig. 89), which indicates a bookcase of the same type as those at Corpus Christi

---

[1] Reparaciones facte circa libros qui continentur in libraria supra capellam domini prioris videlicet in le new byndyng and bordyng cum coopertoriis and le claspyng and chenyng eciam cum diuersis libris ex dono eiusdem prioris videlicet Anno domini M° cccc° viij° and Anno Regni Regis henrici vij° xxiii.

[2] This word seems to have been used at Canterbury to denote any piece of joinery. We have already seen it applied to a carrell (p. 99).

College, Oxford. If we may suppose that each of these cases was two feet wide and eight feet long like those at Merton

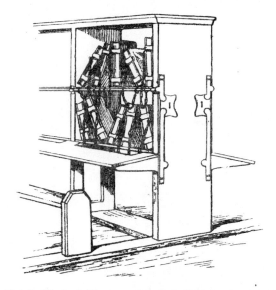

Fig. 89.   Sketch of the probable appearance of a bookcase, and a reader's seat, in the Library at Christ Church, Canterbury.

College, we can accommodate eight cases on each side of the room (fig. 88), with the same interval between each pair as at that college.

Let us now consider whether the library as thus arranged would have had sufficient shelf-room. Each bookcase being 8 feet long would contain 32 feet of shelving, and the 16 cases a total of 512 feet. The catalogue made in the time of Prior Henry of Eastry (1285—1331) enumerates 1850 volumes[1]. If we allow two feet and a half for every ten of these we shall require 462½ feet; or in other words we can arrange the whole collection in 14 stalls, leaving 2 over for the additions which must have been made in the interval between the middle of the 14th century and the date of Brother Ingram's researches.

If the sketch here given of the probable aspect of the library at Christ Church, Canterbury, be compared with the view of the

[1] See above, p. 102. The catalogue has been printed by Edwards, *Memoirs of Libraries*, I. pp. 122—235.

library at Merton College, Oxford (fig. 82), a fairly correct idea of
a great conventual library will be obtained. A very slight effort
of imagination is needed to make the necessary changes in the
shelves, and to replace academic students by Benedictine monks.
Then, if we conceive the shelves to be loaded with manuscripts,
many of which were written in the early days of the English
Church, we shall be able to realise the feelings of Leland on
entering the library at Glastonbury:

> I had hardly crossed the threshold when the mere sight of books
> remarkable for their vast antiquity filled me with awe, or I might almost
> say with bewilderment: so that for a moment I could not move a step
> forward[1].

I propose in the next place to print a translation of the
Introduction to the catalogue[2] of the Benedictine Priory of
S. Martin at Dover, which was a cell to Canterbury made
in 1389 by John Whytfeld. This catalogue does not indicate
the stall-system; in fact I am at a loss to define the precise
system which it does indicate. I print it in this place on
account of its internal interest, and the evidence which it
affords of the care taken in the last quarter of the fourteenth
century to make books easily accessible to scholars.

> The present Register of the Library of the Priory of Dover, compiled
> in the year of the Lord's Incarnation 1389 under the presidency of
> John Neunam prior and monk of the said church, is separated into
> three main divisions. The object is that the first part may supply
> information to the precentor of the house concerning the number of
> the books and the complete knowledge of them: that the second part
> may stir up studious brethren to eager and frequent reading: and that
> the third part may point out the way to the speedy finding of individual
> treatises by the scholars. Now although a brief special preface is
> prefixed to each part to facilitate the understanding of it, to this first
> part certain general notes are prefixed, to begin with, for the more
> plain understanding of the whole Register.
> Be it noted, then, first, that this whole Library is divided into nine
> several classes (Distinctions), marked according to the nine first letters
> of the alphabet, which are affixed to the classes themselves, in such
> a way that A marks out to him who enters the first Class, B the second,

---

[1] Vix certè limen intraveram cum antiquissimorum librorum vel solus conspectus
religionem, nescio an stuporem, animo incuteret meo; eâque de causâ, pedem
paullulum sistebam. Leland, *De Script. Brit.* ed. Hall, I. 41.

[2] This catalogue is in the Bodleian Library (MSS. 920). I am indebted to my
friend Dr James for the admirable translation which I here print.

C the third, and so on in order. Each of the said nine classes, moreover, will be seen to be divided into seven shelves (grades), which are also marked off by the addition of Roman numeral figures, following the letters which denote the classes. We begin the numbering of the shelves from the bottom, and proceed upwards so that the bottom shelf, which is the first, is marked thus, I; the second thus, II; the third thus, III; and so the numbering goes on up to seven[1].

In addition to this, the books of the Library are all of them marked on each leaf with Arabic numerals, to facilitate the ascertaining of the contents of the volumes.

Now since many of the volumes contain a number of treatises, the names of these treatises, although they have not always been correctly christened, are written down under each volume, and an Arabic numeral is added to each name shewing on what leaf each tract begins. To this number the letter A or B is subjoined, the letter A here denoting the first page of the leaf, and the letter B the second. The books themselves, furthermore, have their class-letters and also their shelf-marks inserted not only outside on their bindings, but also inside, accompanying the tables of contents at the beginning. To such class-letters a small Arabic figure is added which shews clearly what position the book occupies in the order of placing on the shelf concerned.

On the second, third, or fourth leaf of the book, or thereabouts, on the lower margin the name of the book is written. Before it are entered the above-mentioned class-letters and shelf-numbers, and after it (a small space intervening) are immediately set down the words with which that leaf begins, which I shall call the proof of investigation (*probatorium cognitionis*). The Arabic figures next following will state how many leaves are contained in the whole volume; and finally another numeral immediately following the last clearly sets forth the number of the tracts contained in the said volume.

If then the above facts be securely entrusted to a retentive memory it will be clearly seen in what class, shelf, place and order each book of the whole Library ought to be put, and on what leaf and which side of the leaf the beginnings of the several treatises may be found. For it has been the object of the compiler of this present register [and] of the Library, by setting forth a variety of such marks and notations of classes, shelves, order, pagination, treatises and volumes, to insure for his monastery security from loss in time to come, to shut the door against the spite of such as might wish to despoil or bargain away such a treasure, and to set up a sure bulwark of defence and resistance. And in truth the compiler will not be offended but will honestly love anyone who shall bring this register—which is still faulty in many respects—into better order, even if he should see fit to place his own name at the head of the whole work.

In the first part of the register, therefore, we have throughout at the top, between black lines ruled horizontally, first the class-letter, in red, and, following it, the shelf-mark, in black characters (*tetris*

---

[1] The words thus translated are: "Incipiendo graduum computacionem a loco inferiori in altum procedendo videlicet ut gradus infimus qui primus est sic signetur I."

signaculis). Then again between other lines ruled in red, vertically: first, on the left a numeral shewing the place of the book in order on its shelf; then the name of the volume; thirdly, the number of the "probatory" leaf; fourthly, the "probatory" words (in the case of which, by the way, reference is made to the text and not to the gloss); fifthly, the number of leaves in the whole volume; and, lastly, the number of the treatises contained in it—all written within the aforesaid lines. In addition there will be left in each shelf of this part, at the end, some vacant space, in which the names of books that may be subsequently acquired can be placed[1].

The meaning of the word "distinction" is the principal difficulty in the way of understanding the above description. I thought at first that it denoted merely difference of subject, and that *gradus*, as in the catalogue of Queens' College, Cambridge, was a side of a lectern. But the statement that the grades are numbered "from the bottom and proceed upwards" can hardly be reconciled with any arrangement of lecterns. *Distinctio* probably denotes a bookcase or press, divided into 7 grades, and probably placed against the wall, the word *gradus* here meaning a flat shelf, instead of one set at an angle as in former instances. If this explanation be correct we have here a very early instance of shelves in such a position.

My second example of a monastic library fitted up according to the stall-system is the library at Clairvaux. As I have already printed a full description of it[2], I need not do more in this place than translate the passage referring to the fittings:

This library is 189 feet long, by 51 feet wide[3]. In it are 48 seats (*bancs*), and in each seat 4 shelves (*poulpitres*) furnished with books on all subjects, but chiefly theology....The building that contains the said library is magnificent, built of stone, and excellently well lighted on both sides with five large windows, well glazed.

As there were so many as 48 bookcases, that is, 24 on each side, the bookcases were evidently spaced without reference to

---

[1] Dr James has pointed out (*Camb. Ant. Soc. Oct. Publ.*, No. XXXII.) that there are six MSS. from Dover Priory among Archbishop Parker's MSS. at Corpus Christi College, Cambridge. The first of these—a Bible in two volumes—is entered in the catalogue of the Priory as A. I. 2, 3—that is to say it was in *distinctio* A, *gradus* I, and the volumes stood second and third in the *gradus*.

[2] See above, p. 112.

[3] The words are: "contient de longueur LXIII passées, et de largeur XVII passées." I have taken one pace = 3 feet.

the lateral windows, which were probably raised high above the floor.

The catalogue, from which I have already quoted the verses commemorating the building of the library, contains much useful information respecting the arrangement of the books. The verses are succeeded by the following introductory note :

Repertorium omnium librorum in hac Clarevallis biblioteca existentium a fratre Mathurino de cangeyo eiusdem loci monacho non sine magno labore editum.

Lege

Pro intelligentia presentis tabule seu Repertorii, sciendum est quod a parte aquilonari collocantur libri quorum litere capitales nigre sunt, quorum vero rubre a parte australi. Et omnes in ea ordine alphabetico scribuntur.

Utriusque autem partis primum analogium per litteram A signatur, secundum per litteram B, tercium per litteram C, quartum per litteram D, quintum per litteram E. Et consequenter cetera analogia per sequentes litteras alphabeticas.

Quodlibet autem analogium quatuor habet partes, quarum prima signatur per litteram A, secunda per B, tercia per C, quarta per D.

Prime partis primi analogii primus liber signatur per A. a. 1, secundus per A. a. 2, tercius per A. a. 3, et consequenter.

Secunde partis primus liber signatur per A. b. 1, secundus per A. b. 2 ; et de consequentibus similis est ordinatio.

Tercie partis primus liber signatur per A. c. 1, secundus per A. c. 2 ; et consequenter.

Quarte partis primus liber signatur per A. d. 1, secundus per A. d. 2 ; et consequenter.

[In this way five "analogia" are enumerated.]

Et eadem est disciplina et ordinacio de ceteris analogiis prout habetur in novissimo quaternione eiusdem tabule, immo et in fronte cuiuslibet analogii in tabella eidem appendente.

Hanc tabulam seu repertorium scripsit quondam frater Petrus mauray de Arecis oriundus. Vivus vel defunctus requiescat in bona semper pace. Amen.

The most important passage in the above note may be thus translated :

Read

For the right understanding of the present table or method of finding books (*tabule seu repertorii*), you must know that on the north side are ranged those books whereof the capital letters are black : on the south side those whereof the capital letters are red. All are set down in alphabetical order.

On each side the first desk (*analogium*) is marked by the letter A; the second by the letter B ; [and so forth].

Each desk has four divisions, the first of which is marked by the letter *a*, the second by the letter *b*, the third by the letter *c*, the fourth by the letter *d*. The first book on the first shelf of the first desk is marked A. a. i ; the second A. a. ii ; [and so forth].

The catalogue as well as the description makes it perfectly clear that each desk, that is to say, each bookcase, had four shelves ; and further, as the authors of the *Voyage Littéraire* (1708) mention chains[1], it may be concluded that there were desks, and seats for readers, between each pair of bookcases. If we place two shelves on each side of the case we get a piece of furniture precisely similar to that in use at Canterbury.

---

[1] *Voyage Littéraire*, ed. 1717, Part I. p. 102.

CHAPTER VI.

THE LECTERN-SYSTEM IN ITALY. LIBRARIES AT CESENA, AT
THE CONVENT OF S. MARK, FLORENCE, AND AT MONTE
OLIVETO. VATICAN LIBRARY OF SIXTUS IV. DUCAL
LIBRARY AT URBINO. MEDICEAN LIBRARY, FLORENCE.
SYSTEM OF CHAINING THERE USED. CHARACTERISTICS
OF MEDIEVAL LIBRARIES. NAMES OF MEDIEVAL BOOK-
CASES AND BOOKSHELVES.

HILE the "stall-system" was being generally
adopted in England and in France, a different
plan was being developed in Italy. It consisted
in a return to the "lectern-system," with the
addition of a shelf below the lectern, on which
the books lay on their sides when not wanted;
and an ingenious combination of a seat for the reader with the
desk and shelf.

The earliest library fitted up in this manner that I have been
able to discover is at Cesena, a city of north Italy between
Forli and Ravenna. It is practically in its original condition.

In the fifteenth century Cesena was governed by the powerful
family of Malatesta, one of whom, Domenico Malatesta Novello,
built the library in 1452, and placed it under the charge of the
convent of S. Francesco. Two burghers were associated with
the Friars in this duty. The library was always public. It was
designed by Matteo Nuzio of Fano, a celebrated architect of
the day, as we learn from an inscription originally inserted into
the wall on the right of the door of entrance, but now placed
inside the library:

MATHEVS . NVTIVS .
FANENSI EX VRBE . CREATVS .
DEDALVS ALTER . OPVS .
TANTVM . DEDVXIT . AD VNGVEM .

The general plan and arrangement will be readily understood
from the ground-plan (fig. 90), and the longitudinal section

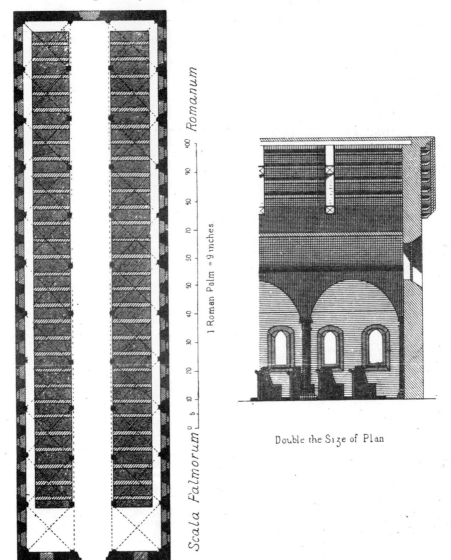

Figs. 90, 91. Ground-plan and section of Library at Cesena.

(fig. 91), copied on a reduced scale from those given by the
learned Giuseppe Maria Muccioli, who published a catalogue of

Fig. 92. General view of the Library at Cesena.

From a photograph.

the MSS. in the library in 1780[1]; and also from the general view
of the interior (fig. 92). It is a long narrow building, 133 ft. 4 in.
long, by 34 ft. broad[2], standing east and west, so that its windows
face north and south. It is on the first floor, being built over
some rooms which once belonged to the convent, and is entered
at the west end through a lofty marble doorway. Internally it
is divided into three aisles, of which the central is the narrowest,
by two rows of ten fluted marble columns. Against the side-
walls and partly engaged in them, are two rows of similar
columns. The aisles are divided by plain quadripartite vaults,
resting partly on the central columns, partly on those engaged
in the side-walls, into eleven bays, each lighted by two windows
(fig. 91). These aisles are about 12 ft. wide. The central aisle,
8 ft. 3 in. wide between the columns, has a plain barrel vault,
extending from end to end of the building.

The influence of the Renaissance may readily be detected in
the ornamentation of the columns, but traces of medieval forms
still linger in the room. If the central alley were wider it might
be taken for the nave of a basilica.

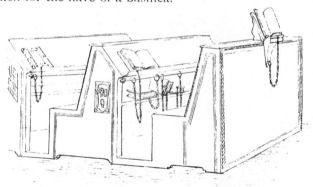

Fig. 93. Bookcases at west end of south side of Library, Cesena.

There are 29 bookcases in each aisle. Between each pair of
cases there is a wooden floor, raised 3½ in. above the general
level of the room; and there is an interval of 2 ft. 3 in. between
the cases and the wall, so that access may be readily obtained
to them from either end. The room is paved with unglazed tiles.

The westernmost bay is empty (fig. 90), being used as a

[1] Catalogus Codicum Manuscriptorum Malastestianæ Cæsenatis Bibliothecæ
fratrum minorum fidei custodiæque concreditæ....Auctore Josepho Maria Mucciolo
ejusdem ordinis fratre et Ravennatis cœnobii alumno. 2 vols. fol. Cæsenæ, 1780—84.

[2] These measurements were taken by myself, with a tape, in September, 1802

vestibule, and the first bookcase, if I may be allowed the expression, on each side, is really not a bookcase but a seat (fig. 93)[1].

The construction of these cases is most ingenious, both as
regards convenience and economy of space.   If they were

Fig. 94. Part of a bookcase at Cesena to shew the system of chaining.

designed by the architect who built the room, he must have
been a man of no ordinary originality.   Each piece of furniture
consists of a desk to lay the books on when wanted for use,
a shelf for those not immediately required, and a seat for the
reader, whose comfort is considered by a gentle slope in the
back (fig. 93).   At the end next the central alley is a panel
containing the heraldic devices of the Malatesta family.

[1] The desk bearing a single volume shewn on this seat (fig. 93) is modern.

The principal dimensions of each case are as follows:

Length	10 ft. 2½ in.
Height	4 ft. 2¼ in.
Width of seat	3 ft. 1 in.
Width of foot-rest	11 in.
Height ,, . . .	3½ in.
Height of seat from ground . .	1 ft. 10½ in.
Width ,, ...	1 ft. 4 in.
Distance from desk to desk . .	4 ft. 1 in.
Angle of slope of desk . . .	45°.

The books are still attached to the desks by chains. The bar which carries them is in full view just under the ledge of the desk (fig. 94), inserted into massive iron stanchions nailed to the underside of the desk. There are four of these: one at each end of the desk, and one on each side of the central standard. The bar is locked by means of a hasp attached to the standard in which the lock is sunk.

The chains are of a novel form (fig. 95). Each link, about 2¼ in. long, consists of a solid central portion, which looks as though it were cast round a bent wire, the ends of which project beyond the solid part. The chain is attached to the book by an iron hook screwed into the lower edge of the right-hand board near the back.

The volume which I figure next (fig. 96), entitled *Lumen animae seu liber moralitatum*,

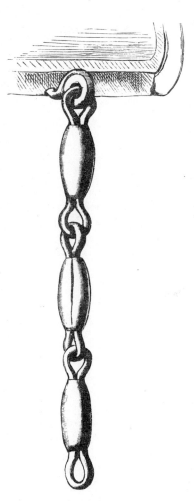

Fig. 95.   Piece of a chain, Cesena.

was printed at Eichstädt in Bavaria, in 1479. M. Ferd. Vander Haeghen, librarian of Ghent, bought it in Hungary a few years since, and gave it to the library which he so ably directs. The chain is just 24 in. long. The links, of which there are ten, are slightly different from any which I have figured, each link being

Fig. 96. Chained book at Ghent.

compressed in the middle so that the two sides touch each other. There is no ring, but a link, rather larger than the rest, is passed round the bar. It will be observed that the chain is fastened to the left-hand board, and not to the right-hand board as in Italy. The presence of a title written on parchment kept in place by strips of leather, and five bosses of copper, shew that the left-hand board was uppermost on the desk.   The position of the chain shews that when it was attached the book was intended to lie on a desk, where the bar must have been in front of, or below, the desk ; but there is also a scar on the upper edge of the right-hand board, which shews that at some previous period it lay on a desk of what I may call the Zutphen type, where the bar was above the sloping surface.

With the library at Cesena may be compared that attached to the Dominican Convent of S. Mark at Florence, built in 1441 for Cosmo dei Medici—the first public library in Italy.   It is on the first floor, and is approached by a staircase from the cloister. It is 148 ft. long by 34 ft. 6 in. wide[1], divided into three aisles by two rows of eleven columns.   The central aisle, 9 ft. wide between the columns, has a plain barrel vault ; the side aisles, 11 ft. wide, have quadripartite vaults.   In each of the side-walls there are twelve windows.   In all these details the library re-sembles that at Cesena so closely that I cannot help suspecting that Malatesta or his architect may have copied it.

The original fittings have been removed, but we learn from the catalogue[2] that the books were originally contained in 64 *banchi*, half of which were on the east side and half on the west side of the room.   There was an average of about sixteen books to each *banchus*.   The catalogue also mentions a Greek library, which had seven *banchi* on each side.   This was probably a separate room.

There is a similar library at the Benedictine Convent of Monte Oliveto, near Siena, but it is on a much smaller scale. Like the others, it is divided into three aisles by two rows of six columns.   The central aisle has a barrel vault, and the side aisles quadripartite vaults.   It is 85 ft. long by 32 ft. broad.   There are seven windows on one side only.   At the end of the library, approached by a flight of thirteen stairs, is a room of the same width and 21 ft. long, which may have been used as an inner

---

[1] These measurements were taken by myself with a tape, in April 1898, and verified in April 1899.

[2] This catalogue is in the State Archives at Modena.

library. An inscription over the door of entrance records that this library was built in 1516[1].

While discussing the arrangements of Italian libraries, I must not omit that at the Convent of S. Francis at Assisi[2]. The catalogue, dated 1 January, 1381, shews that the library, even at that comparatively early date, was in two divisions: (1) for the use of the brethren; (2) for loans to extraneous persons. This catalogue, after a brief preface stating that it includes "all the books belonging to the library of the Holy Convent of S. Francis at Assisi, whether they be chained, or whether they be not chained," begins as follows:

In the first place we make a list of the books which are chained to benches (*banchi*) in the Public Library as follows, and observe that all the leaves of all the books which are in this catalogue, whether they are in quires of 12, 10, 8, or any other number of leaves larger or smaller,—every one of these books contains the denomination of the quires, as appears in the first quire of each book on the lower margin : all the quires being marked at beginning and end in black and red with the figure here shewn, and the number of the quire within it.

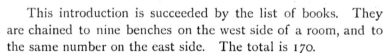

Moreover, the letters of the alphabet that are placed on the top of the covers ought all to be fairly large and entirely black, as marked below [in this catalogue] at the end of each book[3].

This introduction is succeeded by the list of books. They are chained to nine benches on the west side of a room, and to the same number on the east side. The total is 170.

---

[1] I visited Monte Oliveto 19 April, 1899.

[2] See *Ueber Mittelalterliche Bibliotheken*, v. T. Gottlieb. 8vo. 1890, p. 181. I have twice visited Assisi and examined the Catalogue here referred to. My best thanks are due to Professor Alessandri for giving me every assistance in my researches.

[3] Inprimis facimus inventarium de libris in libraria publica ad bancos cathenatis in hunc modum. Et nota, quod omnia folia omnium librorum, qui sunt in isto inuentario sive per sexternos vel quinternos aut quaternos seu quemvis per alium numerum maiorem vel minorem omnes quotquot sunt, nomina quaternorum tenent, ut apparet in quolibet libro in primo quaterno in margine inferiori ; quare omnes sunt ante et retro de nigro et rubeo per talem figuram intus cum suo numero signati. Item lictere alphabeti, qui desuper postes ponuntur, omnes debent esse aliquantulum grosse et totaliter nigre, sicut inferius in fine cuiuslibet libri signatur. The spots round this figure are alternately black and red.

The second part of the catalogue has the following heading:

In the name of the Lord, Amen. Here begins the list of all the books which are in the Reserved Library (*libraria secreta*) of the Holy Convent of S. Francis at Assisi, appointed to be lent to prelates, masters, readers, bachelors, and all other brethren in orders, according as the amount of knowledge or line of study of each demands them.

This part of the collection is contained in eleven presses (for which the unusual word *solarium*[1] is used) arranged along the east and west walls of a room, but whether the same as the last we are not informed. The number of manuscripts is 530.

A considerable number of the manuscripts here registered still exists. They are well taken care of in the Town Hall, and a list of them has been privately printed. Several are in their original condition, bound in boards about a quarter of an inch thick, covered with white leather. The title, written on a strip of parchment, is pasted on the top of the right-hand board. It usually begins with a capital letter in red or black, denoting the desk or press in which a given MS. would be found, thus:

F Postilla Magistri
Nicolai de lyra super psalmos
reponatur uersus orientem in banco vj°.

In the next place I will tell at length the story of the establishment of the Vatican Library by Pope Sixtus IV., as it is both interesting in itself and useful for my present purpose[2].

---

[1] Ducange s. v. *solarium* shews that occasionally it=*armarium*.

[2] I have to thank Father C. J. Ehrle, *S. J.*, Prefect of the Vatican Library, for the very great kindness with which he has assisted me in these researches during three visits to Rome in 1898, 1899, 1900; and also the officials who allowed me to examine parts of the palace not usually accessible to strangers.

Further, I wish it to be clearly and distinctly understood that my researches are based upon an essay by M. Paul Fabre, *La Vaticane de Sixte IV.*, which had appeared in the *Mélanges d'Archéologie et d'Histoire* of the *École Française de Rome* for December 1895, but of the existence of which I had never heard until Father Ehrle shewed it to me. On reading it, I found that M. Fabre had completely anticipated me; he had done exactly what I had come to Rome to do, and in such a masterly fashion that I could not hope to improve upon his work. After some consideration I determined to verify his conclusions by carefully examining the locality, and to make a fresh ground-plan of it for my own use. I have also studied the authorities quoted by M. Eugène Müntz (*Les Arts à la Cour des Papes*) from my own point of view.

There are two works to which I shall frequently refer: *Les Arts à la Cour des Papes pendant le xve et le xvie siècle*, par Eugène Müntz: Part III. 1882 (Bibl. des Écoles Françaises d'Athènes et de Rome, Fasc. 28): and *La Bibliothèque du Vatican*

The real founder of the Vatican Library, as we understand the term, was Nicholas V. (1447—1455), but he was unable to do more than collect books, for which no adequate room was provided till the accession of Sixtus IV. in 1471. In December of that year, only four months after his election, his chamberlain commissioned five architects to quarry and convey to the palace a supply of building-stone "for use in a certain building there to be constructed for library-purposes[1]"; but the scheme for an independent building, as indicated by the terms here employed, was soon abandoned, and nothing was done for rather more than three years. In the beginning of 1475, however, a new impulse was given to the work by the appointment of Bartolommeo Platina as Librarian (28 February)[2]; and from that date until Platina's death in 1481 it went forward without let or hindrance. This distinguished man of letters seems to have enjoyed the full confidence of the Pope, to have been liberally supplied with funds, and to have had a free hand in the employment of craftsmen and artists to furnish and decorate his Library. It is pleasant to be able to record that he lived to see his work completed, and all the books under his charge catalogued. The enumeration of the volumes contained in the different stalls, closets, and coffers, with which the catalogue of 1481 concludes, is headed by a rubric, which records, with pathetic simplicity, the fact that it was drawn up "by Platina, librarian, and Demetrius of Lucca his pupil, keeper, on the 14th day of September, 1481, only eight days before his death[3]."

au xve Siècle, par Eugène Müntz et Paul Fabre; Paris, 1887 (Ibid. Fasc. 48). The former will be cited as "Müntz"; the latter as "Müntz et Fabre." My paper, of which an abstract only is here given, has been published in the Camb. Ant. Soc. Proc. and Comm. 6 March 1899, Vol. X. pp. 11—61.

[1] This document, dated 17 December, 1471, has been printed by Müntz, p. 120. I am afraid that this order can have but one meaning: viz. the excavation and destruction of ancient buildings.

[2] This is the date assigned by Platina himself. See below, p. 231.

[3] MS. Vat. Lat. 3947, fol. 118 b. Notatio omnium librorum Bibliothecæ palatinæ Sixti quarti Pont. Max. tam qui in banchis quam qui in Armariis et capsis sunt a Platyna Bibliothecario et Demetrio Lucense eius alumno custode die xiiii. mensis Septemb. M.CCCC.LXXXI facta. Ante vero eius decessum dierum octo tantummodo. This Notatio has been printed, Müntz et Fabre, p. 250, but without the catalogue to which it forms an appendix. This, so far as I know, still remains unprinted.

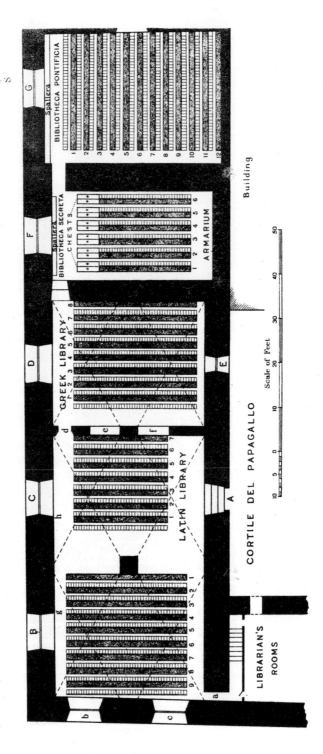

Fig. 98. Ground-plan of the rooms in the Vatican Palace fitted up for library-purposes by Sixtus IV.

It is evident that the Library had suffered considerably from the negligence of those in whose charge it had been. Many volumes were missing, and those that remained were in bad condition. Platina and his master set to work energetically to remedy these defects. The former engaged a binder, and bought materials for his use[1]; the latter issued a Bull (30 June) of exceptional severity[2]. After stating that "certain ecclesiastical and secular persons, having no fear of God before their eyes, have taken sundry volumes in theology and other faculties from the library, which volumes they still presume rashly and maliciously to hide and secretly to detain"; such persons are warned to return the books in question within forty days. If they disobey they are *ipso facto* excommunicated. If they are clerics they shall be incapable of holding livings, and if laymen, of holding any office. Those who have knowledge of such persons are to inform against them. The effect produced by this document has not been recorded; nor are we told what the extent of the loss was. It could hardly have been very extensive, for a catalogue which Platina prepared, or perhaps only signed, on the day of his election, enumerates 2527 volumes, of which 770 were Greek and 1757 Latin[3]. The number of the latter had more than doubled in the twenty years that had elapsed since the death of Nicholas V., an augmentation due, in all probability, to the activity of Sixtus himself.

The place selected to contain this extensive collection was the ground-floor of a building which had been erected by Nicholas V. and subsequently used as a provision store. The position of it, and its relations to neighbouring structures, will be understood from the accompanying plan (fig. 97), which I borrow from M. Fabre's paper. In order to shew how the building was arranged when it was first built, before other structures abutted against it, I have prepared a second plan (fig. 98) drawn from measurements taken by myself.

The floor is divided into four rooms by party-walls which are probably older than 1475, but which are proved, by the catalogue of 1481, to have been in existence at that period.

---

[1] Müntz et Fabre, pp. 148—150, *passim*.   [2] *Ibid.* p. 32.
[3] *Ibid.* p. 141. The catalogue is printed pp. 159—250.

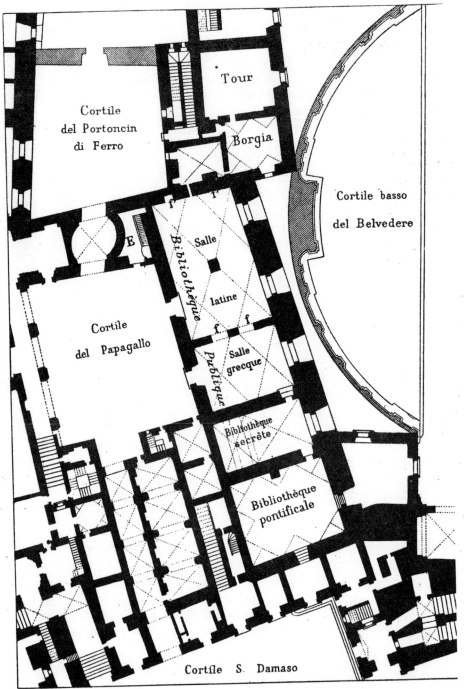

Fig. 97. Ground-plan of part of the Vatican Palace, shewing the building of Nicholas V., as arranged for library purposes by Sixtus IV., and its relation to the surrounding structures.

From Letarouilly, *Le Vatican*, fol. Paris, 1882, as reproduced by M. Fabre.

The first of these rooms, entered directly from the court, contained the Latin Library; the second, the Greek Library. These two, taken together, formed the Common, or Public, Library (*Bibliotheca communis, B. publica*, or merely *Bibliotheca*). Next to this room, or these rooms, was the *Bibliotheca secreta* or Reserved Library, in which the more precious MSS. were kept apart from the others. The fourth room, which was not fitted up till 1480 or 1481, was called *Bibliotheca pontificia*. In addition to MSS. it contained the papal archives and registers (*Regesta*). In the catalogue dated 1512 it is called *Intima et ultima secretior bibliotheca*, and seems to have contained the most valued treasures. This quadripartite division is commemorated by Aurelio Brandolini (Epigram XII.)[1]. After alluding to the founders of some of the famous libraries of antiquity, he says in conclusion :

> Bibliotheca fuit, fateor, sua cuique, sed vna.
> Sixte pater vincis: quatuor vnus habes.

Thanks to the care with which Platina set down his expenditure, we are able to follow step by step the gradual transformation of the rooms. His account-books[2], begun 30 June 1475, record, with a minuteness as rare as it is valuable, his transactions with the different artists and workmen whom he thought proper to employ. It was evidently intended that the library should be beautiful as well as useful, and some of the most celebrated artists of the day were set to work upon it.

The librarian prudently began in August, 1475, by increasing the light, and a new window was made "on the side next the court." It seems to have been impossible to get either workmen or materials in Rome ; both were supplied from a distance. For the windows, glass, lead and solder were brought from Venice, and a German, called simply Hormannus, i.e. Hermann, was hired to glaze them. For the internal decoration two well-known Florentine artists—the brothers Ghirlandajo—were engaged, with

---

[1] MS. Vat. 5008.

[2] These accounts, now preserved in the State Archives at Rome, have been printed with great accuracy (so far as I was able to judge from a somewhat hasty collation) by Müntz, *Les Arts à la Cour des Papes*, Vol. III. 1882, p. 121 sq.; and by Müntz and Fabre, *La Bibliothèque du Vatican au xve Siècle*, 1887, p. 148 sq.

Melozzo da Forli, who was painting there in 1477[1]. In 1476 the principal entrance was decorated with special care. Marble was bought for the doorcase, and the door itself was studded with 95 bronze nails, which were gilt, as were also the ring and knocker, and the frame of trellised ironwork (*cancellus*), which hung within the outer door.

The building is entered from the *Cortile del Papagallo*[2] through a marble doorway (fig. 98, A) in the classical style surmounted by the arms of Sixtus IV. On the frieze are the words SIXTUS PAPA IIII. The doorcase is doubtless that made in 1476; but the door, with its gilt nails and other adornments, has disappeared. Within the doorway there has been a descent of three steps at least to the floor of the Library[3]. The four rooms of which it was once composed are now used as the *Floreria* or *Garde-meuble* of the Vatican Palace; a use to which they have probably been put ever since the new Library was built at the end of the sixteenth century.

The Latin Library, into which the door from the court opens directly, is a noble room, 58 ft. 9 in. long, 34 ft. 8 in. wide, and about 16 ft. high to the spring of the vault. In the centre is a square pier, which carries the four plain quadripartite vaults, probably of brick, covered with plaster. The room is at present lighted by two windows (B, C) in the north wall, and by another, of smaller size, above the door of entrance (A). That this latter window was inserted by Sixtus IV., is proved by the presence of his arms above it on a stone shield. This is probably the window "next the court" made in 1475. The windows in the north wall are about 8 ft. high by 5 ft. broad, and their sills are 7 ft. above the floor of the room. Further, there were two windows in the west wall (*b, c*) a little smaller than those in

---

[1] The entries referring to these purchases are given in full, with translations, in my paper above referred to.

[2] The name is derived from the frescoes with which its external walls were decorated during the reign of Pius IV. (1559—1565). They represented palm trees, on which parrots (*papagalli*) and other birds were perching. Fragments of these frescoes are still to be seen. The court beyond this " del Portoncin di Ferro" was so called from an iron gate by which the passage into it from the Cortile del Papagallo could be closed.

[3] The difference of level between the floor of the court and the floor of the library is eighteen inches. An inclined plane of wood now replaces the steps.

the north wall, and placed at a much lower level, only a few feet above the floor. These were blocked when the Torre Borgia was built by Alexander VI. (1492—1503), but their position can still be easily made out. This room must have been admirably lighted in former days.

The room next to this, the Greek Library, is 28 ft. broad by 34 ft. 6 in. long. It is lighted by a window (fig. 98, D) in the north wall, of the same size as those of the Latin Library, and by another (*ibid.*, E) a good deal smaller, opposite to it. This room was originally entered from the Latin Library by a door close to the north wall (*d*). But, in 1480[1], two large openings (*e, f*) were made in the partition-wall, either because the light was found to be deficient, or because it was thought best to throw the two rooms into one as far as possible. At some subsequent date the door (*d*) was blocked up, and the opening next to it (*e*) was carried down to the ground, so as to do duty as a door. The other opening (*f*), about 7 ft. 6 in. square, remains as constructed.

The decorative work of the brothers Ghirlandajo can still be made out, at least in part, though time has made sad havoc with it. The edges of the vaulting were made prominent by classical moldings coarsely drawn in a dark colour; and at the key of each vault is a large architectural ornament, or coat of arms, surrounded by a wreath of oak-leaves and acorns, to commemorate the Della Rovere family. They are tied together on each side with long flaunting ribbons, which, with their shadows, extend for a considerable distance over the vaults. The semi-circular lunettes in the upper part of the wall under the vaults are all treated alike, except that those on the sides of the room, being larger than those at the ends (fig. 98), contain two subjects instead of one. The lower part, for about 3 feet in height, is painted to represent a solid marble balcony, behind which a Doctor or Prophet is supposed to be standing. He is visible from rather below the waist upwards, and holds in his hand a scroll bearing an appropriate text. On each side of the figure in the smaller lunettes, resting on the balcony, is a large

---

[1] Item pro purganda bibliotheca veteri et asportandis calcinaciis duarum fenestrarum factarum inter græcam et latinam b. xx die qua supra, i.e. 20 Aug. 1480. Müntz, p. 132.

vase of flowers; and behind it a clear sky. Round the upper
edge of the lunette is a broad band of oak-leaves, and fruits
of various kinds.   The figures, of which there were evidently
twelve originally, are the following, beginning with the one at
the north-east corner over the door leading into the Greek
Library, and proceeding to the right:

1. HIERONYMUS. *Scientiam scripturarum ama, et vitia carnis
   non amabis.*
2. GREGORIUS. *Dei sapientiam sardonyco et zaphyro non confer.*
3. THOMAS. *Legend illegible.*
4. BONAVENTURA. *Fructus scripturæ est plenitudo æternæ felici-
   tatis.*
5. ARISTOTELES.
6. DIOGENES.
7. CLEOBULUS.
8. ANTISTHENES.   *Legends illegible.*
9. SOCRATES.
10. PLATO.
11. AUGUSTINUS. *Nihil beatius est quam semper aliquid legere
    aut scribere.*
12. AMBROSIUS. *Diligentiam circa scripturas sanctorum posui.*

Jerome and Gregory occupy the east wall; Thomas Aquinas
and Bonaventura the first lunette on the south wall, over the
door of entrance; Aristotle and Diogenes the next, succeeded
by Cleobulus and Antisthenes on the west wall; on the first
lunette on the north wall are Socrates and Plato; in the second
Augustine and Ambrose, facing Aquinas and Bonaventura. Thus
the eastern half of the library was presided over by doctors of
the Christian Church, the western by pagan philosophers.

The space on the north wall (*gh*), nearly opposite to the door
of entrance, was occupied by the fresco on which Melozzo da
Forli was working in 1477. It was intended to commemorate
the establishment of the Library in a permanent home by
Sixtus the Fourth. The Pope is seated on the right of the
spectator. On his right stands his nephew, Cardinal Pietro
Riario, and before him, his head turned towards the Pope, to
whom he seems to be speaking, another nephew, Cardinal
Giuliano della Rovere, afterwards Pope Julius the Second.
At the feet of the Pope kneels Bartolommeo Platina, the newly

appointed Librarian, who is pointing with the forefinger of his right hand to the inscription below the fresco. Behind Platina are two young men with chains of office round their necks. The inscription, said to have been written by Platina himself, is as follows :

TEMPLA, DOMUM EXPOSITIS[1], VICOS, FORA, MŒNIA, PONTES,
    VIRGINEAM TRIVII QUOD REPARARIS AQUAM,
PRISCA LICET NAUTIS STATUAS DARE MUNERA PORTÛS,
    ET VATICANUM CINGERE, SIXTE, JUGUM,
PLUS TAMEN URBS DEBET ; NAM QUÆ SQUALORE LATEBAT
    CERNITUR IN CELEBRI BIBLIOTHECA LOCO.

The fresco is now in the Vatican picture-gallery. It was transferred to canvas soon after 1815, when the present gallery was formed, and has suffered a good deal from what is called restoration[2].

The decoration of the Greek Library is not alluded to in the Accounts[3]; but it is easy to see that the lunettes have been ornamented on the same system as those of the Latin Library, but without figures; for their decoration still exists, though much damaged by time and damp. Below the lunettes the walls are covered with whitewash, under which some decoration is evidently concealed. The whitewash has peeled off in some places, and colour is beginning to make its appearance.

The *Bibliotheca secreta* is 20 ft. wide by 38 ft. 6 in. long. It is lighted by a single window in the north wall (fig. 98, F), of the same size and shape as the rest. The light is sufficient, even under present conditions.

The fourth and last room—spoken of in 1480 as "that addition which our Master lately made"—is 29 ft. wide by 40 ft. 6 in. long. It is at present lighted by only a single window in the north wall (fig. 98, G), and is very gloomy. But

---

[1] A Foundling Hospital, alluding to the Ospedale di Santo Spirito founded by Sixtus IV.

[2] Fabre, *La Vaticane*, p. 464. Bunsen, *Die Beschreibung der Stadt Rom*, ed. 1832, Vol. II. Part 2, p. 418.

[3] The following entry is curious: Habuere Paulus et Dionysius pictores duos ducatos pro duobus paribus caligarum quas petiere a domino nostro dum pingerent cancellos bibliothecæ et restituerent picturam bibliothecæ græcæ, ita n. Sanctitas sua mandavit, die XVIII martii 1478. Müntz, p. 131.

in former days, before Julius II. (1503—1513) built the *Cortile di San Damaso*, it had another window in the middle of the east wall (*ibid.*, H), where there is now a door.   Nothing certain can be made out about its decoration.

It is much to be regretted that so little is said about the glazing of the windows throughout the Library.   Great care was evidently bestowed upon them, and the engagement of foreign artists, with the purchase of glass at Venice, are proofs that something specially beautiful was intended.   Coloured glass is mentioned, which may have been used either for coats of arms— and we know that the Papal Arms were to be set up in the *Bibliotheca secreta*—or for subjects.   But, in forming conjectures as to the treatment of these windows, it should be remembered that the transmission of light must always have been the first consideration, and that white glass must have preponderated.

The rooms for the Librarian and his assistants were in a small building which abutted on the Library at its S.W. corner, and stood between the two courts, obtaining light from each. Over the door of entrance was the inscription :

SIXTUS . IIII . PONT . MAX.

BIBLIOTECARIO . ET . CVSTODIBVS . LOCVM . ADDIXIT[1].

The accommodation provided was not magnificent, two rooms only being mentioned.   A door (fig. 98, *a*), now blocked, gave access to the Library from this building.   It is interesting to note, as a proof of the richness of all the work, that it was of inlaid wood (*pino intarsiata*).

The work of fitting up this Library occupied about six years.   It began in September 1475, and proceeded continuously to January 1477, when Melozzo's fresco was in progress.   In December of that year the windows of the *Bibliotheca secreta* were begun; but during 1478 and 1479 nothing was done. In 1480 work was resumed, and the last payment to painters was made in 1481.

Let us now consider how these rooms were fitted up for the reception of books.   I will first collect the notices in the Accounts respecting desks, or *banchi*, as they are called, and

---

[1] Fabre, *La Vaticane*, p. 465, citing Bandini, *Bibliothecæ Mediceo-Laurentianæ catalogus*, I. p. xxxviii.

then compare them with the rooms themselves, and with the descriptions in the catalogues, which are fortunately extremely full; and I think that it will be possible to give a clear and consistent picture of the arrangements.

Platina ordered the desks for the Latin Library first, in 1475. This is set down in the following terms:

I have counted out, in the presence of Clement, steward of the household of His Holiness our Master, Salvatus the library-keeper (*librarius*), and Demetrius the reader (*lector*), 45 ducats to Francis the carpenter of Milan, now dwelling in the fishmarket of the city of Rome, towards making the desks in the library; and especially ten desks which stand on the left hand, the length of which is 38 palms or thereabouts; and so having received a part of the money, the total of which is 130 ducats, he promises and binds himself to do that which it is his duty to do, this 15th day of July, 1475[1].

The full name of this carpenter is known, from his receipts, to have been Francesco de Gyovane di Boxi da Milano. He received in all 300 ducats instead of the 130 mentioned in the first agreement, and when the last payment was made to him, 7 June, 1476, the following explanatory note is given:

Moreover I have paid to the same [Francis the carpenter] 30 ducats for what remains due on 25 desks for the Library: for the longer ones, which are 10 in number, there were paid, as entered above, 130 ducats; for the rest there were paid 170 ducats, making a total of 300 ducats, and so he has been paid in full for all the desks, this 7th day of June, 1476[2].

In 1477 the furniture for the next room, the *Bibliotheca secreta* or Inner Library, was begun. The work was entrusted to a Florentine, called in the Accounts merely *Magister Joanninus faber lignarius de Florentia*, but identified by M. Fabre

---

[1] Enumeravi, præsente Clemente synescalcho familiæ s. d. n., Salvato librario, et Demetrio lectore, ducatos XLV Francischo fabro lignario mediolanensi habitatori piscinæ urbis Romæ pro banchis Bibliothecæ conficiendis, maxime vero decem quæ ad sinistram jacent, quorum longitudo est XXXVIII palmorum, vel circa, et ita accepta parte pecuniarum, cujus summa est centum et XXX ducatorum, facturum se debitum promittit et obligat, die XV Julii 1475. Müntz, p. 121.

[2] Item solvi eidem ducatos XXX pro reliquo XXV banchorum bibliothecæ: pro longioribus autem qui sunt X solvebantur centum et triginta, ut supra scriptum est; pro reliquis solvebantur centum et septuaginta; quæ summa est tricentorum ducatorum: atque ita pro banchis omnibus ei satisfactum est, die VII Junii 1476. Müntz, p. 126. The rest of the money had been paid to him by instalments between 15 July, 1475, and this date.

with Giovannino dei Dolci, one of the builders of the Sistine chapel. The most important entry referring to him is the following :

> Master Giovannino, carpenter of Florence, had from me Platyna, librarian of His Holiness our Master, for making the desks in the inner library, for the great press, and the settle, in the said room—all of which were estimated by Master Francis of Milan at one hundred and eighty ducats—he had, as aforesaid, sixty-five ducats and sixty groats on the 7th May, 1477[1].

The last payment on this account was made 18 March, 1478, on which day he also received eight ducats for three frames "to contain the names of the books," and for some repairs to old desks[2]. These frames were painted by one of Melozzo da Forli's workmen[3]. In February, 1481, 12 book-chests were supplied[4].

The desks for the fourth room or *Bibliotheca pontificia* were ordered in 1480—81. The workmen employed were Giovannino and his brother Marco.

> Master Giovannino of Florence and Master Marco his brother, a carpenter, received xxv ducats in part payment for the desks which are being made in the library now added by His Holiness our Master, 18 July, 1480[5].

These workmen received 100 ducats up to 7 April, 1481, but the account was not then settled. Up to this period the bookcases had cost the large sum of 580 ducats or, if the value

---

[1] Magister Joanninus faber lignarius de Florentia habuit a me Platyna s. d. n. bibliothecario pro fabrica banchorum Bibliothecæ secretæ, pro Armario magno et Spaleria ejusdem loci, quæ omnia extimata fuerunt centum et octuaginta ducat' a magistro Francisco de Mediolano ; habuit, ut præfertur, ducatos sexaginta quinque et bononenos sexaginta die VII maii 1477. Müntz, p. 130. There were 100 bononeni in each ducat.

[2] Habuit ultimo ducatos octo pro tribus tabulis ex nuce cornisate (?) ad continenda nomina librorum e per le cornise de tre banchi vechi ex nuce die supradicta ; nil omnino restat habere ut ipse sua manu affirmat, computatis in his illis LX bononenis qui superius scribuntur. Müntz, p. 130.

[3] Dedi Joanni pictori famulo m. Melotii pro pictura trium tabularum ubi descripta sunt librorum nomina carlenos XVIII die X Octobris 1477. *Ibid.*, p. 131.

[4] Item pro XII capsis latis in bibliothecam secretam. Müntz et Fabre, p. 158.

[5] Magister Joanninus de Florentia et m. Marcus ejus frater faber lignarius habuere ducatos XXV pro parte solucionis banchorum quæ fiunt in bibliotheca addita nunc a Sᵐᵒ. d. nostro, die XVIII Julii 1480. Müntz, p. 134.

of the ducat be taken at six shillings and sixpence, £188 10*s.* of our money.

The purchase of chains began in January 1476[1]. It is worth notice that so simple an article as a chain for a book could not be bought in Rome, but had to be sent for from Milan ; where, by the way, the dues exacted by the government made the purchase irksome and costly.   The total number of chains bought was 1728, and the total cost 102 ducats, or rather more than £33.   The rings were found to be too small, and were altered in Rome.   Nothing is said about the place from which the rods came (*ferramenta quibus catenæ innituntur*).

In 1477 (14 April) "John the chain-maker (*Joannes fabricator catenarum*)" supplies "48 iron rods on which the books are strung on the seats[2]" and also 48 locks, evidently connected with the same number of rods supplied before.   In the same year a key-maker (*magister clavium*) supplies 22 locks for the seats and cupboards in the *Bibliotheca secreta*[3] ; and in 1480, when the *Bibliotheca pontificia* was being fitted up, keys, locks, chains, and other ironwork were supplied by Bernardino, nephew of John of Milan[4].

For further information we must turn to the catalogues. For my present purpose the first of these[5] is that by Platina, of which I have already spoken, dated 14 September, 1481.   It is a small folio volume, written on vellum, with gilt edges, and in plain binding that may be original.   The first page has a lovely border of an enlaced pattern with the arms of Sixtus IV. in a circle at the bottom.

The compiler of the catalogue goes through the library case by case, noting (at least in the Latin Library) the position of the case, the subjects of the books contained in it, and their titles.   This is succeeded by an enumeration of the number of volumes, so as to shew, in a couple of pages, how many the

---

[1] Müntz, pp. 124—126.

[2] Magister Joannes fabricator catenarum habuit a me die XIIII aprilis 1477 ducatos decem, ad summam centum et quinque ducatorum quos ei debebam pro tribus miliaribus et libris octingentis ferri fabrefacti ad usum bibliothecæ, videlicet pro quadraginta octo virgis ferreis ad quas in banchis libri connectuntur [etc.]. Müntz, p. 128.

[3] *Ibid.*, p. 127.   [4] *Ibid.*, p. 135.

[5] MSS. Vat. 3947.

whole Library contained. MM. Müntz and Fabre print this enumeration, but, so far as I know, the catalogue itself has not as yet been printed by any one. For my present purpose I shall combine the headings of the catalogue, the subjects, and the number of the volumes, as follows:

Inventarium Bibliothecæ Palatinæ Divi Sexti Quarti Pont. Max.

[I. LATIN LIBRARY.]

Ad sinistram ingredientibus

In primo banco. *[Bibles and Commentaries]* . .	51
In secundo banco. *Hieronymus. Augustinus* . .	55
In tertio banco. *Augustinus. Ambrosius. Gregorius*	47
In quarto banco. *Ioannes Chrysostomus* . . .	50
In quinto banco. *Thomas*	47
In sexto banco. *In Theologia. In divino officio* .	54
In septimo banco. *Ius canonicum* . . .	43
In octauo banco. *Ius canonicum* . . .	41
In nono banco. *Ius civile*	42
	— 430

In primo banco ad dextram ingredientibus. *Philosophi*	53
In secundo banco. *Astrologi. In Medicina* . .	48
In tertio banco. *Poetæ*	41
In quarto banco. *Oratores*	43
In quinto banco. *Historici*	33
In sexto banco. *Historici ecclesiastici* . . .	48
In septimo banco. *Grammatici*	47
	— 313

[II. GREEK LIBRARY.]

In primo banco Bibliothecæ Grecæ. *Testamentum vetus et novum*	42
In secundo banco. *Auctores clariores [Fathers]* .	31
In tertio banco. *Auctores clariores*	46
In quarto banco. *Auctores clariores*	49
In quinto banco. *Ius civile et canonicum* . . .	58
In sexto banco. *In Philosophia*	59
In septimo banco. *Oratores et Rhetores* . . .	57
In octauo banco. *Historici. Poetæ et Grammatici* .	58
	— 400

[III. INNER LIBRARY.]

[A. BANCHI.]

In primo banco Bibliothecæ Secretæ. [*Bibles, Fathers, etc.*]   29
In secundo banco. *In Theologia*   37
In tertio banco. *In Philosophia*   41
In quarto banco. *Ius canonicum*   20
In quinto banco. *Concilia*   34
In sexto banco. *In Astrologia. In Hebraico. In Dalmatico. In Arabico*   29
                                                                ——— 190

[B. ARMARIUM.]

In primo armario Bibliothecæ Secretæ. *Libri sacri et in divino officio*   173
In secundo armario. *Ius canonicum. Ius civile* .   148
In tertio armario. *Expositiones. In sententiis. Poetæ. Grammatici et Historici Greci* .   .   .   242
In quarto armario. *In medicina. Mathematici et Astrologi. Ius canonicum et civile. Oratores et Rhetores. Platonis Opera. In Philosophia* .   186
In quinto armario. *Auctores clariores* .   .   189
                                                                ——— 938

[C. CAPSÆ.]

In prima capsa primi banchi Bibliothecæ Secretæ. *In Theologia*   107
In secunda capsa primi banchi. *Diversa facultas* [*Miscellanea*]   66
In prima capsa secundi banchi. [*Privileges and Royal Letters in 3 volumes*]   3
In secunda capsa secundi banchi. [*Miscellanea*] .   124
In prima capsa tertii banchi. *Philosophi* .   .   90
In secunda capsa tertii banchi .   .   .   .   [oo]
In prima capsa quarti banchi. *Historici* .   .   65
In secunda capsa quarti banchi .   .   .   [oo]
In prima capsa quinti banchi. [*Official forms*] .   43
In secunda capsa quinti banchi. *In Arabico* .   23
In prima capsa sexti banchi. *In Historia ecclesiastica. Ceremonialia*   67
In secunda capsa sexti banchi. *Libri sine nomine ad quinquaginta parvi et modici quidem valoris* .   50
                                                                ——— 638

[D. SPALERA.]

In prima capsa spaleræ Bibliothecæ Secretæ. *In Poesi. Oratores Rhetores*   69
In secunda capsa. *In divino officio et sermones* .   59
In tertia capsa. *Concilia et Canon. De potestate ecclesiastica*   54
In quarta et ultima capsa. *In Medicina. In Astrologia* 34
                                                                ——— 216

[IV. Bibliotheca Pontificia.]

[A. Banchi.]

In primo banco Bibliothecæ Pontificiæ. *Testamentum vetus et novum*	19
In secundo banco. *Expositores*	22
In tertio banco. *Augustinus*	14
In quarto banco. *Hieronymus*	23
In quinto banco. *In Theologia*	22
In sexto banco. *In Theologia*	18
In septimo banco. *Thomas*	23
In octavo banco. *In Philosophia*	29
In nono banco. [*Greek and Latin Classics*] . .	25
In decimo banco. *Ius canonicum*	28
In undecimo banco. [*Civil Law*]	17
In duodecimo banco. [*New Testament. Fathers*] .	19

——— 259

[B. Spalera.]

Regestra Pontificum hic descripta in capsis Spaleræ Bibliothecæ Pontificiæ per Platinam Bibliothecarium ex ordine recondita et in capsa prima .	21
In secunda capsa Spaleræ Bibliothecæ Pontificiæ .	47
In tertia capsa Bibliothecæ Pont. Regestra recondita par Platynam Bibliothecarium	16
In quarta capsa Spaleræ Bibliothecæ Pontificiæ Regestra recondita	16
In quinta capsa Spaleræ Bibliothecæ Pontificiæ Regestra recondita	15

These lists give the following results:

Latin Library,	left hand,	9 seats	430	
,,	,, right	,, 7 ,,	313	
				743
Greek Library		8 ,,		400
Inner ,,		6 ,,	190	
		Armaria	938	
		Capsæ	638	
		Spalera	216	
				1982
Bibliotheca Pontificia		12 seats	259	
		5 Capsæ (Regestra)	115	
				374
		Total		3499

Before proceeding farther, it should be noticed that, on a rough average, each seat in the Latin Library, left hand, contained 47 volumes, and in the same Library, right hand, 43 volumes. In the Greek Library, each seat contained 50 volumes; in the Inner Library, 31 volumes; in the *Bibliotheca pontificia*, 21 volumes.

In the next place I will give the results of the examination of a catalogue[1] of the Library, which M. Fabre, with much probability, assigns to the year 1512[2]. It begins as follows with the Latin Library:

Ad sinistra' Pontificis bibliothecam introeuntibus
In primo scanno supra   . . . . . [27]
    „   „   infra   . . . . . [27]
Finis primi scanni sub et supra   . . . [54]

The nine seats (*banchi*) of the left side of the Latin Library are gone through in the same way as the first, with the result that each is shewn to have two shelves. The total number of books is 457, or 27 more than in 1481.

On the opposite, or right-hand side of the Library, the first two seats have three shelves, and are described as follows:

In primo scanno supra   . . . . . [22]
    „   „   infra   . . . . [27]
  „ eodem scanno inferius siue sub infra . . [26]
Finis primi scanni sub et subter   . . . [75]

On this side of the Latin Library the number of books has risen to 360 as against 313 of the previous catalogue.

In the Greek Library there are similarly two shelves to each seat, and the total number of volumes is 407 as against 400.

The account of the Inner Library begins as follows:

In secretiori bibliotheca
In iij°. scanno supra.   . . . . . [16]
  „   „   infra .   . . . . . [17]
  „   „   inferius siue sub infra   . . [21]

Three of the seats have three shelves; the rest two; and the total number of volumes has become 222 as against 190: or, an average of 37 to each seat.

---

[1] MSS. Vat. 7135.   [2] *La Vaticane*, etc., p. 475

The *Bibliotheca pontificia* is introduced with the following heading :

In intima et ultima secretiori bibliotheca ubi libri sunt pretiosiores.

Each seat has two shelves, and the total number of volumes is 277 as against 259 in 1481. Among the MSS. occurs " Virgilius antiquus litteris maiusculis "—no doubt the Vatican Virgil (*Codex romanus*), a volume which fully justifies its place among those termed *libri pretiosiores*.

This catalogue closes with the following sentence :

Finis totius Bibliothece Pontificie : viz. omnium scamnorum tam Latinorum quam Grecorum in prima, secunda, tertia, et quarta eius distinctione et omnium omnino librorum : exceptis armariis et capsis : et iis libris, qui Græci ex maxima parte, in scabellis parieti adherentibus in intima ac penitissima Bibliothece parte sunt positi. Deo Laudes et Gratias.

The increase between 1481 and 1512 in the number of volumes in the parts of the Library defined in the above catalogue will be best understood from the following table, which shews that 131 volumes had been added in 31 years.

	1481	1512
Latin Library	743	817
Greek „	400	407
Bibliotheca secreta	190	222
„ pontificia	259	277
Total	1592	1723

Another catalogue, unfortunately without date[1], but which has every appearance of belonging to the same period, notes the rooms as the *Bibliotheca magna publica*, i.e. the Latin and Greek Libraries taken together, the *Bibliotheca parva secreta*, and the *Bibliotheca magna secreta*.

The catalogue drawn up by Zenobio Acciaioli, 12 October, 1518[2], offers no peculiarity except that in the Inner Library each seat is noted as having three rows of books, thus :

In primo bancho bibliothece parve secrete
Infra in secundo ordine
„   tertio   „

[1] MS. Vat. 3946.   [2] MS. Vat. 3948.

Fig. 99. Interior of the Library of Sixtus IV., as shewn in a fresco in the Ospedale di Santo Spirito, Rome.

From a photograph taken by Danesi.

We may now proceed to arrange the Library in accordance with the information derived from the Accounts and the catalogues, compared with the ground-plan (fig. 98).

These authorities shew that in each of the rooms the books were arranged on what are called *banchi*, or as they would have been termed in England, desks, or seats, to which the books were attached by chains. It is obvious, therefore, that there must have been also seats for readers. A piece of furniture fulfilling these conditions and constructed twenty-five years earlier, is still to be seen at Cesena, as I have just explained. Further, I have examined a good many manuscripts now in the Vatican Library which formed part of the older collection; and wherever the mark of the chain has not been obliterated by rebinding, it is in the precise position required for the above system.

If I am right in supposing that the cases at Cesena are a survival of what was once in general use, we should expect to find another example of them in the Vatican; and that such was the case, is proved by the evidence of a fresco in the Ospedale di Santo Spirito at Rome, representing the interior of the library. This hospital was rebuilt by Sixtus IV. on an enlarged scale[1], and after its completion in 1482, one of the halls on the ground floor was decorated with a series of frescoes representing the improvements which he had carried out in the city of Rome. Recent researches[2] make it probable that the earlier pictures in the series of which the library is one, were selected by Platina, and executed before his death in 1481. I am able to present to my readers a reduced copy of this invaluable record (fig. 99) executed for me by Signor Danesi, under the kind superintendence of Father Ehrle.

The artistic merit of such a work as this is not great, but I feel sure that the artist faithfully reproduced what he saw with the limitations prescribed by his own want of skill. The desks bear a general resemblance to those at Cesena; they are plainer than the Accounts would warrant, but this may be due

---

[1] For an account of what Sixtus accomplished at Santo Spirito see Pastor, *History of the Popes*, Eng. Tran. IV. 460—462.

[2] Brockhaus, *Janitschek's Repertorium für Kunstwissenschaften*, Band VII. (1884); Schmarsow, *Melozzo da Forli* (1886), pp. 202—207.

C. L.   15

to want of skill on the part of the artist. The chains have also been omitted either for the same reason or from a wish to avoid detail. It will be noticed that each desk is fully furnished with volumes laid out upon it, and that these vary in number and size, and have different bindings. It may be argued that the artist wished to compliment his patrons by making the most of their property; but I should be inclined to maintain that this was the normal condition of the Library, and that the books, handsomely bound and protected by numerous bosses of metal, usually lay upon the desks ready for use.

If this fresco be compared with the earlier work of Melozzo da Forli, it is not difficult to identify four of the persons present in the Library (other than the readers). The central figure is obviously Sixtus IV., and the Cardinal to whom he is speaking is, I think, meant for Giuliano della Rovere, afterwards Julius II. The figure immediately behind the Pope may be intended for Pietro Riario, and the figure behind him is certainly Platina. The others, I take it, are simply attendants.

Nor must it be forgotten that, important as this fresco is in connexion with the Library of the Vatican, it is of even greater interest as a contemporary representation of a large fifteenth century library.

The arrangement of each room is not quite so simple as might appear at first sight; and, besides the desks, there are other pieces of furniture to be accounted for. We will therefore go through the rooms in order with the ground-plan (fig. 98). On this plan the cases are coloured gray, the readers' seats are indicated by transverse lines, and the intervals are left white.

Latin Library. The Accounts tell us that there were 10 seats on the left hand of the Latin Library, and that these were longer than the rest, measuring 38 palms each, or about 27 ft. 9 in. English[1].

As the distance from the central pier to the west wall is just 27 ft. 6 in., it is obvious that the cases must have stood north and south—an arrangement which is also convenient for readers, as the light would fall on them from the left hand. For this reason I have placed the first desk against the pier,

---

[1] I have taken 1 palm = mètre 0·223; and 1 mètre = 39·37 in.

the reader's seat being westward of it.   A difficulty now arises. It is stated in the Accounts that *ten banchi* are paid for, but all the catalogues mention only *nine*.   I suggest that the explanation is to be found in the fact that ten pieces of furniture do occur between the pier and the wall, the first of which is a shelf and desk, and the last a seat only.   This arrangement is to be seen at Cesena and in the Medicean Library at Florence. The room being 34 ft. 8 in. wide, space is left for a passage along the south wall to the door (*a*) of the Librarian's room, and also for another along the opposite ends of the desks.

For the arrangement of the rest of the Library, the Accounts give a most important piece of information.   They tell us that the whole of the seats for the Common Library, i.e. the Latin and Greek Libraries taken together, 25 in number, cost 300 ducats, of which sum the 10 long seats above mentioned absorbed 130 ducats, leaving 170 to pay for the remaining 15. From these data it is not difficult to calculate the cost of each palm, and from that the number of palms that 170 ducats would buy.   I make this to be 510 palms, or about 373 feet[1].

It is, I think, obvious that there must have been some sort of vestibule just inside the door of entrance, where students could be received, and where they could consult the catalogue or the Librarian.   Further, the catalogues shew that the seven desks arranged in this part of the Library were in all probability shorter than those of the opposite side, for they contained fewer volumes.   If we allow each of them 21 ft. 4 in. in length, we shall dispose of 149 ft., which leaves 224 ft. for the 8 desks of the Greek Library, or 28 ft. for each, with one foot over.

Greek Library.   In this room there were eight seats, and, as explained above, each was about 28 ft. long.   The room being 28 ft. wide, this number, with a width of 3 ft. for each, is very convenient, and leaves a passage 4 ft. wide along the west wall.   The length, moreover, does not interfere with the

---

[1] My calculation works out as follows.   Each of 10 seats was 38 palms long : total length, 380 palms.   As these 10 seats cost 130 ducats, each palm cost ¹³⁰⁄₃₈₀ ducats = ⅓ of a ducat nearly.

As the total paid was 300 ducats, this first payment, viz. 130 ducats, left 170 ducats still due for the 15 remaining seats.   As each palm cost a third of a ducat, 170 ducats would buy 510 palms = 113·73 metres = 4477 inches (nearly) — 373 feet.

passage from door to door, and leaves a short interval between the ends of the desks and the opposite wall.

Inner Library. In this room space has to be provided for (1) six seats, each holding on an average about 30 volumes; (2) a press (*armarium*) with five divisions, and holding 938 volumes; (3) a settle (*spalera*); (4) 12 chests or coffers (*capsæ*).

I have placed the *armarium* at the end of the room, opposite the window. In this position it can be allowed to be 20 ft. in width with 5 divisions, each, we will suppose, about 4 ft. wide. Let us suppose further that it was 7 ft. high, and had 6 shelves. If we allow 8 volumes to each foot, each shelf would hold 32 volumes, and each division six times that number, or 192. This estimate for each division will give a total of 960 volumes for the five divisions, a number slightly in excess of that mentioned in Platina's catalogue.

After allowing a space 5 ft. wide in front of the press, there is plenty of room left for 6 desks, each 21 ft. long. I have placed the *spalliera*, with its four coffers (*capsæ*) under the seat, below the window. This piece of furniture, in modern Italian *spalliera*, French *épaulière*, is common in large houses at the present day. It usually stands in an ante-room or on a landing of one of the long staircases. A portion at least of the *spalliere* used in this Library are still in existence. They stood in the vestibule of the present Vatican Library until a short time ago, when the present Pope had them removed to the Appartamento Borgia, where they stand against the wall round one of the rooms. There are two distinct designs of different heights and ornamentation. The photograph here reproduced (fig. 100) was taken specially for my use. The *spalliere* have evidently been a good deal altered in the process of fitting up, and moreover, as it is impossible to discover whether we have the whole or only a part of what once existed, it is useless to make any suggestion, from the length of the portions that remain, as to which room they may once have fitted. They are excellent specimens of inlaid work. That on the right, with the row of crosses along the cornice, is 6 ft. 2 in. high, and 66 ft. long. That on the left is 5 ft. 10 in. high, and 24 ft. 7 in. long. The *capsæ* project from the wall 1 ft. 4 in., and are 2 ft. high. Their lids vary a little in length, from 3 ft. 11 in. to 4 ft. 10 in.

Fig. 100. The library-settles (*spalliere*) once used in the Vatican Library of Sixtus IV., and now in the Appartamento Borgia.

From a photograph.

But the presence of a *spalliera* is not the only peculiarity in the furniture of this room. Platina's catalogue shews that, connected in some manner with each seat, were two coffers (*capsæ*); and we have seen that 12 such chests were brought into the Library in 1481. I have placed these in pairs at the ends of the desks opposite the settle (*spalliera*).

Innermost Library, or *Bibliotheca pontificia*. This Library contained 12 desks. These, from their number, must have stood east and west. There was also a *spalliera*, which held the Papal Registers. I have placed it in the recess on the north side of the room, which looks as though made for it.

It should be noted that there was a map of the world in the Library, for which a frame was bought in 1478[1]; and a couple of globes—the one celestial, the other terrestrial. Covers made of sheepskin were bought for them in 1477[2]. Globes with and without such covers are shewn in the view of the Library of the University of Leyden taken in 1610 (fig. 69); and M. Fabre reminds us that globes still form part of the furniture of the Library of the Palazzo Barberini in Rome, fitted up by Cardinal Francesco Barberini, 1630—40[3].

Comfort was considered by the provision of a brazier on wheels "that it may be moved from place to place in the Library[4]."

The following curious rule, copied, as it would appear, in the Library itself, by Claude Bellièvre of Lyons, who visited Rome about 1513, shews that order was strictly enforced:

Nonnulla quæ collegi in bibliotheca Vaticani. Edictum S. D. N. Ne quis in bibliotheca cum altero contentiose loquatur et obstrepat, neve de loco ad locum iturus scamna transcendat et pedibus conterat,

---

[1] Per lo tellaro del mappamondo b. 52. Müntz, p. 129. Habuere pictores armorum quæ sunt facta in duabus sphæris solidis et pro pictura mappemundi ducatos III, die XII decembris 1477. Müntz et Fabre, p. 151. This map had probably been provided by Pius II. (1458—1464), who kept in his service Girolamo Bellavista, a Venetian maker of maps. Müntz et Fabre, 126.

[2] Expendi pro cohopertura facta duobus sphæris solidis quarum in altera est ratio signorum, in altera cosmographia, ducatos IIII videlicet cartenos XVI in octo pellibus montoninis, cartenos XXV in manifactura; sunt nunc ornata graphio cum armis s. d. n., die XX decembris 1477. Müntz et Fabre, p. 152. M. Fabre quotes an extract in praise of the map and globes from a letter written from Rome in 1505, *La Vaticane de Sixte IV.*, p. 471 *note*.

[3] *Ibid.*   [4] Müntz, p. 130.

atque libros claudat et in locum percommode reponat. Ubique volet perlegerit. Secus qui faxit foras cum ignominia mittetur atque hujusce loci aditu deinceps arcebitur[1].

Before concluding, I must quote an interesting description of this Library by Montaigne :

Le 6 de Mars [1581] je fus voir la librerie du Vatican qui est en cinq ou six salles tout de suite. Il y a un grand nombre de livres atachés sur plusieurs rangs de pupitres ; il y en a aussi dans des coffres, qui me furent tous ouverts ; force livres écris à mein et notamment un Seneque et les Opuscules de Plutarche. J'y vis de remercable la statue du bon Aristide[2] à tout une bele teste chauve, la barbe espesse, grand front, le regard plein de douceur et de magesté : son nom est escrit en sa base très antique...[3]

Je la vis [la Bibliothèque] sans nulle difficulté ; chacun la voit einsin et en extrait ce qu'il veut ; et est ouverte quasi tous les matins, et si fus conduit partout, et convié par un jantilhomme d'en user quand je voudrois[4].

Sixtus IV. intended the library attached to the Holy See to be of the widest possible use. In the document appointing Demetrius of Lucca librarian, after Platina's death, he says distinctly that the library has been got together "for the use of all men of letters, both of our own age, or of subsequent time[5]"; and that these are not rhetorical expressions, to round a phrase in a formal letter of appointment, is proved by the way in which manuscripts were lent out of the library, during the whole time that Platina was in office. The Register of Loans, beginning with his own appointment and ending in 1485, has been printed by Müntz and Fabre, from the original in the Vatican Library[6], and a most interesting record it is. It is headed by a few words of warning, of which I give the general sense rather than a literal translation.

Whoever writes his name here in acknowledgment of books received on loan out of the Pope's library, will incur his anger and his curse unless he return them uninjured within a very brief period.

[1] Bibl. Nat. Paris, MSS. Lat. 13123, fol. 220, quoted by Müntz et Fabre, p. 140.

[2] This statue, found in Rome in the middle of the sixteenth century, represents Aristides Smyrnæus, a Greek rhetorician of the second century after Christ. It is still in the Vatican Library, at the entrance to the Museo Cristiano.

[3] In the omitted passage Montaigne describes a number of books shewn to him.

[4] *Journal du voyage de Michel de Montaigne en Italie*, ed. Prof. Alessandro d'Ancona. 8vo. Città di Castello, 1895, p. 269. I owe this quotation to M. Fabre.

[5] Müntz et Fabre, p. 299.

[6] *Ibid.*, pp. 269—298. MSS. Vat. Lat. 3964.

This statement is made by Platina, librarian to his Holiness, who entered upon his duties on the last day of February, 1475[1].

Each entry records the title of the book lent, with the name of the borrower. This entry is sometimes made by the librarian, but more frequently by the borrower himself. When the book is returned, Platina or his assistant notes the fact, with the date. The following entry, taken almost at random, will serve as a specimen:

Ego Gaspar de Ozino sapientissimi domini nostri cubicularius anno salutis MCCCCLXXV die vero XXI Aprilis confiteor habuisse nomine mutui a domino Platina Lecturam sive commentum in pergameno super libris x Etticorum Aristotelis, et in fidem omnium mea propria manu scripsi et supscripsi. Liber autem pavonatio copertus est in magno volumine.——Idem Gaspar manu propria.——Restituit fideliter librum ipsum et repositus est inter philosophos die XXVIII April 1475.

It is occasionally noted that a book is lent with its chain, as for instance:

Christoforus prior S. Balbine habuit Agathium Historicum ex banco VIII° cum cathena...Restituit die XX Octobris post mortem Platyne.

When no chain is mentioned are we to understand that the book was not so protected, and that there were in the library a number of books without chains, perhaps for the purpose of being more conveniently borrowed?

A few words should be added on the staff of the library. At first—that is during the year 1475—Platina had under his orders three subordinates, Demetrius, Salvatus, and John. These are called writers (*scriptores*) or keepers (*custodes*); and Salvatus is once called librarian (*librarius*), but it will be shewn below that this word means a writer rather than a librarian, as we understand the word. The position of these persons was extremely humble; and Salvatus was so indigent that his shoes were mended at the Pope's expense, and a decent suit of clothes provided for him at the cost of eight ducats[2]. Besides these

---

[1] Quisquis es qui tuum nomen hic inscribis ob acceptos commodo libros e bibliotheca pontificis, scito te indignationem ejus et execrationem incursurum nisi peropportune integros reddideris. Hoc tibi denuntiat Platyna, S. suæ bibliothecarius, qui tantæ rei curam suscepit pridie Kal. Martii 1475.

[2] Dedi die XIII Septembris 1475 ducatum unum Salvato scriptori pro emendis calligis. Item expendi pro veste una Salvati scriptoris seminudi et algentis ducatos VIII de mandato sancti domini nostri. Müntz et Fabre, p. 148.

there was a bookbinder, also called John.   In the following
year two keepers only are mentioned, Demetrius and Josias.
The latter died of the plague in 1478.   The salary of the
librarian was at the rate of ten ducats a month, and that of each
of his subordinates at the rate of one ducat for the same period.
This arrangement appears to have been confirmed by a Bull of
Sixtus IV. before the end of 1477[1].

These officers and Platina appear to have lived together in
the rooms adjoining the Latin Library, as shewn by the accounts
for the purchase of beds, furniture, and the like[2]; and when
Josias falls ill of the plague, Platina sends away Demetrius
and John the bookbinder, "for fear they should die or infect
others[3]."

All articles required for the due maintenance of the library
were provided by Platina.   The charges for binding and lettering
are the most numerous.   Skins were bought in the gross—on
one occasion as many as 600—and then prepared for use.   All
other materials, as gold, colours, varnish, nails, horn, clasps, etc.,
were bought in detail, when required; and probably used in
some room adjoining the library.   Platina also saw to the
illumination (*miniatio*) of such MSS. as required it.

Comfort and cleanliness were not forgotten.   There are
numerous charges for coals, with an amusing apology for their
use in winter "because the place was so cold"; and for juniper
to fumigate (*ad suffumigandum*).   Brooms are bought to clean
the library, and fox-tails to dust the books (*ad tergendos libros*[4]).

It should further be mentioned that Sixtus assigned an
annual income to the library by a brief dated 15th July, 1477.
It is therein stipulated that the fees, paid according to custom

---

[1] Habui ego Platyna sanctissimi domini nostri bibliothecarius ducatos triginta pro
salario meo, quod est decem ducatorum in mense, ab idibus Julii usque ad idus
Octobris 1477, quemadmodum apparet in bulla de facultatibus officiis et muneribus
a sanctissimo domino nostro papa Sixto IIII facta.   *Ibid.* p. 150.

[2] Müntz, pp. 129, 133.

[3] Item dedi ducatos quinque pro quolibet Demetrio et Johanni ligatori librorum
quos ex mandato domini nostri foras misi, mortuo ex peste eorum socio, ne ipsi
quoque eo loci interirent vel alios inficerent, die VIII junii 1478.   Müntz et Fabre,
p. 153.

[4] The entries alluded to in this account will all be found in Müntz and Fabre,
pp. 148—158.

by all officials appointed to any office vacated by resignation, should thenceforward be transferred to the account of the library[1].

While Sixtus IV. was thus engaged in Rome, a rival collector, Federigo da Montefeltro, Duke of Urbino (1444—1482), was devoting such leisure as he could snatch from warfare to similar pursuits. The room in which he stored his treasures is practically unaltered. It differs materially in arrangement from the other libraries of the same period. This difference is perhaps due to its position in a residence which was half palace, half castle. It is on the ground floor of a building which separates the inner from the outer court. It measures 45 ft. in length, by 20 ft. 9 in. in width. The walls are about 14 ft. high to the spring of the barrel-vault which covers the whole space. There are two large windows at the north end of the room, and one at the south end. These are about 7 ft. from the ground. The original entrance was through a door into the inner court, now blocked. In the centre of the vault is a large eagle in relief with F.D. on each side of its head; round it is a wreath of cherubs' heads; and outside of all a broad band of flames and rays. The vault is further decorated with isolated flames, gilt, on a white ground[2].

The books are said to have occupied eight presses, or sets of shelves, set against the east and west walls, but our information on the subject of the fittings is provokingly meagre. It is chiefly contained in the following passage of a description written by Bernardino Baldi, and dated 10 June, 1587. Baldi, as a native of Urbino, and in later life attached to the service of the Duke, must have been well acquainted with the room and its contents.

La stanza destinata a questi libri è alla mano sinistra di chi entra nel Palazzo contigua al vestibolo, o andito...le fenestre ha volte a Tramontana, le quali per esser alte dal pavimento, ed in testa della stanza, e volte a parte di cielo che non ha sole, fanno un certo lume rimesso, il quale pare col non distraer la vista con la soverchia abbondanza della luce, che inviti ed inciti coloro che v' entrano a studiare. La state è freschissima, l' inverno temperatamente calda. Le scanzie de' libri sono accostate alle mura, e disposte con molto bell' ordine.

In questa fra gli altri libri sono due Bibbie, una latina scritta a penna e miniata per mano di eccellentissimi artefici, e l' altra Ebrea

---

[1] The document is printed by Müntz and Fabre, p. 300.

[2] I visited Urbino for the purpose of studying this library 28 April, 1900.

antichissima scritta pure a mano...Questa si posa sopra un gran leggivo d' ottone, e s' appoggia all' ale d' una grande aquila pur d' ottone che aprendole la sostiene.   Intorno alle cornici che circondano la libreria si leggono scritti nel fregio questi versi[1].

In the preface to the catalogue of the library published at Rome in 1895, the author, after quoting the above passage, adds "There were eight presses each containing seven shelves[2].   The architectural decorations have all disappeared, with the exception of a fragment of a pediment at the south end of the room, on which F. E. DVX is still visible.   The lectern is in the choir of the cathedral.

The Biblioteca Laurenziana, or Medicean Library, at Florence, is the last Italian library which I intend to describe.

After the death of Pope Leo X. in 1521, his executor Cardinal Giulio dei Medici, afterwards Pope Clement VII., restored to Florence the books which their ancestors had got together, and commissioned Michelangelo to build a room for their reception.   The work was frequently interrupted, and it was not until 1571 (11 June) that the library was formally opened.

The great architect, supported by the generosity of the Pope, constructed an apartment which for convenience and for appropriate decoration stands alone among libraries.   It is raised high above the ground in order to secure an ample supply of light and air, and is approached by a double staircase of marble.   It is 151 ft. 9 in. long, by 34 ft. 4 in. broad, and was originally lighted by 15 windows in each of the side-walls at a height of about 7 ft. 6 in. from the floor.   There is a flat roof of wood, carved; and a pavement of terra-cotta consisting of yellow designs on a red ground.

When the room was first fitted up there were 44 desks on each side, but when the reading-room was built at the beginning

---

[1] *Memorie concernenti la Citta di Urbino.* Fol. Rome, 1724, p. 37. See also Vespasiano, *Federigo Duca d' Urbino*; ap. Mai, *Spicilegium Romanum*, I. pp. 124—128; Dennistoun, *Memoirs of the Dukes of Urbino*, 8vo. 1851, I. pp. 153—160. The duties of the librarian, which remind us in many particulars of those of the monastic *armarius*, are translated by Dennistoun (p. 159) from Vat. Urb. MSS. No. 1248, f. 58.

[2] *Codices Urbinates Graeci Bibl. Vat.* 4to. Rome, 1895, p. 12. For this statement, the writer cites Raffaelli, *Imparziale istoria dell' unione della Biblioteca ducale di Urbino alla Vaticana di Roma.* Fermo, 1877, p. 12.

of the last century, four were destroyed. This reading-room also blocks four windows. The glass was supplied by Giovanni da Udine in 1567 and 1568. The subjects are heraldic. In each window the arms of the Medici occupy a central position, and are surrounded by wreaths, arabesques, and other devices of infinite grace and variety, in the style which the genius of Raphael had introduced into the Vatican.

Fig. 101. Bookcases in the Medicean Library, Florence.

The bookcases (fig. 101) are of walnut-wood, a material which is said to have been prescribed by the Pope himself. They were executed, if we may believe Vasari[1], by Battista del

1 *Vasari*, ed. 1856, vol. XII. p. 214.

Cinque and Ciapino, but they are now known to have been
designed by Michelangelo. A rough outline in one of his

Fig. 102. Copy, slightly reduced, of a sketch by Michelangelo for one of the
bookcases in the Medicean Library, Florence.

sketch-books, preserved in the Casa Buonarotti at Florence
with other relics illustrating his life, and here reproduced
(fig. 102), unquestionably represents one of these desks. The
indication of a human figure on the seat proves the care
which he took to ensure a height convenient for readers.

These desks are on the same general plan as those at
Cesena, but they are rather higher and more richly ornamented.
Each is 11 ft. 3 in. long, and 4 ft. 4 in. high. It must be
admitted that the straight back to the reader's seat is not so
comfortable as the gentle slope provided in the older example.
A frame for the catalogue hangs on the end of each desk next
the central alley. In order to make clear the differences in the
construction of the desks at Cesena and at Florence I append
an elevation of each (figs. 103, 104).

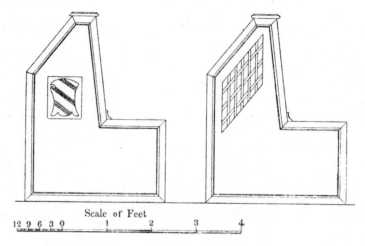

Fig. 103. Elevation of desks at Cesena.

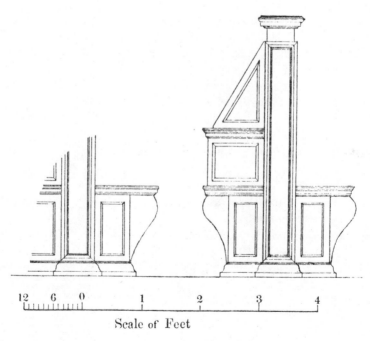

Fig. 104. Elevation of desks at Florence.

It will be seen from the view of one of the desks (fig. 101) that the books either lie on the sloping desk or are packed away on the shelf under it. There is an average of 25 books on each desk. The chains, as at Cesena, are attached to the lower edge of the right board, at distances varying from 2 in. to 4 in. from the back of the book (fig. 105). The staple is sunk into the wood.

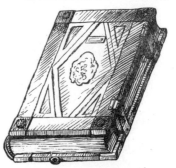

Fig. 105. A book in the Medicean Library, to shew attachment of chain.

The chains are made of fine iron bars about one-eighth of an inch wide, but not quite so thick, flattened at the end of each link, and rounded in the centre, where a piece of the same iron is lapped round, but not soldered. Each chain (fig. 106) is 2 ft. 3 in. long. So far as I could judge all the chains in the library are of the same length. There is a ring at the end of the chain next to the bar, but no swivel.

The ironwork by which these chains are attached to the desk is somewhat complicated. By the kindness of the librarian, Signor Guido Biagi, I have been allowed to study it at my leisure, and to draw a diagrammatic sketch (fig. 107) which I hope will make it clear to my readers. The lock is sunk in the central support of the desk. The bar passes through a ring on each side of this support, and also through a ring near each end of the desk. These rings are

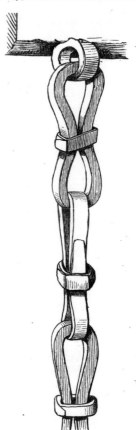

Fig. 106. Piece of chain in the Medicean Library, of the actual size.

fixed to the lower edge of the desk just under the molding.   A

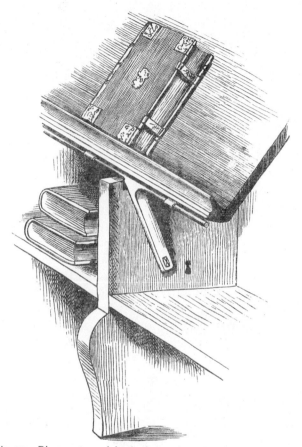

Fig. 107.   Diagram to explain the ironwork at the Medicean Library.

flat piece of iron is forged on to the bar near the centre.   This
iron is pierced near the key-hole with an oblong slit through
which passes a moveable piece
of iron, here shewn in outline
of its actual size (fig. 108).
The bolt of the lock passes
through a hole in this piece,
and holds the bar firmly in
its place.

The bar is not quite so

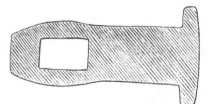

Fig. 108.   Outline of bolt forming part
of ironwork.

long as the desk; consequently, when it has been unlocked, and the iron bolt sketched above withdrawn, it can be turned round by taking hold of the central iron, and pushed to the right or to the left, past the terminal rings. The chains can then be readily unstrung, or another strung upon the bar.

In the next chapter I shall describe the changes in Library arrangements adopted during the period which succeeded the Middle Ages; but, before ending this present chapter, there are a few points affecting the older libraries and their organization to which I should like to draw attention.

In the first place all medieval libraries were practically public. I do not mean that strangers were let in, but even in those of the monasteries, books were let out on the deposit of a sufficient caution; and in Houses such as S. Victor and S. Germain des Près, Paris, and at the Cathedral of Rouen, the collections were open to readers on certain days in the week. The Papal library and those at Urbino and Florence were also public; and even at Oxford and Cambridge there was practically no objection to lending books on good security. Secular corporations followed the example set by the Church, and lent their manuscripts, but only on security. A very remarkable example of this practice is afforded by the transaction between the École de Médecine, Paris, and Louis XI. The king wanted their copy of a certain work on medicine; they declined to lend it unless he deposited 12 marks worth of plate and 100 gold crowns. This he agreed to do; the book was borrowed; duly copied, and 24 January, 1472, restored to the Medical Faculty, who in their turn sent back the deposit to the king[1].

As a general rule, these libraries were divided into the lending library and the library of reference. These two parts of the collection have different names given to them. In the Vatican Library of Sixtus IV. we find the common library (*Bibliotheca communis*) or public library (*B. publica*), and the reserved library (*B. secreta*). The same terms were used at Assisi. At Santa Maria Novella, Florence, there was the library, and the lesser library (*B. minor*). In the University Library, Cambridge, there was "the public library." which contained the more ordinary books and was open to everybody, and "the

---

[1] Franklin, *Anc. Bibl. de Paris*, II. 22.

private library" where the more valuable books were kept and to which only a few privileged persons were admitted[1]. At Queens' College, in the same university, the books which might be lent (*libri distribuendi*) were kept in a separate room from those which were chained to the shelves (*libri concatenati*), and at King's College there was a public library (*B. magna*) and a lesser library (*B. minor*). In short, in every large collection some such division was made, either structural, or by means of a separate catalogue[2].

I have shewn that two systems of bookcases, which I have called lectern-system and stall-system, were used in these libraries; but, as both these have been copiously illustrated, I need say no more on that part of the subject. Elaborate catalogues, of which I have given a few specimens, enabled readers to find what they wanted in the shortest possible time, and globes, maps, and astronomical instruments provided them with further assistance in their studies. Moreover in some places the library served the purpose of a museum, and curiosities of various kinds were stored up in it.

No picture of a medieval library can be complete unless it be remembered that in many cases beauty was no less an object than utility. The bookcases were fine specimens of carpentry-work, carved and decorated; the pavement was of encaustic tiles worked in patterns; the walls were decorated with plaster-work in relief; the windows were filled with stained glass; and the roof-timbers were ornamented with the coat-armour of benefactors.

Of these embellishments the most distinctive was the glass. At St Albans the twelve windows contained figures illustrating the subjects of the books placed near them. For instance, the second window represented Rhetoric and Poetry; and the figures selected were those of Cicero, Sallust, Musaeus, Orpheus. Appropriate verses were inscribed beneath each. The whole scheme recalls the library of Isidore, Bishop of Seville, which I have

---

[1] This statement rests on the authority of Dr Caius, *Hist. Cant. Acad.* p. 89. Cum duæ bibliothecæ erant, altera priuata seu noua, altera publica seu vetus dicebatur. In illa optimi quique; in hac omnis generis ex peiori numero ponebantur. Illa paucis, ista omnibus patebat.

[2] *Arch. Hist.* III. p. 401.

C. L.   16

already described[1]. In the library of Jesus College, Cambridge, each light contains a cock standing on a globe, the emblem of Bishop Alcock the founder, with a label in his beak bearing a suitable text, and under his feet an inscription containing half the designation required. For instance, the first two bookcases contained works on Physic, and in the window is the word PHI-SICA divided between the two lights[2]. In Election Hall at Eton College—a room originally intended for a library—we find the Classes of Civil Law, Criminal and Canon Law, Medicine, etc., illustrated by medallions shewing a church council, an execution, a physician and his patient, and the like[3]. At the Sorbonne, Paris, the 38 windows of the library were filled with the portraits of those who had conferred special benefits on the college[4]; at Froidmont[5] near Beauvais the authors of the *Voyage Littéraire* remark the beautiful stained glass in the library; and in Bishop Cobham's library at Oxford, according to Hearne, there "was brave painted glass containing the arms of the benefactors, which painted glass continued till the times of the late rebellion[6]."

Lastly, I will collect the different terms used to designate medieval bookcases. They are—arranged alphabetically—*analogium, bancus* or *banca, descus, gradus, stallum, stalla, stallus* or *staulum*, and *sedile*. I have sometimes thought that it would be possible to determine the form of the bookcase from the word used to describe it; but increased study has convinced me that this is impossible, and that the words were used quite loosely. For instance, *bancus* designates the cases in the Vatican Library which represent a variety of the lectern-system; and its French equivalent *banc* the cases at Clairvaux which were stalls with four shelves apiece. Again "desk" (*descus*) is used interchangeably with "stall" (*stallum*) in a catalogue of the University Library, Cambridge, dated 1473, to designate what I strongly suspect were lecterns; in 1693 by Bishop Hacket when de-

---

[1] See above p. 45. Dr James has printed the verses from Bodl. MSS. Laud. 697, fol. 27, *verso*, in *Camb. Ant. Soc. Proc. and Comm.* VIII. 213.

[2] The whole series is given in *Arch. Hist.* III. p. 461.

[3] I quote this account of the glass at Eton from Dr James, *ut supra*, p. 214.

[4] De Lisle, *Cabinet de Manuscrits*, vol. II. p. 200.

[5] *Voyage Littéraire*, ed. 1717, II. 158.

[6] Bliss, *Reliquiæ Hearnianæ*, II. 693; *ap.* Macray, *Annals*, p. 4.

scribing the stalls which Dean Williams gave to the library at Westminster Abbey[1]; and in 1695 by Sir C. Wren to describe bookcases which were partly set against the walls, partly at right-angles to them.

It has been already shewn that *gradus* means a shelf, or a lectern, or a side of a lectern[2]; and *sedile* is obviously only the Latin equivalent for "seat," which was sometimes used, as at S. John's College, Cambridge, in 1623[3], to designate a bookcase. It was also used at Christ Church, Canterbury, for what I have shewn to be a stall with four shelves[4]. The word *analogium* was used in France to signify a lectern[5]. The word "class" (*classis*) is used at the University Library, Cambridge, in 1584, instead of the ancient "stall," and afterwards superseded it entirely. For instance, when a Syndicate was appointed in 1713 to provide accommodation for Bishop Moore's Library, the bookcases are described as *Thecæ sive quas vocant classes.* Gradually the term was extended until it reached its modern signification, namely, the shelves under a given window together with those on the sides of the bookcases to the right and left of the spectator facing it[6].

We sometimes meet with the word *distinctio.* For instance, an Apocalypse in the library of Corpus Christi College, Cambridge, which once belonged to St Augustine's College, Canterbury, is noted as having stood "*distinctione prima gradu tertio*"; and the same word is used in the introduction to the catalogue of Dover Priory to signify what I am compelled to decide was a bookcase. The word *demonstratio,* on the other hand, which occurs at the head of the catalogue of the library of Christ Church, Canterbury, made between 1285 and 1331, probably denotes a division of subject, and not a piece of furniture.

Until the lectern-system had gone out of fashion, a word to denote a shelf was not needed. When shelves had to be referred to, *textus*[7] was used at Canterbury, and *linea*[8] at Citeaux. On

---

[1] See above, p. 188.
[2] See Index.
[3] *Arch. Hist.* Vol. II. p. 270.
[4] See above, p. 192.
[5] See Index.
[6] *Arch. Hist.* Vol. III. p. 30. Conyers Middleton, *Bibl. Cant. Ord. Meth.* Works, Vol. III. p. 484.
[7] See above, p. 192.
[8] See above, p. 105.

the other hand, at Saint Ouen at Rouen, this word indicates a
row of bookcases, probably lecterns.   In a record of loans[1] from
that library in 1372 and following years, the books borrowed are
set down as follows (to quote a few typical instances):

> Item, digestum novum, linea I, E, ii.
> Item, liber de regulis fidei, cum aliis, linea III, L, viii.
> Item, Tulius de officiis, linea II a parte sinistra, D, ii.

These extracts will be sufficient to shew that the cases were
arranged in three double rows, each double row being called a
linea.   Each lectern was marked with a letter of the alphabet,
and each book with the number of the row, the letter of the
lectern to which it belonged, and its number on the lectern.
Thus, to take the first of the above entries, the Digest was to be
found in the first row, on lectern E, and was the second volume
on the said lectern.   It is evident that there was a row of lecterns
on each side of a central alley or passage, and that a book was
to be found on the right hand, unless the left hand was specially
designated.

A catalogue has been preserved of the books in the castle
of Peñiscola on the east coast of Spain, when the anti-pope
Benedict XIII. retired there in 1415.   They were kept in presses
(*armaria*), each of which was subdivided into a certain number
of compartments (*domuncule*), each of which again contained
two shelves (*ordines*)[2].   I suggest that this piece of furniture
resembled, on a large scale, Le Chartrier de Bayeux, which I
have already figured (fig. 26).

In conclusion, I will quote a passage in which the word
library designates a bookcase.   It occurs in an inventory of
the goods in the church of S. Christopher le Stocks, London,
made in 1488:

> On the south side of the vestrarie standeth a grete library with ij
> longe lecturnalles theron to ley on the bokes[3].

I need hardly remind my readers that the French word
bibliothèque has the same double meaning.

---

[1] *Du prêt des livres dans l'abbaye de Saint Ouen, sous Charles V.* par L. Delisle.
Bibl. de l'École des Chartes, ser. III. Vol. I. p. 225.   1849.

[2] *Le Librairie des Papes d'Avignon*, par Maurice Faucon. Tome II. p. 43, in
Bibl. des Écoles Françaises d'Athènes et de Rome, Fasc. 50.

[3] *Archæologia*, Vol. 47, p. 120.   I have to thank my friend Mr P. T. Micklethwaite,
architect, for this quotation.

CHAPTER VII.

CONTRAST BETWEEN THE FIFTEENTH AND SIXTEENTH CENTURIES. SUPPRESSION OF THE MONASTERIES. COMMISSIONERS OF EDWARD VI. SUBSEQUENT CHANGES IN LIBRARY FITTINGS. S. JOHN'S COLLEGE, AND UNIVERSITY LIBRARY, CAMBRIDGE. QUEEN'S COLLEGE, OXFORD. LIBRARIES ATTACHED TO CHURCHES AND SCHOOLS. CHAINING IN RECENT TIMES. CHAINS TAKEN OFF.

 HAVE now traced the evolution of the bookcase from a clumsy contrivance consisting of two boards set at an angle to each other, to the stately pieces of furniture which, with but little alteration, are still in use; and I hope that I have succeeded in shewing that the fifteenth century was emphatically the library-era throughout Europe. Monasteries, cathedrals, universities, and secular institutions in general vied with each other in erecting libraries, in stocking them with books, and in framing liberal regulations for making them useful to the public.

To this development of study in all directions the sixteenth century offers a sad and startling contrast. In France the Huguenot movement took the form of a bitter hostility to the clergy—which, after the fashion of that day, exhibited itself in a very general destruction of churches, monasteries, and their contents; while England witnessed the suppression of the Monastic Orders, and the annihilation, so far as was practicable, of all that belonged to them. I have shewn that monastic libraries were the public libraries of the Middle Ages; more

than this, the larger houses were centres of culture and education, maintaining schools for children, and sending older
students to the Universities. In three years, between 1536 and
1539, the whole system was swept away, as thoroughly as
though it had never existed. The buildings were pulled down,
and the materials sold; the plate was melted; and the books
were either burnt, or put to the vilest uses to which waste
literature can be subjected. I will state the case in another
way which will bring out more clearly the result of this
catastrophe. Upwards of eight hundred monasteries were suppressed, and, as a consequence, eight hundred libraries were
done away with, varying in size and importance from Christ
Church, Canterbury, with its 2000 volumes, to small houses with
little more than the necessary service-books. By the year 1540
the only libraries left in England were those at the two Universities, and in the Cathedrals of the old foundation. Further,
the royal commissioners made no attempt to save any of the
books with which the monasteries were filled. In France in
1789 the revolutionary leaders sent the libraries of the convents
they pillaged to the nearest town: for instance, that of Citeaux
to Dijon; of Clairvaux to Troyes; of Corbie to Amiens. But
in England at the suppression no such precautions were taken;
manuscripts seem to have been at a discount just then, for
which the invention of printing may be to some extent responsible; their mercantile value was small; private collectors
were few. So the monastic libraries perished, save a few
hundred manuscripts which have survived to give us an imperfect notion of what the rest were like.

How great the loss was, has probably been recorded by
more than one writer; but for the moment I can think of
nothing more graphic than the words of that bitter protestant
John Bale, a contemporary who had seen the old libraries, and
knew their value. After lamenting that "in turnynge ouer of
yᵉ superstycyouse monasteryes so lytle respect was had to theyr
lybraryes for the sauegarde of those noble and precyouse monumentes" (the works of ancient writers), he states what ought to
have been done, and what really happened.

Neuer had we bene offended for the losse of our lybraryes beynge
so many in nombre and in so desolate places for the most parte, yf the

chiefe monumentes and moste notable workes of our excellent wryters had bene reserued.

If there had bene in every shyre but one solempne lybrary, to the preseruacyon of those noble workes, it had bene yet sumwhat. But to destroy all without consydyracyon is and wyll be vnto Englande for euer a moste horryble infamy amonge the graue senyours of other nacyons. A greate nombre of them whych purchased those super-stycyouse mansyons, reserued of those bokes some to...scoure theyr candelstyckes, and some to rubbe theyr bootes. Some they sold to the grossers and sopesellers, and some they sent ouer see to the boke bynders, not in small nombre, but at times whole shyppes full, to the wonderynge of the foren nacyons. I know a merchaunt man which shall at this tyme be namelesse, that boughte the contentes of two noble lybraryes for .xl. shyllynges pryce, a shame it is to be spoken. This stuffe hath he occupyed in the stede of graye paper by the space of more than these .x. yeares, and yet he hath store ynough for many yeares to come[1].

The Universities, though untouched by the suppression, were not allowed to remain long at peace. In 1549, commissioners were sent by Edward the Sixth to Oxford and Cambridge. They considered that it fell within their province to reform the libraries as well as those who used them ; and they did their work with a thoroughness that under other circumstances would have been worthy of commendation. Anthony Wood[2] has told us in eloquent periods, where sorrow struggles with indignation, how the college libraries were treated ; how manuscripts which had nothing superstitious about them except a few rubricated initials, were carried through the city on biers to the market-place and there consumed. Of the treatment meted out to the public library of the University he gives an almost identical account[3]. This library—now the central portion of the Bodleian—had been completed about 1480. It was well stocked with manuscripts of value, the most important of which, in number about 600[4], had been given by Humphrey Duke of Gloucester, between 1439 and 1446. His

---

[1] *The laboryouse Journey and Serche of Johan Leylande for Englandes Antiquitees...* by Johan Bale. London, 1549.

[2] *History and Antiquities of University of Oxford*, Ed. Gutch, 4to. 1796, Vol. II. p. 106. Wood (b. 1632, d. 1695) gives these facts as "credibly reported from antient men and they while young from scholars of great standing."

[3] *Ibid.* Vol. II. Pt. 2, p. 918.

[4] This number is given on the authority of Macray, *Annals of the Bodleian Library*, Ed. II. p. 6.

collection was that of a cultivated layman, and was comparatively poor in theological literature. Yet in this home of
all that was noble in literature and splendid in art (for the
Duke's copies are said to have been the finest that could be
bought) did this crew of ignorant fanatics cry havoc, with
such fatal success that only three MSS. now survive; and on
January 25, 1555—56, certain members of the Senate were
appointed "to sell, in the name of the University, the book-
desks in the public library. The books had all disappeared;
what need then to retain the shelves and stalls, when no one
thought of replacing their contents, and when the University
could turn an honest penny by their sale[1]?"

I suppose that in those collegiate and cathedral libraries of
which some fragments had been suffered to remain, the gaps
caused by the destruction of manuscripts were slowly filled up
by printed literature. No new bookcases would be required for
many years; and in fact, nearly a century passed away before
any novelty in the way of library-fittings makes its appearance.
Further, when new libraries came to be built, the provision of
suitable furniture was not easy. The old stall, with two shelves
loaded with books attached to them by chains, and a desk and
seat for the use of the reader, was manifestly no longer adequate,
when books could be produced by the rapidity of a printing-
press, instead of by the slowness of a writer's hand. And yet,
as we shall see, ancient fashions lingered.

So far as I know, the first library built and furnished under
these new conditions in England was that of S. John's College,
Cambridge. This "curious example of Jacobean Gothic[2]" was
built between 1623 and 1628, at the sole charge of Bishop
Williams, whose work at Westminster during the same period
has been already recorded. The site selected was the ground
between the second court of the college and the river, the
library-building being constructed as a continuation of the
north side of that court, with the library on the first floor,
and the chambers intended for the Bishop's Fellows and
Scholars on the ground floor.

The room, after the fashion of the older libraries, is long and

[1] Macray, *ut supra*, p. 13.
[2] These words were used by Professor Willis, *Arch. Hist.* Vol. III. p. 451.

narrow, 110 ft. in length by 30 ft. in breadth.   Each side-wall is
pierced with ten lofty pointed windows of two lights with tracery
in the head.   The sills of these windows are raised 4 ft. above the
floor, and the interval between each pair of windows is 3 ft. 8 in.
There is also a western oriel, the foundations of which are laid

Fig. 109.   West oriel of the Library at S. John's College, Cambridge.

in the river which washes its walls (fig. 109).   The name of the
founder is commemorated on the central gable by the letters
I. L. C. S., the initials of *Johannes Lincolniensis Custos Sigilli*,
the Bishop being at that time keeper of the Great Seal, or, as we
should say, Lord Chancellor.   The date 1624 marks the completion of the shell of the building[1].

---

[1] For the history of this building see Professor Willis, *ut supra*, Vol. II.
pp. 264—271.

The beautiful fittings (fig. 110), which are still in use, were completed before 1628. Medieval arrangement was not wholly discarded, but various modern features were introduced. The side-walls and window-jambs are panelled to a height of 8 ft.; and the cornice of this panel-work is continuous with that of the taller cases—which, as in the older examples, stand at right

Fig. 110. Bookcases in the Library of S. John's College, Cambridge.

angles to the walls between each pair of windows. Before these fittings were constructed, chaining had been practically abandoned, so that it was not necessary to provide either desk or seat. In the place, therefore, of the reader's seat, a low bookcase was set in front of each window. These cases were originally 5 ft. 6 in. high, with a sloping desk on the top on which books could be laid for study. Stools also were provided for the convenience of readers. The larger cases or, as the building-account of the library calls them, "the greater seats," have been a good deal altered in order to accommodate more books. Originally the plinth ran round the sides of the case; as did also the broad member which is seen on the end above the arches. By this arrangement there were in all only four shelves, namely, one below the broad member and three above it. Further, there was a pilaster in the middle, below the central bracket. It should be noted that the medieval habit of placing a list of the books contained in each case at the end of the case is here maintained.

It might have been expected that these splendid cases would have invited imitation, and in those at Clare College the general style was undoubtedly copied. But, as I have already explained[1], those cases were originally genuine specimens of the stall-system, with desks. In other libraries, while a new style of bookcase was put up, we shall find no innovation comparable to that seen at S. John's. This was due, in great measure, to the medieval character of the rooms to be fitted up.

The library at Peterhouse was lengthened in 1633. It is 75 ft. long by 25 ft. broad, and each of its side-walls is pierced by a range of three-light windows. The cases (fig. 111) were put up between 1641 and 1648. Like those at S. John's, they stand at right angles to the walls between the windows, but they are detached, and not continuous with the panelwork. Originally they were just eight feet high, but have since been heightened to accommodate more books. Each case is still divided by a central pilaster. So far they do not present any striking peculiarity, but I wish to draw attention to a curious contrivance, which we shall find subsequently reproduced in various forms, though not exactly as it is seen here; for these cases were evidently admired, and imitated in several other colleges. The chains had been taken off the books at Peterhouse in 1593—94, when they were first moved into the new library; so that desks attached to the cases were not required. Nor were lower cases, with desks at the top of them, provided. But the convenience of the reader was considered, up to a certain

---

[1] See above p. 186.

point, by the provision of a seat, 12 in. wide and 23 in. high, extending along the side of each case, and returned along the wall between it and the case next to it.   This arrangement may still be seen in the two compartments at the west end of the room, one on each side of the door of entrance.   The ends of the seat or 'podium,' are concealed by boldly carved wings[1].

Fig. 111.   Bookcases in the Library of Peterhouse, Cambridge.

The convenience of this type of case was evidently recognised at once, for we find it copied, more or less exactly, in the south room of the University Library (1649); at Jesus College (1663); at Gonville and Caius College (1675); at Emmanuel College (1677); and at Pembroke College (1690).

The south room of the University Library, on the first floor, is 25 ft. wide and was originally 67 ft. long.   It was lighted by eight windows in the north wall, and by nine windows in the south wall, each of two lights.   There was also a window of four lights in the east gable, as we learn from Loggan's print, and probably a window in the west gable also[2].   It was entered by a

---

[1] *Arch. Hist.* ut supra, Vol. I. p. 33, and Vol. III. p. 454.

[2] When the new façade was built in the middle of the 18th century this room was shortened by about 8 feet, so that now there are only 8 windows on the south side and 7½ on the north side.

Fig. 112. Bookcases in the south room of the University Library, Cambridge.

door, in the north-east corner, approached by a " vice," or turret-stair. This door was fortunately left intact when the east building was erected in 1755. The room has been but little altered, and still preserves the beautiful roof, the contract for which is dated 25 June, 1466[1].

We do not know anything about the primitive fittings, but, having regard to the fact that the spaces between the windows are barely two feet wide, it is probable that they were lecterns. Moreover, a catalogue, dated 1473, enumerates eight stalls on the north side each containing on an average 21 books, and nine on the south side, each containing 18 books[2]. These numbers, compared with those mentioned above at Zutphen, indicate lecterns.

In the next century this room was assigned to teaching purposes, and the lecterns were either removed or destroyed. In 1645 the University petitioned Parliament to put them in possession of Archbishop Bancroft's library, which he, by will dated 28 October, 1610, had bequeathed to the Public Library of the University of Cambridge, should certain other provisions not be fulfilled. The request was granted, 15 February, 1647, and the books arrived in 1649. The room in question, then used as the Greek School, was ordered, 3 September, 1649, to be " fitted for the disposeall of the said books " without delay. The existing cases were supplied at once, for Fuller, writing in the following year, speaks of them with commendation[3]. Their exact date is therefore known.

These cases (fig. 112) are 8 ft. high from the floor to the top of the horizontal part of the cornice, and 22 in. broad. They have the central pilaster ; but the seat has been cut down to a step, which is interrupted in the middle, so as to allow the central pilaster to rise directly from the ground. The wing, however, was too picturesque a feature to be discarded, so it was placed at the end of the step, and carried up, by means

---

[1] The contract is printed and explained in *Arch. Hist.* Vol. III. pp. 92—6.

[2] *Camb. Ant. Soc. Proc.* Vol. II. p. 258. The catalogue is printed, with remarks, by H. Bradshaw, M.A., University Librarian. It should be noted that on the south side of the room, the first case only is called 'stall,' the remaining eight are called 'desks.'

[3] *History of University of Cambridge*, ed. Prickett and Wright, p. 160. See also *Arch. Hist.* Vol. III. p. 27.

of a long slender prolongation, as far as the molding which separates the two panels on the end of the stall.

These cases were exactly copied at Gonville and Caius College; and again at Emmanuel College; but in both those examples the step is continuous. At Jesus College the same type is maintained, with the central pilaster and continuous step; but the work is extremely plain, and there is neither wing nor pediment. At Pembroke College there is a further modification of the type. The step disappears, and, instead of it, a plinth extends along the whole length of the case. The wing, however, remains, as a survival of the lost step, and helps to give dignity to the base of the standard, which is surmounted by a semicircular pediment, beneath which is a band of fruit and flowers in high relief[1].

I will now describe a very interesting bookcase at King's College, Cambridge (fig. 113), which was put up in 1659, with a bequest from Nicholas Hobart, formerly Fellow[2]. It remains in its original position in one of the chapels on the south side of the choir, which were used for library-purposes till the present library was built by Wilkins in 1825. It has several details in common with those at S. John's College, as originally constructed, and will help us to understand their aspect before they were altered. There is a lofty plinth, a broad member interposed between the first and second shelf, a central vertical pilaster; and, as at Peterhouse, and elsewhere, a step or 'podium' with a wing. But, with these resemblances to cases in which books are arranged as at present, it is curious to find the usual indications of chaining, which we know from other sources was not given up in this library until 1777. There are locks on the end of the case just below each of the two shelves, and scars on the vertical pilasters caused by the attachment of the iron-work that carried the bar. Further, just below the broad band, a piece of wood of a different quality has been inserted into the pilasters, evidently to fill up a vacancy caused by the removal of some part of the original structure, probably a desk or shelf.

---

[1] These descriptions are all borrowed from Professor Willis, *Arch. Hist.* Vol. III. pp. 454—458, 460, 465.

[2] *Arch. Hist.* Vol. I. p. 538.

The antiquary William Cole, writing in 1744, describes these chapels when used as libraries. Each chapel held five bookcases, "two at the extremities, which are but half-cases, and three in the body, of which the middlemost is much loftier than the rest." In the chapel fitted up by Hobart, Cole tells us that "at

Fig. 113. Bookcase in the old Library of King's College, Cambridge, made with the bequest of Nicholas Hobart, 1659.

the end of the biggest middle class is wrote in gold letters LEGAVIT NICOLAUS HOBART 1659[1]." As the chapel is only 20 ft. long, the intervals between the cases could hardly have exceeded 2 ft., and as the books were chained they must have been consulted standing.

A similar return to ancient forms is to be found in the library of Queen's College, Oxford, begun in 1692. The architect is said

[1] *Arch. Hist.* 1. p. 539.

to have been Nicholas Hawkesmoore, to whom the fittings, put up in the first fourteen years of the eighteenth century[1], are also ascribed. This library is 123 ft. long by 30 ft. wide. There are ten bookcases on each side at right angles to the walls between the windows. Each case is about 11 ft. high, and 2 ft. 6 in. wide; but, though their ornamentation is in the style of the period, of which they are splendid examples, their general design exactly reproduces the old type. In their original state they were provided with desks, though there is no evidence that the books were chained; they had only two shelves above that which was on the level of the top of the desk; and there was a double seat between each pair of cases. The space above the second shelf, between it and the cornice, was occupied by a cupboard, handsomely ornamented with carved panels, for small books or manuscripts[2]. In fact, the only innovation which the designer of these remarkable cases permitted himself to employ was to make the moldings of their cornices continuous with that of the panelwork which he carried along the sides of the room, and into the jambs of the windows. The space below the desk was utilised for books, but, as these were found to be inconvenient of access, the desks and seats were taken away in 1871, and dwarf bookcases provided in front of the windows.

When the Dean and Chapter of Canterbury built their library, now called the Howley-Harrison Library, in 1669—70, they constructed a room on strictly medieval lines. It is 65 ft. long by 21 ft. broad, with seven equidistant windows in the north wall and six in the south wall. The bookcases, which are plain medieval stalls, project from the walls at right angles between the windows.

There is another class of libraries which must be briefly mentioned in this chapter, namely, those connected with parish

---

[1] This date is given on the authority of the present Provost, John Richard Magrath, D.D.

[2] A view of the Library in its original state is given in Ingram's *Memorials*, Queen's College, p. 12. An article in *Notes and Queries*, 6th Ser. IV. 442, by the Rev. Robert Lowes Clarke, M.A., Fellow and Librarian, contains the following passage: "The bookcases were fitted with reading desks, as at the Bodleian, and there were fixed oak seats in each recess. These were convenient in some ways, and helped to make the room seem a place for study rather than a store for materials, but they made the lower shelves hard of access, and were removed in 1871 to give room for new cases."

churches and grammar-schools. I suppose that after the destruction of monastic libraries all over the country, the dearth of
books would be acutely felt, and that gradually those who had
the cause of education at heart established libraries in central
situations, to which persons in quest of knowledge might resort.

SOUTH AISLE OF CHURCH

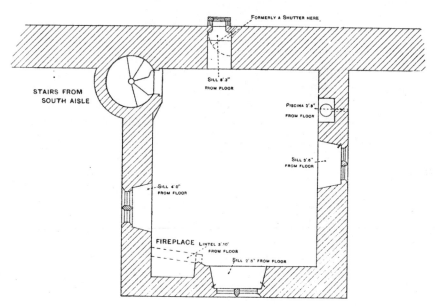

Fig. 114.   Ground plan of Library, Grantham, Lincolnshire.

Scale one quarter of an inch to one foot.

The library (fig. 114) at Grantham in Lincolnshire occupies a
small room, 16 feet from north to south by 14 feet from east to
west, over the south porch of the parish church, approached by a
newel stair from the south aisle. It was founded in 1598 by
the Reverend Francis Trigg, rector of Wellbourn ; and in 1642,
Edward Skipworth "out of his love and well-wishing to learning,
and to encourage the vicars of Grantham to pursue their studies
in the winter-time, gave fifty shillings, the yearly interest thereof
to provide firewood for the library fire."   From this language I
conclude that the original gift of books was made for the benefit
of the vicar for the time being.

There are three bookcases set against the walls, each about 6 ft. high and 6 ft. long. A considerable number of the books still bear their chains, which are composed of long flat links closely resembling those at Guildford, with a ring and swivel next to the bar. The library—room, bookcases, and books—was carefully restored and repaired in 1894[1].

At Langley Marye or Marish in Buckinghamshire near Slough, a library was founded in 1623 by Sir John Kederminster "as well for the perpetual benefit of the vicar and curate of the parish of Langley, as for all other ministers and preachers of God's Word that would resort thither to make use of the books therein." He placed it under the charge of the four tenants of his almshouses, who were to keep safe the books, and the key of the room, under stringent penalties[2].

The library is a small room on the south side of the church, entered through the squire's pew, to which there is a separate door in the south wall. The fittings are of an unusual character, and have been preserved unaltered. The whole room is panelled at a distance of 15 in. from the wall, so as to make a series of cupboards, in which the books are contained. The doors of these cupboards are divided into panels, alternately square and oblong. Each of the former contains a small figure painted in colours on a black ground ; each of the latter a shield, or some heraldic device. The inner surface of these doors is similarly divided into panels, on each of which is painted an open book. Above the cupboards, just under the flat ceiling, is a series of more or less imaginary landscapes, doing duty as a frieze. Over the fireplace is a very beautiful piece of decoration consisting of a large oval shield with various coats of arms painted on it. It is set in an oblong panel, in the spandrels of which are painted seated figures of Prudence, Justice, Temperance, Fortitude, with their emblems and suitable mottoes[3].

In 1629, the following entry occurs in what is called "the Church Book" of Cartmel, in Lancashire :

---

[1] For these details I have to thank the late Canon H. Nelson. I visited Grantham in 1895 with my friend Mr T. D. Atkinson, architect, who drew the above plan.

[2] *Report of Comm. for Inquiring concerning Charities*, Vol. II. pp. 95—100.

[3] This description of the library is partly from my own notes, taken 7 July, 1901, partly from Hornby's *Walks about Eton*, 1894.

14 July, 1629. It is ordered and agreed upon that the church-wardens seate in the body of the churche shall be enlarged both in the wideness and in the deske that the bookes given unto the church may bee more convenientlie laid and chained to remain there according to the directions of the donors[1].

The will of Humphry Chetham, a wealthy merchant of Manchester, dated 16 December, 1651, directs £200 to be spent on certain specified books,

> to be, by the discretion of my Executors, chained upon Desks, or to be fixed to the Pillars, or in other convenient Places, in the Parish Churches of *Manchester* and *Boulton in the Moors*, and in the Chapels of *Turton*, *Walmesley*, and *Gorton*, in the said County of *Lancaster*[2].

The bookcase at Gorton[3] is a cupboard of oak, 7 ft. long by 3 ft. high and 19 in. deep, raised upon four stout legs, 22 in. high. On opening the doors, the interior is seen to be divided into two equal parts by a vertical partition, and again by a horizontal shelf. The shelf and the partition are both 9 in. deep, so as to leave a considerable interval in front of them. The bars—of which there is one for each division—rest in a socket pierced in a small bracket screwed to each end of the case, in such a position that the bar passes just in front of the shelf. A flat piece of iron, nailed to the central division, carries a short hasp, which passes over the junction of the bars, and is there secured by a lock. By this arrangement no person could withdraw either bar without the key. The chains, of iron, tinned, are of the same type as those at Hereford, but the links are rather longer and narrower. They are attached to the volume in the same manner, either near the bottom of the right board, or near the top of the left board. There are scars on the lower edge of the case, and on the legs, which seem to indicate that there might once have been a desk. Otherwise, the books, when read, must have rested on the reader's knees. The whole piece of furniture closely resembles one dated 1694 at Bolton in Lancashire to be described below (fig. 116).

The bookcase at Turton[4] resembles that at Gorton so closely

---

[1] *Old Church and School Libraries of Lancashire*, by R. C. Christie, Chetham Soc., 1885, p. 76.

[2] *The last will of Humphry Chetham*, 4to. Manchester, n. d. p. 42.

[3] This bookcase stood in the National School-room when I examined it in 1885. In 1898 the books were thoroughly repaired.

[4] The front of this bookcase is figured on the title-page of *Bibliographical notices of the Church Libraries at Turton and Gorton*. Chetham Soc., 1855, p. 3.

that it needs no particular description. The doors are richly
carved, and on the cornice above them is the following inscription, carved in low relief:

THE GIFT OF HUMPHRY CHETHAM ESQVIRE. 1655.

Besides these parochial libraries Mr Chetham directed the
foundation (among other things) of "a Library within the Town
of *Manchester*, for the Use of Scholars, and others well affected,
to resort unto... the same Books there to remain as a public
Library for ever ; and my Mind and Will is, that Care be taken,
that none of the said Books be taken out of the said Library at
any Time... the same Books [to] be fixed or chained, as well as
may be, within the said Library, for the better Preservation
thereof."   In order to carry out these provisions the executors
bought an ancient building called the *College*, which is
known to have been completed before 1426 by Thomas Lord
de la Warre, as a college in connexion with the adjoining
collegiate church, now the Cathedral[1].   The library was placed
in two long narrow rooms on the first floor, the original destination of which is uncertain.   They are at right angles to each
other, and have a united length of 137 ft. 6 in., with a
breadth of 17 ft.   The south and west walls are pierced with
fourteen three-light windows, probably inserted by Chetham's
executors; the east and west walls are blank.

The existing fittings, though they have been extensively
altered[2] from time to time, are in the main those which were
originally put up. The bookcases, of oak, are placed in medieval
fashion at right angles to the windows. They are 10 ft. long,
2 ft. wide, and were originally 7 ft. high, but have been
pieced apparently twice, so that they now reach as high as the
wall-plate. Each pair of cases is 6 ft. apart, so as to make
a small compartment, closed by wooden gates, which now open

---

[1] The architectural history of these buildings has been admirably worked out, in
Old Halls in Lancashire and Cheshire, by Henry Taylor, Architect, 4to. Manchester,
1884, pp. 31—46.

[2] These alterations probably began when the following Order was made :
"Tuesday, 24 July, 1787. That a Committee be appointed to inspect the Library
along with the Librarian, consisting of the Treasurer [etc.]; And that such
Committee shall have power to repair and make such Alterations in the Library as
they may think proper."   No Order for taking off the chains has been discovered.

in the middle; but a lock attached to one side of the end of each case indicates that originally the gates were in one piece. The cases are quite plain, with the exception of a few panels at the end. On the uppermost of these, which is oblong, and extends from side to side of the case, the subjects of the works are written: as, PHILOSOPHIA; and beneath, in smaller characters, *Mathematica, Physica, Metaphysica.* All indications of chaining have been obliterated, but a reference to the earliest account-book which has been preserved, that beginning 20 April, 1685, shews that the founder's directions were obeyed:

20 Apr. 1685.	To James Wilson for Cheining ten books..	0	2	6
,,　　1686.	—————————— for making 26 large Claspes and Cheining 26 bookes....................................	0	4	4
9 Mar. 1686—87.	—————————— for Cheining and Clasping 12 doz. bookes............	00	18	00

Chains were evidently kept as a part of the stock-in-trade of the library, to be used as required, for, at the end of an Inventory taken 18 November, 1684, we find:

Alsoe in the Library two globes; three Mapps; two queres of larg paper to make tables; a paper fol-booke; A Ruleing penn; 24 dossen Chains; A geniological roul; and a larg serpent or snaks skin.

At Wimborne Minster the books are placed in a small room, about fifteen feet square, over the vestry, a building in the Decorated style, situated between the south transept and the south aisle of the choir. Access to this room is obtained by a turret-stair at the south-west corner. It was fitted up as a library in 1686, when the greater part of the books were given by the Rev. William Stone. There are two plain wooden shelves, carried round three sides of the room. The chains are attached to the right-hand board of each book, instead of to the left-hand board, and they are made of iron wire, twisted as shewn in the sketch (fig. 115). The swivel, instead of being

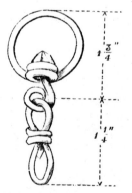

Fig. 115.　Ring and link of chain: Wimborne Minster.

central, plays in a twist of the wire which forms the ring
attached to the book. The iron bars are supported on eyes,
and are secured by a tongue of iron passed over a staple fixed
into the bracket which supports the shelf. The tongue was
originally kept in its place by a padlock, now replaced by
a wooden peg. No desk was attached to the shelves, but in
lieu of it a portable desk and stool were provided[1].

A library was built over the porch of the parish church at
Denchworth[2], Berks, in 1693, and "stocked with 100 books well
secured with chains," presumably for the use of the vicar and
his successors; and in 1715, William Brewster, M.D., bequeathed
285 volumes to the churchwardens of All Saints' Church, Hereford, for the same purpose[3]. The books were placed in the
vestry, where they still are. They are all chained on a system
copied from that in use at the Chapter Library.

In addition to collections of books, which varied in extent
according to the taste, or the means, of the donor, single volumes
are often found chained in churches. These do not come within
the scope of this Essay, and I will therefore pass on to notice
some libraries connected with Grammar Schools.

At Abingdon in Berkshire, the school, founded 1563, had
a library, some volumes of which, bearing their chains, are still
preserved. There was a similar collection at Bicester in Oxford-
shire, where a school is said to have been in existence before
1570. In 1571 James Pilkington, Bishop of Durham (1561—
1577), by will dated 4 February in that year, bequeathed his
books to the school at Rivington in Lancashire. The following
extracts from the statutes, said to have been made shortly after
the arrival of the books, remind us of monastic provisions[4].

The Governors shall the first day of every quarter when they come
to the School take an account of all such books as have been given to

---

[1] *Sketches of English Literature*, by Clara Lucas Balfour, 12mo. Lond. 1852.
Introduction. In the description of the library there given the padlocks are specially
mentioned. Compare also, *A History of Wimborne Minster*, 8vo. Lond. 1860; and
Hutchins' *Dorsetshire*, ed. 1803, Vol. II. p. 554.

[2] *Notes and Queries*, Series 6, Vol. IV. p. 304. The library was destroyed in
1852 when the Church was restored by Mr George Street, Architect.

[3] *The History of All Saints' Church, Hereford*, by Rev. G. H. Culshaw, M.A.,
8vo. Hereford, 1892.

[4] *Old Church and School Libraries of Lancashire*, by R. C. Christie, Chetham
Soc., 1885. p. 189.

the School, and if any be picked away torn or written in they shall cause him that so misused it to buy another book as good and lay it in the place of it and there to be used continually as others be.

The Schoolmaster and Usher whensoever the Scholars go from the School shall cause all such books as have been or shall be given to the School and occupied abroad that day to be brought into the place appointed for them, and there to be locked up; and every morning shall cause the dictionaries, or such other books as are meet to be occupied abroad by the Scholars, that have none of their own, to be laid abroad, and see that none use to write in them, pull out leaves, nor carry them from the School; and if any misuse any book, or pick it away, the Governours shall cause him to buy another as good, to be laid in the stead of it, and occupied as the other was.

And for the books of divinity, the Schoolmaster and Usher and such as give themselves to study divinity, shall occupy them, that they may be the more able to declare any article of the catechism or religion to the scholars; and in the church to make some notes of the Chapters that be read that the people may better understand them and remember what is read. And yet these books they shall not carry out of the School, without license of the Governours, and on pain to bring it again, or else to buy one as good, in its stead, and to be allowed out of the Master's or Usher's wages.

If any preacher come and desire to have the use of some of those books, they shall let him have the use of them for a time so that they see them brought in again; none other shall carry them from the School except they have license of half the Governours and be bound to bring it safe again.

In 1573 John Parkhurst, Bishop of Norwich (1560—1575), bequeathed "the most part" of his Latin books to his native town Guildford, to be placed in "the Lybrarie of the same Towne ioyning to the Schole." These books, after some legal difficulties had been overcome, were brought to Guildford, and placed in a gallery which connected the two wings of the school, and had been begun in 1571. The books were fastened to the shelves with chains, one of which has been already figured (fig. 58). There is evidence that the library was well cared for, and augmented by various donations, which were regularly chained as they came in, down to the end of the 17th century[1].

Henry Bury, founder of the free school at Bury in Lancashire in 1625, directed in his will that a convenient place should be found for the library, because, as he proceeds to say:

[1] *Cam. Ant. Soc. Proc. and Comm.* Vol. VIII. pp. 11—18. In 1899 the books which remained were put in order and set on new shelves by the care and at the cost of H. A. Powell, Esq.

I have already geven...in trust for the use of Bury Parish and the countrie therabouts, of ministers also at ther metinge and of schole maisters and others that seek for learninge and knowledge, above six hundreth bookes, and some other such things as I thought might helpe for their delight, and refresh students, as globes mappes pictures and some other things not every wheare to bee seene.

This language shews that this provident benefactor intended his library to be public. It is pleasant to be able to record that some of the books which he gave are still in existence[1].

Lastly I will figure (fig. 116) the press given in 1694 by "James Leaver citison of London," to the Grammar School at Bolton in Lancashire. It closely resembles those given by Humphry Chetham to Turton and Gorton. The system of ironwork by which the bars are kept in place is exactly the same; and it retains the desk, traces of which exist at Gorton.

In my enumeration of the libraries attached to schools and churches, I have drawn special attention to the fact that in nearly all of them the books were chained. In explanation of this it might be argued that these libraries were in remote places, to which new ideas would not easily penetrate, but I am about to shew that this method of protection, which began in a remote past, was maintained with strange persistency down to modern times. I shall collect some further instances of the chaining of books in places where it might have been expected that such things would be no longer thought of; and in conclusion I shall record some dates at which the final removal of chains took place.

In the library of the Faculty of Medicine, Paris, the books were ordered to be chained in 1509, in consequence of some thefts; and these chains were still attached to certain books in 1770[2]. At Corpus Christi College, Cambridge, in 1554, it was ordered that the books bequeathed by Peter Nobys, D.D. (Master 1516—23), should be taken better care of for the future, and, if the chains were broken, that they should be repaired at the expense of the college[3]. In 1555, Robert Chaloner, Esq., bequeathed his law books to Gray's Inn, with forty shillings in

[1] *Old Church and School Libraries of Lancashire*, by R. C. Christie, Chetham Soc. p. 139.

[2] Franklin, *Anc. Bibl.* Vol. II. p. 25.

[3] Masters, *History*, p. 62.

Fig. 116. Bookpress in the school at Bolton, Lancashire.
From *Bibliographical Miscellanies* by William Blades.

money, to be paid to his cousin, "to th' entent that he maie by cheines therwith and fasten so manye of them in the Librarye at Grauisin [Gray's Inn] as he shall think convenyente[1]."

At S. John's College, Cambridge, in 1563—4, three shillings were paid to "Phillip Stacyoner for cornering, bossing, and chayninge *Anatomiam Vessalii etc.*[2]" In 1573, Dr Caius directs by will twelve copies of his own works to be given to his college, "there to be kepte as the other bokes are, and to be successivelye tyed with chaynes in the Librarye of the same College[3]." Dr Perne, Master of Peterhouse, by will dated 25 February, 1588, directs that all his books therein bequeathed "be layed and chayned in the old Librarie of the Colledge[4]." At Trinity College, Cambridge, in 1601, Mr Peter Shaw gave £5 towards the "cheyning and desking of his bookes given to the newe liberarie[5]." In 1638—9, when a new library was completed for the Barber Surgeons of London, £6. 18s. were spent on binding and chaining, as for instance:

Paid for 36 yards of chaine at 4d. the yard and 36 yards at 3d. the yard cometh to xxijs. vjd.
Paid to the coppersmith for castinge 80 brasses to fasten the chaines to the bookes—xiijs. iiijd.[6]

Sir Matthew Hale, who died in 1676, directed in his will that certain manuscripts should be given to the Honourable Society of Lincoln's Inn: "My desire," he said, "is that they be kept safe and also in remembrance of me. They were fit to be bound in leather and chained and kept in archives[7]." In the will of Matthew Scrivener, Rector of Haslingfield in Cambridge-shire, dated 4 March, 1687, the following passage occurs: "I give fifty pounds in trust for the use of the public Library [at Cambridge], either by buying chains for the securing the books at present therein contained, or for the increase of the number

---

[1] *The Guild of the Corpus Christi, York*, ed. Surtees Society, 1872, p. 206, *note*.
[2] S. John's College Audit-Book, 1563—4, *Exp. Necess.*
[3] *Commiss. Docts.* (Cambridge), II. 309.
[4] *Arch. Hist.* III. 454.
[5] Sen. Burs. Accounts, 1600—1, *Recepta.*
[6] *Memorials of the Craft of Surgery in England*, ed. D'Arcy Power, 8vo. London 1886, p. 230.
[7] Herbert, *Inns of Court*, p. 303.

of them[1]." At the church of S. Gatien at Tours it is recorded in 1718 that the library which occupied one alley of the cloister was well stocked with manuscripts, chained on desks, which stood both against the wall and in the middle of the room[2]. Lastly, in 1815, John Fells, mariner, gave £30 to found a theological library in the church of S. Peter, Liverpool. "The books were originally fastened to open shelves in the vestry with rods and chains[3]."

Towards the end of the eighteenth century the practice was finally abandoned. At Eton College in 1719 it was "Order'd to take yᵉ Chains off yᵉ Books in yᵉ Library, except yᵉ Founder's Manuscripts[4]"; at the Bodleian Library, Oxford, the removal of them began in 1757[5]; at King's College, Cambridge, the books were unchained in 1777[6]; at Brasenose College, Oxford, in 1780[7]; and at Merton College in 1792[8].

In France the custom was evidently abandoned at a much earlier date, for the authors of the *Voyage Littéraire*, who visited more than eight hundred monasteries at the beginning of the eighteenth century, with the special intention of examining their records and their libraries, rarely allude to chaining, and when they do mention it, they use language which implies that it was a curious old fashion, the maintenance of which surprised them[9].

---

[1] *Documents relating to St Catharine's College*, ed. H. Philpott, D.D., p. 125.

[2] *Voyage Liturgique de la France*, by Le Sieur de Moléon, 1718. I have to thank Dr James for this reference.

[3] *Old Church Libraries, ut supra*, p. 102.

[4] Eton College Minute Book, 19 December, 1719.

[5] Macray, *ut supra*, p. 86. The inconvenience of chaining had long been felt for in *The Foreigner's Companion through the Universities*, by Mr Salmon, 1748, it is objected that "the books being chain'd down, there is no bringing them together even in the Library," p. 27.

[6] King's College Mundum Book, 1777: *Smith's work*. "To a man's time 9 Dayes to take the Chains of the books £1. 7s. 0d."

[7] Churton's *Lives of Smyth and Sutton*, p. 311, *note*.

[8] Henderson's *History*, p. 237.

[9] *Voy. Litt.*, ed. 1724, Vol. III. p. 24.

CHAPTER VIII.

HILE in England we were struggling with the difficulties of adapting medieval forms of libraries and bookcases to the ever-increasing number of volumes, a new system was initiated on the continent, which I propose to call the wall-system.

It seems so natural to us to set our bookshelves against a wall instead of at right angles to it, that it is difficult to realize that there was a time when such an arrangement was an innovation. Such however was the case. I believe that this principle was first introduced into a library at the Escōrial, which Philip the Second of Spain began in 1563, and completed 13 September, 1584. I do not mean by this sentence that nobody ever set bookshelves against a wall before the third quarter of the sixteenth century. I have shewn above, when discussing the catalogue of Dover Priory[1], that the books stood on pieces of furniture which were probably so treated ; and it is not uncommon in illuminated manuscripts to see a writer's books standing on one or more shelves set against the wall near his desk. Further, in the accounts of the library arranged

---

[1] See above, p. 196.

in the Vatican by
Sixtus IV., shelves
set against the wall
of one of the four
rooms are specially
mentioned[1]; and in
the description of the
library of the Dukes
of Urbino, it is ex-
pressly stated that
" the shelves for the
books are set against
the walls (*le scanzie
de' libri sono accostate
alle mura*)[2]." What
I wish to enforce is
that before the Es-
cōrial was built, no
important library
was fitted up in that
manner from the
beginning by the
architect.

The library of
the Escōrial[3] occu-
pies a commanding
position over the por-
tico through which
the building is en-
tered. It is 212 ft.

[1] See above, p. 224.
[2] See above, p. 233.
[3] For the history of the
Escōrial, see Ford, *Handbook for Spain*, Ed. 1855,
pp. 749—763, and *Descrip-
cion...del Escorial*, Fra de
los Santos, fol. Madrid,
1657, with the English
translation by G. Thomp-
son, 4to. London, 1760.

Fig. 118.   Bookcases in the Library of the Escōrial on an
enlarged scale.

Fig. 117. General view of the Library of the Escōrial, looking north.

long, by 35 ft. broad and about 36 ft. high. The roof is a barrel-vault, gorgeously painted in fresco, as are the wall-spaces above the bookcases, and the semicircular lunettes at the ends of the room. In that at the north end is Philosophy, in that at the south end is Theology, while between them are personifications of Grammar, Rhetoric, Logic, Music, etc. On the walls, forming a gigantic frieze, are various his-torical scenes, and figures of celebrated persons real and imaginary, as for instance, the first Nicene Council, the School of Athens, Solomon and the Queen of Sheba, Cicero, David, Orpheus, etc. The general appearance of this splendid room will be understood from the view (fig. 117). It is lighted by five windows on the east side and seven on the west side, to which is added on the east side a range of five smaller windows just under the vault. The principal windows are quite different from those of any other library I have been considering, for they are nearly 13 ft. high, and extend down to the floor.

The wall-spaces between each pair of windows have book-cases fitted to them, of a very original and striking design. They are divided into compartments by fluted Doric columns supporting an entablature with projecting cornice, above which again is a sort of second entablature. The bases of the columns rest upon an extremely lofty plinth, intersected, at about three-quarters of its height from the ground, by a shelf, behind which is a sloping desk. The material used for these cases is mahogany, inlaid with ebony, cedar, and other woods. They were designed by Juan de Herrera, the architect of the building, in 1584, and I am assured that they have escaped alteration, or serious damage from the numerous fires which have occurred in the palace.

In order to exhibit the distinctive peculiarities of these remarkable cases as clearly as possible, I give (fig. 118) an enlargement of part of the former view; and further, an elevation of one of them drawn accurately to scale (fig. 119), for which I have to thank a Spanish architect, Don Ricardo Velasquez.

These bookcases have a total height of rather more than 12 ft., measured from the floor to the top of the cornice. The desks are 2 ft. 7 in. from the floor, a height which corresponds with that of an ordinary table, and suggests that they must have been intended for the use of seated readers, though seats are not provided in the library at present. The section of the

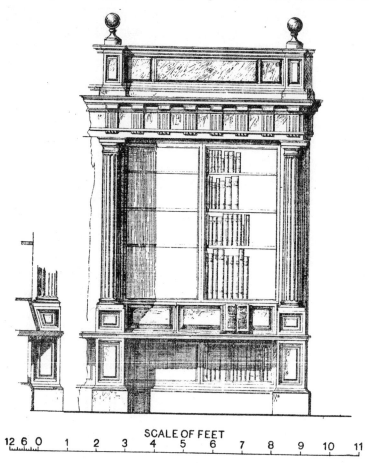

SCALE OF FEET
12 6 0   1   2   3   4   5   6   7   8   9   10   11

Fig. 119.   Elevation of a bookcase, and section of a desk in the Library of the Escōrial.

shelf and desk placed beside the elevation shews that there is a convenient slope to lay the books against. The uppermost of the four shelves is at a height of 9 ft. from the ground, so that a ladder is required to reach the books. The two photographs which I have reproduced (figs. 117, 118) shew that they have the fore-edge turned outwards, according to what is, I am informed, the usual custom in Spain.

I believe that the work done in the Escōrial had a very

Fig. 121. Interior of the Ambrosian Library at Milan.

From a photograph taken in 1899.

definite effect on library-fittings elsewhere; but, like other important inventions, the scheme of setting shelves against a wall instead of at right angles to it occurred to more than one person at about the same period; and therefore I cannot construct a genealogical tree, as I once thought I could, with the Escōrial at the root, and a numerous progeny on the branches.

Between 1603 and 1609—only 25 years afterwards—Cardinal Federigo Borromeo built, endowed, and furnished the Biblioteca Am- brosiana at Milan. A plain Ionic portico, on the cornice of which are the words BIBLIOTHECA AMBROSIANA, gives access to a single hall, on the ground floor, 74 ft. long by 29 ft. broad (fig. 120). The walls are lined with bookcases about 13 ft. high, separated, not by columns, but by flat pilasters, and protected by wire-work of an unusually large mesh, said to be original. At each corner of the hall is a staircase, leading to a gallery, 2 ft. 6 in. wide. The cases in this gallery are about 8 ft. 6 in. high. Above them again is a frieze consisting of a series of portraits of saints in oblong frames. The roof is a barrel-vault, orna- mented with plaster-work. Light is admitted through two enormous semi-circular windows at each end of the room. No alteration, I was informed when I visited the library in 1898, has been permitted. Even the floor of plain tiles, with four

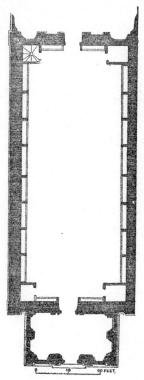

Fig. 120. Ground-plan of the Am- brosian Library at Milan.

Reduced from that given by P. P. Boscha.

tables (one at each corner), and a central brazier, is left as the Cardinal arranged it.

A good idea of the appearance of this noble room will be obtained from the general view (fig. 121)[1]. The way in which

---

[1] I have to thank the librarian, Monsignore Ceriani, for kindly allowing this photograph to be taken for my use.

the books were arranged was evidently thought remarkable at
the time, for a contemporary writer says of it "the room is not
blocked with desks to which the books are tied with iron chains
after the fashion of the libraries which are common in monasteries, but it is surrounded with lofty shelves on which the
books are sorted according to size[1]."

This library was part of a larger scheme which included a
college of doctors, a school of art, a museum, and a botanic
garden; all of which were amply endowed. The library was
to be open not merely to members of the college, but to the
citizens of Milan and all strangers who came to study there;
but the severest penalties awaited those who stole a volume,
or even touched it with soiled hands; and only the Pope
himself could absolve them from such crimes[2].

Before many years were over these novelties in library
arrangement and library administration found a ready welcome
in France, where Cardinal Mazarin was engaged in the formation
of a vast collection of books intended to surpass that of his
predecessor Richelieu[3]. Even then his library was public; all
who chose to come might work in it on Thursdays from 8 to 11
in the morning, and from 2 to 5 in the afternoon. At a later
period of his life, when he had removed to a palace now
included in the Bibliothèque Nationale, he was able to build
a library in accordance with his magnificent ideas. An accident
of construction placed this room over the stables, a conjunction which afforded endless amusement to the pamphleteers of
the time. It was finished at the end of 1647; and in the
following year the Cardinal threw it open, the first public
library given to Paris. *Publicè patere voluit, censu perpetuo
dotavit, posteritati commendavit*, said the inscription which he
placed over the door of entrance. I need not attempt to
recover from the somewhat conflicting accounts of admiring
contemporaries the exact dimensions and arrangements of this
gallery, for the bookcases still exist almost unaltered in the

---

[1] *Gli Istituti Scientifici etc. di Milano.* 8vo. Milan, 1880, p. 123, note.

[2] Boscha, *De Origine et statu Bibl. Ambros.* p. 19; *ap.* Grævius, *Thes. Ant. et
Hist. Italic*, Vol. IX. part 6; see also the Bull of Paul V., dated 7 July 1608, approving
the foundation and rehearsing the statutes, in *Magnum Bullarium Romanum*, 4to.
Turin, 1867, Vol. XI. p. 511.

[3] For the history of the Bibliothèque Mazarine see Franklin, *Anc. Bibl. de Paris*,
Vol. III. pp. 37—160.

Fig. 122. Bookcases in the Bibliothèque Mazarine, Paris.

From a photograph by Dujardin, 1898.

Bibliothèque Mazarine. One detail deserves notice because it may have been borrowed from the Ambrosian Library. There is said to have been a staircase in each of the four corners of the room by which access to a gallery was obtained[1].

Mazarin died in 1661, and, in accordance with his will, a college, to be called *Le Collège des Quatre Nations*, was founded and endowed, and the library was removed into it. The college was suppressed at the Revolution, and the buildings are now occupied by the *Institut de France*, but the library remains practically intact. It occupies two rooms at right angles to each other with a united length of about 158 ft., and a width of 27 ft. They are admirably lighted by 17 large windows.

The bookcases (fig. 122), from the original library in the Palais Mazarin, were placed round the new room. At first they terminated with the cornice, surmounted by the balustrade which protected the gallery mentioned above, and the roof was arched. In 1739, when additional shelf-room was required, and the roof was in need of repair, it was agreed to construct the present flat ceiling, and to gain thereby wall-space of sufficient height to accommodate 20,000 additional books. The gallery thus formed is approached by two staircases constructed at the same time[2].

If the elevation of these cases (fig. 123) be compared with that of the cases in the Escōrial (fig. 119), I feel sure that my readers will agree with me in admitting that the French example was copied from the Spanish. The general arrangement is the same, and especially the really distinctive features, namely, the division by columns, and the presence of a desk. It will be observed that the French example is the larger of the two, being 18 ft. high from the floor to the top of the cornice. The desk, moreover, is 4 ft. from the floor, so that it was evidently intended to be used standing.

I am aware that Naudé, the librarian employed by Mazarin to collect books for him, did not visit Spain, nor was Mazarin himself ever in that country. There is therefore no evidence to connect his library with that of Philip II., but in justification of

---

[1] Franklin, *Anc. Bibl. de Paris*, Vol. III. pp. 55—6.
[2] The minute of the conservators of the library authorising this change is printed by Franklin, *ut supra*, p. 117.

my theory I submit that the resemblance is too close to be
accidental, and that in all probability the library at the Escŏrial
had been much talked of in the world of letters.

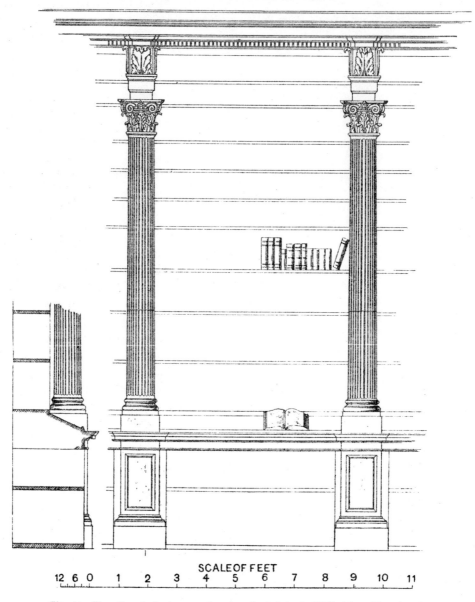

Fig. 123. Elevation of a bookcase and section of a desk in the Bibliothèque Mazarine, Paris.

The convenience of placing book-shelves against a wall was soon accepted in England, but at first in a somewhat half-hearted fashion. The earliest instance of this, so far as I know, is to be met with in the Bodleian Library, Oxford, where the first stone of the eastern wing was laid in 1610, and completed, with the fittings, in 1612[1].

Fig. 124.　A portion of the bookcases set up in the eastern wing of the Bodleian Library, Oxford, built 1610—1612.

From Loggan's *Oxonia Illustrata*, 1675.

Advantage was taken of the whole of the wall-space provided by this extension, and it was lined with a bookcase extending from floor to ceiling. In order to provide easy access to the upper shelves, a light gallery was provided, the pillars of which were utilised to support a seat for the readers, because, the

[1] Macray, *Annals*, ut supra, p. 37.

18—2

books being still chained, desks and seats were indispensable. These cases still exist almost unaltered, but their appearance as first constructed has been preserved to us in Loggan's print, taken about 1675, part of which is here reproduced (fig. 124).

In 1634 (13 May) the first stone was laid of the enlargement of the library towards the west, corresponding exactly to the wing at the opposite end erected twenty-four years before[1]. The fittings were on the same plan, but of a more elaborate and highly finished design, the plain supports of the former work being replaced by Ionic columns supporting arches with frieze and cornice, and a heavy balustrade for the gallery above.

I now come to the influence exercised upon the architecture and fittings of libraries by Sir Christopher Wren, and I shall be able to shew that though he did not actually introduce the wall-system into England, he developed it, adapted it to our requirements, and by the force of his genius shewed what structural changes were necessary in order to meet the increased number of books to be accommodated. Wren never visited Italy, but in 1665 he spent about six months in Paris, where he made the acquaintance of the best painters, sculptors, and architects, among whom was the Italian Bernini. From him he might easily obtain information of what was passing in Italy, though he describes him as "the old reserved Italian" who would hardly allow him a glimpse of a design for which, says Wren, "I would have given my skin." French work he studied enthusiastically, and after giving a list of places he had visited says, "that I might not lose the impressions of them I shall bring you almost all France in paper." Among other things he specially records his admiration for what he terms "the masculine furniture of the Palais Mazarin," though he does not specially mention the library; but, as Mazarin had died four years before, his palace would have been practically dismantled, and the only furniture likely to attract Wren's attention would have been his bookcases[2].

The first piece of library work executed by Wren in England was at Lincoln Cathedral, 1674, where after the Restoration a new library was required. Dr Michael Honywood, who had been appointed Dean in 1660, offered to build one at his own cost,

[1] Macray, *ut supra*, p. 80.
[2] Elmes, *Life of Sir C. Wren*, pp. 180—184. *Parentalia*, p. 261.

Fig. 125.   Entrance to Wren's Library at Lincoln Cathedral, with part of the
bookcase which lines the north wall.

and to present to it the books which he had collected in Holland. The site selected was that formerly occupied by the north alley of the cloister, which, through faulty construction, had fallen down, and lain in ruins for a long period.

The building consists of an arcade of nine semicircular arches supported on eight Doric columns. The upper storey, containing the library, has eleven windows in a similar classical style, and above there is a bold entablature ornamented with acanthus leaves. The library is 104 ft. long by 17 ft. 6 in. wide and 14 ft. high; the ceiling is flat and perfectly plain. In addition to the windows above mentioned there is another at the west end. The entrance is at the east end through a richly ornamented door (fig. 125). The shield in the centre of the pediment bears the arms of Dean Honywood.

Wren placed a continuous bookcase along the north wall of this room, extending from floor to ceiling. At the base there is a plinth (fig. 125), which may have originally contained cupboards, but is now fitted with shelves; and at the top, close to the ceiling, there is a heavy entablature decorated with acanthus leaves and classical moldings above a plain cornice, which bears at intervals oblong tablets inscribed with the subjects of the books beneath. The shelves are disposed in compartments, alternately wide and narrow, the former being set slightly in advance of the latter, so as to break the monotony of a bookcase of uniform width extending the whole length of a long room.

While this work was proceeding Wren planned the New Library for Trinity College, Cambridge[1], begun 23 February, 1675—6. His design is accompanied by an explanation, contained in a rough draught of a letter to some gentleman of Trinity College, probably the Master. It is not signed, but internal evidence shews that it must have been written or dictated by Wren.

This library was placed on a cloister, open both to the east and to the west, at the end of Nevile's Court. The level of the

---

[1] The history of this library has been fully narrated in the *Arch. Hist.*, ut supra, Vol. II. pp. 531—551. Wren's Memoir quoted below has been collated with the original in the library of All Souls' College, Oxford, where his designs are also preserved.

library floor was made to correspond with that of the first floor
of the chambers on the north and south sides of the court. This
is shewn in Wren's design, part of which is here reproduced
(fig. 126), and explained in the following passage of his memoir.

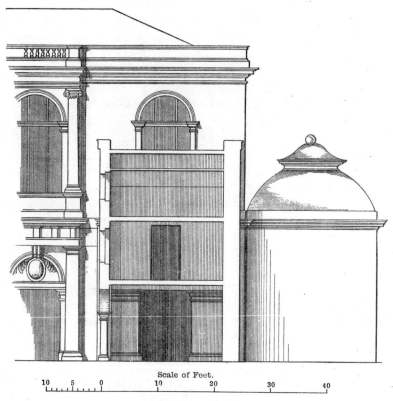

Scale of Feet.

Fig. 126. Part of Wren's elevation of the east side of the Library of Trinity College,
Cambridge, with a section of the north range of Nevile's Court, shewing the door
to the Library from the first floor.

[The design] shewes the face of the building next the court with the
pavillions for the staircases and the Sections of the old buildings where
they joyne to the new....

I haue given the appearance of arches as the Order required fair
and lofty: but I haue layd the floor of the Library upon the impostes,
which answar (*sic*) to the pillars in the cloister and the levells of the old
floores, and haue filled the Arches with relieues of stone, of which I
haue seen the effect abroad in good building, and I assure you where
porches are lowe with flat ceilings is infinitely more gracefull then lowe
arches would be and is much more open and pleasant, nor need the

mason freare (*sic*) the performance because the Arch discharges the weight, and I shall direct him in a firme manner of executing the designe.

Fig. 127.   Elevation of one bay on the east side of the Library of Trinity College, Cambridge, drawn to scale from the existing building.

By this contrivance the windowes of the Library rise high and giue place for the deskes against the walls, and being high may be afforded to be large, and being wide may haue stone mullions and the glasse pointed, which after all inventions is the only durable way in our Climate for a publique building, where care must be had that snowe driue not in....

The general design seems to have been borrowed from that of the Library of S. Mark at Venice, begun by Sansovino in 1536. The Italian architect, like Sir Christopher Wren, raised his library on a cloister, which is in the Doric style, while the superstructure is Ionic. The Venetian example is more ornate, and there are statues upon every pier of the balustrade. The arcades are left open, because there was not the same necessity for accommodating the level of the floor to that of older buildings, and also because the wall opposite to the windows had to be left blank on account of the proximity of other structures. No consideration for fittings such as influenced Wren could have influenced the Italian architect.

The style of Wren's work will be understood from the elevation of a bay on the east side (fig. 127), drawn to scale from the existing building. If this be compared with the original design (fig. 126), it will be seen that the style there indicated has been closely followed.

We will now consider the fittings. A long stretch of blank wall having been provided both along the sides and at the ends of the room, Wren proceeded to design a masterly combination of the old and new methods of arranging bookcases. As he says in another passage of the same memoir, when describing this part of his design :

The disposition of the shelues both along the walls and breaking out from the walls....must needes proue very convenient and gracefull, and the best way for the students will be to haue a litle square table in each Celle with 2 chaires. The necessity of bringing windowes and dores to answer to the old building leaues two squarer places at the endes and 4 lesser Celles not to study in, but to be shut up with some neat Lattice dores for archives.

The bookcases, designed by himself, were executed under his direction by Cornelius Austin, a Cambridge workman. My illustration (fig. 128) shews one of the "4 lesser Celles" with one of its doors open, and next to it a "Celle" for students with

table, revolving desk, and two stools.   These pieces of furniture
were also designed by Wren.

Fig. 128.   Interior of the north-east corner of the Library of Trinity College, Cambridge,
shewing the bookcases, table, desk and chairs, as designed by Sir C. Wren.

The cases are 11 ft. 10 in. high, and the wooden floor upon
which they stand is raised higher than that of the library.   The
great depth of the plinth, which Wren utilised for cupboards,
recalls the plan of some of the older cases, and there is the little
cupboard to contain the catalogue at the end of each standard ;
but, with these exceptions, there is nothing medieval about
them except their position.   On the top of each case is a
square pedestal of wood on which Wren intended to place
a statue, but this part of his scheme was not carried out.
The celebrated Grinling Gibbons supplied the busts which take
the place of Wren's statues, and also the coats of arms and
wreaths of flowers and fruit with which the ends of the cases
are decorated.

It is difficult to decide the source from which an architect
so great as Wren derived any feature of his buildings, but it
seems to me reasonable to ascribe to foreign influence his use
of the side-walls at Trinity College library ; and his scheme for
combining a lofty internal wall with beauty of external design,
and a complete system of lighting, must always command admiration.   In the next example of his library work foreign
influence may be more directly traced, for I feel that the library
of S. Paul's Cathedral suggests reminiscences of the Ambrosian
library at Milan.

Wren placed the library of his new cathedral in the western
transept, with an ingenuity of contrivance and a dignity of
conception peculiarly his own.   On the level of what in a Gothic
church would have been the triforium, he constructed, both on
the north and south side, a large and lofty room.   It was his
intention that each of these rooms should be used as a library,
and that they should be connected by means of the gallery
which crosses the west end of the nave.   Access to them was
to be obtained from the exterior, without entering the church,
by a circular staircase in the south-west corner of the façade.
This plan has not been fully carried out, and the southern
library only has been fitted up.   It is now usually reached by
means of the staircase leading to the dome.

These arrangements will be understood from the ground-
plan (fig. 129)[1].   This plan shews very clearly the library itself,
the two circular staircases at the west end, leading up to the
gallery, the wide geometrical staircase leading down to the
portico, the corridor into which this staircase opens, and from
which a visitor could either ascend by a flight of stairs to the
gallery crossing the nave, or, turning to his right, either enter
the library, or pass eastwards towards the dome.

The library (fig. 130) is a well-lighted room, with an area
measuring 53 ft. by 32 ft., and of sufficient height to admit of
the introduction of a gallery under the vault.   A massive stone
pier projects into the room at each corner, so as to break the
formal regularity of the design in a very pleasing manner.   The
gallery, together with the bookcases, which stand against the

---

[1] This plan has been reduced from one on a larger scale kindly sent to me by
my friend Mr F. C. Penrose, architect to the Cathedral.

Fig. 130. Sir Christopher Wren's Library at S. Paul's Cathedral, London,
looking north-east.

walls, both in the gallery and below it, were either designed by Wren himself, or placed there with his approval. The Building

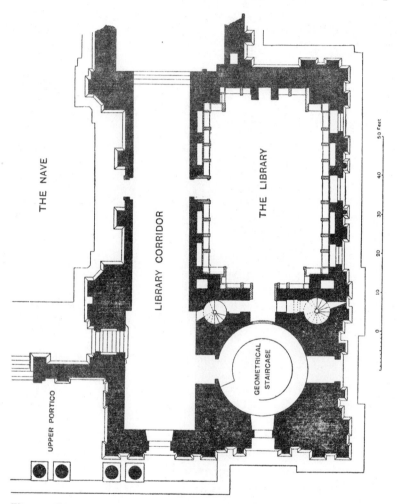

Fig. 129.   Ground plan of Library and adjacent parts of S. Paul's Cathedral, London.

Accounts[1] contain many valuable pieces of information respecting the history of the room and its fittings. The floor "in the south library" was laid down in July, 1708, as was also

---

[1] I have to thank the Dean and Chapter for leave to study these Accounts, and to have a photograph taken of the library.

that in the gallery; the windows "in the north and south library," words which shew very clearly that the corresponding room on the north side was also intended for a library, were painted in December, 1708; and the ornamental woodwork was supplied in March, 1708—9. From the entries referring to these works I will quote the following, as it particularises the most striking feature in the room, namely, the large ornamental brackets which appear to support the gallery:

To Jonathan Maine Carver in the South Library, viz. For carving 32 Trusses or Cantalivers under the Gallary, 3 ft. 8 in. long, and 3 ft. 8 in. deep and 7 in. thick with Leather worke cut through and a Leaf in the front and a drop hanging down with fruit and flowers etc. at 6^l. 10^s. each.

$$208^l. — —-$$

The words "leather work," used in the above entry, are singularly suitable, for the whole composition looks more like something molded out of leather or plaster than cut out of a solid piece of wood. The vertical portion, applied to the pilasters, consists of a bunch of flowers, hops, and corn, somewhat in the manner of Grinling Gibbons, who has been often named as the artist. The above-mentioned pilasters divide the wall-space into 33 compartments, each of which is from 3 ft. 6 in. to 4 ft. wide, and 9 ft. high, exclusive of the plinth and cornice, and fitted with six shelves, which are apparently at the original levels.

The gallery is approached by a staircase contrived in the thickness of the south-west pier. It is 5 ft. wide, and fitted with bookcases ranged against the wall in the same manner as those below, but they are loftier, and of plainer design. The balustrade, a molded cornice of wood, supported on pilasters of the same material, which recall those separating the compartments below, and the great stone piers, enriched with a broad band of fruit, flowers, and other ornaments set in a sunk panel, are striking features of this gallery.

The material used throughout for the fittings is oak, which fortunately has never been painted, and has assumed a mellow tone through age which produces a singularly beautiful effect.

If we now return to Cambridge, we shall find that the influence of Wren can easily be traced in all the library fittings

put up in the course of the 18th century. The first work of
this kind undertaken was the provision of additional fittings to
the library of Emmanuel College[1] between 1702 and 1707. The
tall cases, set up at right angles to the walls in 1679, were moved
forward, and shelves in continuation of them were placed against
the side-walls. The same influence is more distinctly seen in
the library of S. Catharine's Hall[2], which was fitted up, according
to tradition, at the expense of Thomas Sherlock, D.D., probably while Master, an office which he held from 1714 to 1719.
The room is 63 ft. 6 in. long by 22 ft. 10 in. wide; and it
is divided by partitions into a central portion, about 39 ft.
long, and a narrow room at each end, 12 ft. long. Each of
these latter is lighted by windows in the north and south walls;
the former has windows in the south wall only. The central
portion is divided into three compartments by bookcases which
line the walls, and project from them at right angles; in the two
smaller rooms the cases only line the walls, the space being too
narrow for any other treatment.

When the building of the new Senate House had set free
the room called the Regent House, in which the University had
been in the habit of meeting from very early times, it was fitted
up, between 1731 and 1734, as part of the University Library[3].
Wren's example was followed as far as the nature of the room
would permit. Wherever a blank wall could be found, it was
lined with shelves, and the cases placed at right angles to the
side-walls were continued over the narrow spaces left between
their ends and the windows. One of these cases, from the south
side of the room, is here shewn (fig. 131). The shelves under
the windows were added subsequently. A similar arrangement
was adopted for the east room in 1787—90.

At Clare College, at about the same date, the new library
over the kitchen was fitted up with shelves placed against the
walls. These fittings are excellent specimens, ornamented with
fluted Ionic pilasters, an elaborate cornice, and pediments above
the doors. It is worth noting, as evidence of the slowness with
which new fashions are accepted, that the antiquary William

[1] *Arch. Hist.* Vol. II. p. 710.   Vol. III. p. 468.
[2] *ib.* Vol. III. p. 468.
[3] *ib.* Vol. III. pp. 74, 470.

Cole, writing in 1742, calls this library "a very large well-proportion'd Room à la moderne, wth ye Books rang'd all round it & not in Classes as in most of y[e] rest of y[e] Libraries in other Colleges[1]."

Fig. 131.   Bookcase in the north room of the University Library, Cambridge, designed by James Essex, 1731—1734.

The fashion of which I have been tracing the progress in England had been accepted during the same period in France, where some beautiful specimens of it may still be seen. I presume that the example was set by the wealthy convents, most of which had been rebuilt, at least in part, in the then fashionable classical style, during the seventeenth century[2]. At Rheims a library fitted up by the Benedictines of Saint Remi in 1784 now does duty as the chapel of the Hôtel-Dieu. Fluted Corinthian columns supporting an elaborate cornice

---

[1] *Arch. Hist.* Vol. I. p. 113.

[2] See the set of views of French Religious Houses called *Le Monasticon Gallicanum*, 4to. Paris, 1882.   The plates were drawn by Dom Germain 1645—1694.

Fig. 132.   Interior of the Library of the Jesuits at Rheims, now the *Lingerie de l'Hôpital Général.*

divide the walls into compartments, in which the books
are ranged on open shelves. The room is 120 ft. long, by
31 ft. broad, with four windows on each side. With this may
be compared the public library at Alençon, the fittings of which
are said to have been brought from the abbey of the Val Dieu
near Mortain at the Revolution. The room is 70 ft. long by 25 ft.
wide. Against the walls are 26 compartments or presses, alternately open and closed. Each of these terminates in an ogee
arch enriched with scrolls and a central shield. The whole
series is surmounted by a cornice divided by console brackets,
between which are shields, probably intended originally to carry
the names of the subjects of the books.

Lastly, I must mention the libraries of Louis XVI. and
Marie Antoinette at Versailles. The walls are lined with a
double row of presses, each closed by glass doors. The lower
row is about four feet high, the upper row about ten feet high.
The wood-work is painted white, and enriched with wreaths of
leaves in ormolu. As a general rule the books are hidden from
view by curtains of pleated silk.

I mentioned in a previous chapter[1] that additional space was
provided for the library in a French monastery by raising the
roof of an existing building, putting in dormer windows, and
converting the triangular space so gained into a library by
placing in it bookcases of a convenient height, and connecting
them together by a ceiling. I have fortunately discovered
one such library still in existence at Rheims. It belonged
originally to the Jesuits, who had constructed it about 1678,
and when the Order was expelled from France in 1764, and
their House became the workhouse (*hôpital général*) of the
town, it was fortunately made use of as the *lingerie*, or linen-
room, without any material change. Even the table has been
preserved. The view here presented of the interior (fig. 132)
may serve to give a general idea, not merely of this library, but of
others of the same class. The decoration of the ceiling is coarse
but effective. On the coved portion of it, within the shields, are
written the subjects of the books on the shelves beneath. I
made a list of these and have printed them on the margin of my
ground-plan (fig. 133). This plan also shews the arrangement

---

[1] See above, pp. 106, 114.

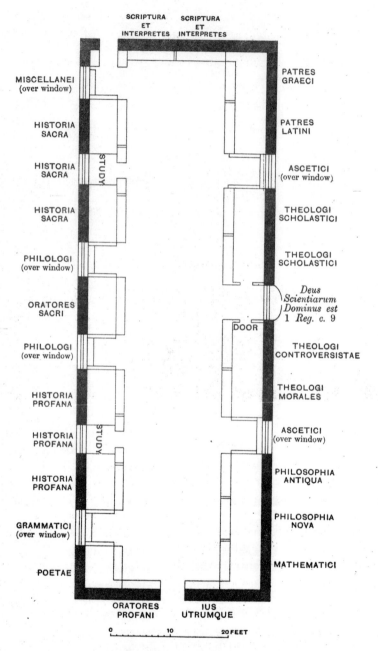

Fig. 133. Ground-plan of the Library of the Jesuits at Rheims.

of the bookcases. They are placed at a distance of five feet from the walls, and are returned to meet each window, thus forming convenient bays for private study. The space between the bookcases and the wall was used as a store-room[1].

The Bibliothèque Sainte-Geneviève, at Paris, offered originally a splendid example of a library arranged in this manner. It consisted of two galleries, at right angles to each other, fitted up in the same style as the library at Rheims. The longest of these galleries was 147 ft. long by 24 ft. wide. The guide-books prepared for the use of visitors to Paris in the middle of the 18th century dwell with enthusiasm on the convenience and beauty of this room. The books were protected by wire-work; between each pair of cases was a bust of a Roman emperor or an ancient philosopher; at the crossing of the two galleries was a dome which seemed to be supported on a palm-tree in plaster-work at each corner, out of the foliage of which peered the heads of cherubs; while the convenience of readers was consulted by the liberality with which the library was thrown open on three days in every week, and furnished with tables, chairs, a ladder to reach the upper shelves, and a pair of globes[2]. This library was begun in 1675, and placed, like that at Rheims, directly under the roof. The second gallery, which is shorter than the first, was added in 1726. It was not disturbed at the Revolution, nor under the Empire, though the rest of the abbey-buildings became the Lycée Napoléon. After the Restoration, when this school became the Collége Henri IV., the presence of the library was found to be inconvenient, and in 1850 it was removed to a new building close to the Pantheon. The galleries are now used as a dormitory for the school-boys, but the dome, with some of its decorations, still survives.

Another example of this arrangement, which seems to have been peculiarly French, is afforded by the library of Saint Germain-des-Près, the gradual extension of which I have already described[3]. The books were contained in oak presses set against the walls. Above them was a series of portraits representing

---

. [1] Jadart, *Les Anciennes Bibliothèques de Reims*, 8vo. Reims, 1891, p. 14.

[2] Franklin, *Anc. Bibl. de Paris*, Vol. I. pp. 71—99. He gives a view of the interior of the library from a print dated 1773.

[3] See above, p. 114.

the most important personages in the Order of S. Benedict. This library was open to the public daily from 9 to 11 a.m. and from 3 to 5 p.m.[1]

I will conclude this chapter with a few words on the library of the most famous of all European monasteries, namely Monte Cassino, the foundation of which was undoubtedly laid by S. Benedict himself. I confess that I had hoped to find there a library which might either by its position or its fittings recall the early days of monasticism ; but unfortunately the piety of the Benedictine Order has induced them to rebuild their parent house in a classical style, and to obliterate nearly every trace of the primitive building. The library, to which I was obligingly conducted by the Prior, is 60 ft. long by 30 ft. broad, with two large windows at the end opposite to the door. The side-walls are lined with bookcases divided by columns into four compartments on each side, after the fashion of Cardinal Mazarin's library. These columns support a heavy cornice with handsome ornaments. A band of woodwork divides the cases into an upper and lower range, but there is no trace of a desk. I could not learn the date at which these fittings had been constructed, but from their style I should assign them to the middle of the seventeenth century[2].

---

[1] Franklin, *ut supra*, I. pp. 107—134.
[2] I visited Monte Cassino 13 April, 1898.

CHAPTER IX.

PRIVATE LIBRARIES. ABBAT SIMON AND HIS BOOK-CHEST. LIBRARY OF CHARLES V. OF FRANCE. ILLUSTRATIONS OF THIS LIBRARY FROM ILLUMINATED MANUSCRIPTS. BOOK-LECTERN USED. IN PRIVATE HOUSES. BOOK-DESKS REVOLVING ROUND A CENTRAL SCREW. DESKS ATTACHED TO CHAIRS. WALL-CUPBOARDS. A SCHOLAR'S ROOM IN THE FIFTEENTH CENTURY. STUDY OF THE DUKE OF URBINO. LIBRARY OF MONTAIGNE. LIBRARY OF MARGARET OF AUSTRIA. CONCLUSION.

N the previous chapters I have sketched the history of library-fittings from the earliest times to the end of the eighteenth century. The libraries to which these fittings belonged were, for the most part, public, or as good as public. But, as in history we have recognised the important fact that a record of battles and sieges and enactments in Parliament gives an imperfect conception of the life of a people, so I should feel that this archeological subject had been insufficiently treated if I made no attempt to shew how private scholars disposed their books, or with what appliances they used them. For instance, in what sort of chair was the author of the *Philobiblon* sitting when he wrote the last words of his treatise, 24 January, 1345, and how was his study in his palace at Auckland furnished? Further, how were private students bestowed in the fifteenth century, when a love of letters had become general? Lastly, how were libraries fitted up for private use in the succeeding century, when the great people of .the earth, like the wealthy Romans of imperial

times, added the pursuit of literature to their other fashions, and considered a library to be indispensable in their luxurious palaces?

In the hope of obtaining reliable information on these interesting questions, I have for some years past let no opportunity slip of examining illuminated manuscripts. I have gone through a large number in the British Museum, where research is aided by an excellent list of the subjects illustrated; in the *Bibliothèque Nationale*, Paris; and in the *Bibliothèque Royale*, Brussels, where the manuscripts are for the most part those which once belonged to the Dukes of Burgundy. I have been somewhat disappointed in this search, for, with the single exception of the illustration from Boethius (fig. 63), I have not found any library, properly so called. This is no doubt strange, having regard to the great variety of scenes depicted. It must be remembered, however, that these are used for the most part to illustrate some action that is going forward, for which a library would be a singularly inappropriate background. Single figures, on the other hand, are frequently shewn with their books about them, either reading or writing. Such illustrations most frequently occur in *Books of Hours*, in representations of the Evangelists; or in portraits of S. Jerome, who is painted as a scholar at his desk surrounded by piles of books and papers; and I think we may safely take these as representations of ordinary scholars, because, by the beginning of the fifteenth century, when most of the pictures to which I refer were drawn, it had become the custom to surround even the most sacred personages with the attributes of common life.

In the twelfth century, when books were few, they were kept in chests, and the owners seem to have used the edge as a desk to lean their book on. My illustration (fig. 134) shews Simon, Abbat of S. Albans 1167—1183, seated in front of his book-chest[1]. The chest is set on a frame, so as to raise it to a convenient height; and the Abbat is seated on one of those folding wooden chairs which are not uncommon at the present day. Simon was a great collector of books: "their number,"

---

[1] MSS. Mus. Brit., MSS. Cotton, Claudius E. 4, part I. fol. 124. I have to thank my friend, Mr Hubert Hall, of the Public Record Office, for drawing my attention to this illustration.

writes his chronicler, "it would take too long to name; but those who desire to see them can find them in the painted aumbry in the church, placed as he specially directed against the tomb of Roger the hermit[1]."

Fig. 134. Simon, Abbat of S. Albans (1167—1183), seated at his book-chest.

From MSS. Cotton.

Chests, as we have seen above at the Vatican library, were used for the permanent storage of books in the fifteenth century; and a book-chest frequently formed part of the travelling luggage of a king. For example, when Charles V. of France died, 16 September, 1380, at the Château de Beauté-sur-Marne, thirty-one volumes were found in his chamber "in a chest resting on two supports, which chest is by the window, near the fireplace, and it has a double cover, and in one of the divisions of the said chest were the volumes that follow." His son, Charles VI., kept the thirteen volumes which he carried about with him in a carved chest, within which was an inlaid box (*escrin marqueté*) to contain the more precious books[2].

The earliest information about the furniture of a medieval private library that I have as yet discovered is contained in a fragment of an account-book recording the cost of fitting up a tower in the Louvre in 1367 and 1368, to contain the books belonging to Charles V. of France. Certain pieces of

---

[1] *Gesta Abbatum*, ed. Rolls series, I. p. 184. I owe this reference and its translation to the Reverend F. A. Gasquet, *Medieval Monastic Libraries*, p. 89, in *Downside Review*, 1891, Vol. X. No. 2.

[2] Henri Havard, *Dict. de l'Ameublement*, s. v. Librairie. The first chest is described in the following words: " Livres estans en la grant chambre dudit Seigneur, en ung escrin assiz sur deux crampons, lequel est à la fenestre emprès la cheminée de ladite chambre, et est a deux couvescles, en l'une des parties dequel coffre estoient les parties qui s'ensuivent." See also J. Labarte: *Inventaire du Mobilier de Charles V.* 4to. Paris, 1879, p. 336.

woodwork in the older library in the palace on the Isle de la Cité are to be taken down and altered, and set up in the new room. Two carpenters are paid (14 March, 1367) for "having taken to pieces all the cases (*bancs*) and two wheels (*roes*), which were in the king's library in the palace, and transported them to the Louvre with the desks (*lettrins*), and the aforesaid wheels, each made smaller by a foot all round; and for having put all together again, and hung up the desks (*lettrins*) in the two upper stages of the tower that looks toward the Falconry, to put the king's books in; and for having panelled the first of those two stories all round on the inside with wood from 'Illande,' at a total cost of fifty francs of gold. Next, because the seats were too old, they were remade of new timber which the aforesaid carpenters brought. Also [they were paid] for two strong doors for the said two stories 7 ft. high, 3 ft. broad, and 3 fingers thick." In the following year (4 May, 1368), a wire-worker (*cagetier*) is paid "for having made trellises of wire in front of two casements and two windows...to keep out birds and other beasts (*oyseaux et autres bestes*), by reason of, and protection for, the books that shall be placed there." The ceiling is said to have been panelled in cypress wood ornamented with carvings[1].

The "tower that looks toward the Falconry" mentioned in the above description has been identified with the north-west tower of the old Louvre. The rooms fitted up as a library were circular, and about 14 feet in diameter[2].

The above description of a library will be best explained by an illumination (fig. 135) contained in Boccacio's *Livre des cas des malheureux nobles hommes et femmes*, written and

---

[1] Franklin, *Anc. Bibl. de Paris*, Vol. II. p. 112. A copy of this account is in the *Bibliothèque de l'Arsenal*, No. 6362. This I have collated with M. Franklin's text. The most important passage is the following: A Jacques du Parvis et Jean Grosbois, huchiers, pour leur peine d'avoir dessemblé tous les bancs et deux roes qui estoient en la librairie du Roy au palais, et iceux faict venir audit Louvre, avec les lettrins et icelles roes estrécies chacune d'un pied tout autour; et tout rassemblé et pendu les lettrins es deux derraines estages de la tour, devers la Fauconnerie, pour mettre les livres du Roy; et lambroissié de bort d'Illande le premier d'iceux deux estages tout autour par dedans, au pris de L. francs d'or, par marché faict à eux par ledit maistre Jacques, XIVᵉ jour de mars 1367.

[2] A. Berty, *Topographie historique du vieux Paris*, 4to. Paris, 1866, Vol. I. pp. 143—146. He considers that the "bort d'Illande" was Dutch oak, 480 pieces of which had been given to the king by the officer called Sénéchal of Hainault.

illuminated in Flanders for King Henry the Seventh, and now
in the British Museum[1]. Two gentlemen are studying at a
revolving desk, which can be raised or lowered by a central
screw. This is evidently the "wheel" of the French King's

Fig. 135. Two men in a library.

From a MS. of *Les cas des malheureux nobles hommes et femmes* in the British Museum.

library. Behind are their books, either resting on a desk
hung against the wall, which is panelled, or lying on a shelf
beneath the desk. This piece of furniture would be properly
described either as a *banc* or a *lettrin*. It should be noted that
care has been taken to keep the wheel steady by supporting it

[1] MSS. Mus. Brit. 14 E. v.

on a solid base, beneath which are two strong cross-pieces of
timber, which also serve as a foot-rest for the readers. The
books on the desk set against the wall are richly bound, with
bosses of metal. Chaining was evidently not thought of, indeed
I doubt if it was ever used in a private library. The window
is glazed throughout. In other examples which I shall figure
below we shall find a wire trellis used instead of glass for part
at least of the window.

My next illustration (fig. 136), also Flemish, is of the same
date, from a copy of the *Miroir historial*[1]. It represents a
Carmelite monk, probably the author of the book, writing in his
study. Behind him are three desks, one above the other, hung
against the wall along two sides of the room, with books bound
and ornamented as in the former picture, resting upon them,
and beneath the lowest is a flat shelf or bench on which a
book rests upon its side. The desk he is using is not uncommon in these illustrations. It is fixed on a solid base,
which is further strengthened, as in the example of the wheel-
desk, by massive planks, to guard against the slightest vibration;
and it can be turned aside by means of a limb—apparently of
iron—which is first vertical, then horizontal, then vertical again.
The Carmelite holds in his left hand an instrument for keeping
the page perfectly flat. This instrument has usually a sharp
point with which any roughness on the page can be readily
removed. The volume he is using is kept open by two strings,
to each of which a weight is attached. Behind the desk, covered
with a cloth, is a chest secured by two locks. On this stands
an object which appears to be a large magnifying glass.

Sometimes the desk was carried round three sides of the
room, with no curtain to keep off dust, and with no shelf beneath it. The illustration (fig. 137) is from a French translation
of Valerius Maximus (1430—75) in the Harleian Collection[2].

I now pass to a series of pictures which illustrate the daily
life of a scholar or a writer who had few books, but who could
live in a certain ease—allowing himself a chair and a desk.
Of these desks there is an infinite variety, dictated, I imagine,

---

[1] MSS. Mus. Brit. 14 E. 1. This miniature has been reproduced by Father Gasquet
in the paper quoted above.

[2] MSS. Mus. Brit., MSS. Harl. 4375, f. 151 b.

Fig. 136. A Carmelite in his study.

From a MS. of *Le Miroir Historial* in the British Museum.

by the fashion prevalent in particular places at particular times. I have tried to arrange them in groups.

Fig. 137.　Three musicians in a library.

From a MS. of a French translation of *Valerius Maximus*, in the British Museum.

In the first place the chair is usually a rather elaborate piece of furniture, with arms, a straight back, and, very frequently, a canopy. A cushion to sit upon is sometimes permitted, but, as a general rule, these chairs are destitute of stuffing, tapestry, or other device to conceal the material of which they are made. Occasionally the canopy is richly carved or painted in a pattern.

The commonest form of desk is a modification of the lectern-system. It consists of a double lectern, beneath which is a row of cupboards, or rather a shelf protected by several doors, one of which is always at the end of the piece of furniture. The triangular space under the lectern is also used for books. This device is specially commended by Richard de Bury in the *Philobiblon*[1]. "Moses," says he, "the gentlest of men, teaches us to make bookcases most neatly, wherein they may be protected from any injury: *Take*, he says, *this book of the law, and put it in the side of the ark of the covenant of the Lord your God.*" My illustration (fig. 138) is taken from an edition of the *Ship of Fools*, printed at Basle by Nicolas Lamparter in 1507. In this example the desk with its cupboards stands on a plinth, and

[1] *The Philobiblon of Richard de Bury:* ed. E. C. Thomas, London, 1888.

this again on a broad step. Both are probably introduced to ensure steadiness.

Fig. 138. A bibliomaniac at his desk.

From the *Ship of Fools*.

The seated figure represents a bibliomaniac who treats his books as mere curiosities from which he derives no mental improvement. He has put on his spectacles and wielded his feather-brush, in order to dust the leaves of a folio with greater care. Under the cut are the following explanatory lines:

Qui libros tyriis vestit honoribus
Et blattas abijt puluerulentulas
Nec discens animum litterulis colit:
Mercatur nimia stulticiam stipe.

I append a rough translation:

Who clothes his books in Tyrian dyes,
Then brushes off the dust and flies,
Nor reads one line to make him wise,
Spends lavish gold and—FOLLY buys.

Such a desk as this was used in the succeeding century in at least two libraries belonging to ladies of high rank. The first belonged to Margaret of Austria, daughter of Maximilian, Emperor of Germany. She had been the wife of Philibert II., Duke of Savoy, and after his death, 10 September, 1504, her father made her regent of the Netherlands. She died at Malines 30 November, 1530, at the age of fifty. She seems to have been a liberal patroness of literature and the arts, and the beautiful church that she built at Brou in memory of her husband bears witness to her architectural taste and skill.

The inventory, out of which I hope to reconstruct her library, is dated 20 April, 1524[1]. It is headed: "Library," and begins with the following entry: "The first desk (*pourpitre*) begins over the door, and goes all round up to the fireplace." On this desk or shelf are enumerated fifty-two volumes, all bound in velvet with gilt bosses. This entry is succeeded by: "here follow the Books of Hours, being on a desk high up in continuation of the preceding one between the windows and the fireplace." This desk contains twenty-six volumes bound in velvet, red satin, or cloth of gold, with gilt bosses.

We come next to "the first desk below (*d'ambas*) beginning near the door at the first seat." This desk carries nine books, presumably on the sloping portion, because we presently come to a paragraph headed "here follow the books covered with leather &c., which are underneath the desks beginning near the door." The author of the inventory then returns to the first desk, and enumerates eleven volumes. He next goes round to "the other side of the said desk," and enumerates thirteen

---

[1] Printed in *Jahrbuch der Kunsthistorischen Sammlungen des Allerhöchsten Kaiserhauses*, Band III. 4to. Wien, 1885.

volumes. In this way six desks are gone through. All have books bound in black, blue, crimson, or violet, velvet laid out upon them, while those in plainer dress are consigned to the shelves beneath. It should be added that the fourth desk is described as being near the fireplace (*empres la chemynée*).

The desks having been gone through, we come to "the books which are within the iron trellis beginning near the door." This piece of furniture contained twenty-seven volumes.

The number of books accommodated in the whole room was as follows :

First shelf			52	
Second shelf			26	78
First desk (sloping portion)		9		
Under desk: one side	11			
,, ,, other side	13	24	33	
Second desk		21		
	11			
	10	21	42	
Third ,, ,,		26		
	13			
	10	23	49	
Fourth ,, ,,		15		
	18			
	14	32	47	
Fifth ,, ,,		19		
	11			
	10	21	40	
Sixth ,, ,,		20		
	9			
	10	19	39	250
Within the trellis-work				27
				355

We will next try to form some idea of the way in which this library was arranged ; and first of the two shelves which begin "over the door." A shelf in this position is shewn in Carpaccio's well-known picture of S. Jerome in his study. It is set desk-wise against the wall supported on iron brackets. As a large proportion of the fifty-two volumes on our shelf are described as of large size (*grant*), we shall be justified in assuming that each was 10 in. broad. The total therefore would occupy 520 in. or say 43 ft. at least, not allowing for intervals between them. This shelf extended from the door round the room to the fireplace, by which I suppose we are to understand that it began on the wall which contained the door, and was carried round the corner of the room up to the fireplace.

The second shelf, at the same height as the preceding, contained only twenty-six volumes, fifteen of which are described as small (*petit*). A space of thirteen feet or even less will therefore be amply sufficient to contain them.

The six desks which stood on the floor were, I imagine, constructed in some such way as that which I have figured above from the *Ship of Fools*. It is evident that books in velvet bindings and adorned with gilt bosses would be set out where they could be seen, and for such a purpose what could be better than a lectern? The table I have given above shews that there were 110 volumes thus disposed, or an average of say 18 to each desk. A careful analysis of the inventory, where the size of each book is always set down, shews me that there were very few small books in this part of the library, but that they were divided between large (*grant*) and medium size (*moien*). If we allow 8 in. for each book, we get an average of 144 in. = 12 ft. for each desk, that is, as the desk was double, the piece of furniture was 6 ft. long. Under the sloping portion it had a shelf on each side. Four such desks stood between the door and the fireplace, and two between the fireplace and the window, which seems to have been opposite the door.

We are not told where the "trellis of iron" was. I suppose these words mean some shelves set against the wall with iron-work in front of them. As the enumeration of the books begins "near the door" the piece of furniture may be placed on the side of the door opposite to the former desks.

The inventory further shews that this library did duty as a museum. It was in fact filled with rare and beautiful objects, and must have presented a singularly rich appearance. In the middle of the hood over the fireplace was a stag's head and horns bearing a crucifix. There was a bust of the Duke of Savoy, in white marble, forming a pendant to one of the Duchess Margaret herself, and in the same material a statuette of a boy extracting a thorn from his foot, probably a copy of the antique in the Ducal Gallery at Florence. There were also twenty oil paintings in the room, some of which were hung round the hood of the fireplace. Besides these works of art there were several pieces of furniture, as, for instance, a large press containing a complete set of armour, a sideboard "à la mode d'Italie," given as a present by the viceroy of Naples ; a square table of inlaid work ; a smaller table bearing the arms of Burgundy and Spain ; three mirrors ; a number of objects in rock-crystal ; and lastly some feather dresses from India (S. America?), presented by the Emperor.

It is provoking that the inventory, minute as it is, should desert us at the most important point, and give insufficient data for estimating the size of the room. I conjecture that it was about 46 ft. long from the following considerations. In the first place, I allow 2 ft. for the width of each desk. Of these there were four between the door and the fireplace = 8 ft. Secondly, I allow 3 ft. each for the five intervals = 15 ft., or a total of 23 ft. from the door to the fireplace. For the fireplace itself I allow 10 ft. Between the fireplace and the wall containing the window or windows, there were two desks and three intervals = 13 ft. I pointed out above that 43 ft. at least might be allowed for the shelf extending from the door to the fireplace. Of this I have absorbed 23 ft., leaving 20 ft. for the distance from the door to the corner of the room. As we are not told anything about the position of the door my estimate of the size of the room cannot be carried further.

A similar arrangement obtained in the library of Anne de France, daughter of Louis XI., or as she is usually called Anne de Beaujeu[1]. Her catalogue made 19 September, 1523, records 314 titles, which I need hardly say represent a far larger number of books. They were arranged like those of the Duchess Margaret, on eleven desks (*poulpitres*). These were set round a room, with the exception of two which were placed in the middle of it. It is interesting to note respecting one of these, that it had a cupboard at the end, for the contents are entered as follows : *au bout dudit poulpitre sont enclos les livres qui s'ensuivent*, and sixteen volumes are enumerated. There was also a shelf set against the wall, described as *le plus hault poulpitre le long de la dite muraille*, which contained fifty-five volumes. This desk

[1] Lerou de Lincey, *Mélanges de la Société des Bibliophiles*, 1850. p. 231.

was probably high up, like the one in the library of the Duchess Margaret. The books upon it are noted as being all covered with red velvet, and ornamented with clasps, bosses, and corner-

Fig. 139. S. John writing his Gospel.

From a MS. *Hours* in the Fitzwilliam Museum, Cambridge.

pieces of metal. There were also in this library an astrolabe, and a sphere with the signs of the Zodiac.

A desk, similar in general character to that figured in the

Ship of Fools, but of a curiously modern type, occurs in an
Hours in the Fitzwilliam Museum, Cambridge, executed about
1445 for Isabel, Duchess of Brittany. The picture (fig. 139)
represents S. John writing his Gospel.

A modification of this form of desk was common in Italy.
It is often used by painters of the fifteenth century in pictures of
the Annunciation, where it does duty as a prie-dieu. The example I have selected (fig. 140) is from a painting by Benedetto
Bonfigli, in the church of S. Peter at Perugia. It represents
S. Jerome writing. A small circular revolving desk, at the
left-hand corner of the larger desk, holds the work he is
copying or referring to. On the desk near the inkstand lies
the pointed *stylus* mentioned above. Below the cupboard containing books is a drawer. Projecting from the top of the
revolving desk, there is a vertical rod of iron with a long
horizontal arm. This is no doubt intended to carry a lantern.
I shall shortly give an example of one in such a position.

I now return to the wheel-desk, of which I have already
figured one specimen (fig. 135). A piece of furniture consisting

Fig. 141. Çircular book-desk.

From a MS. of *Fais et Gestes du Roi Alexandre*, in the British Museum.

Fig. 140. S. Jerome writing.

From an oil painting by Benedetto Bonfigli, in the Church of
S. Peter at Perugia.

of one or more tables which could be raised or depressed by means of a central screw, was very generally used by scholars in the Middle Ages. I shall present a few of the most common forms.

My first specimen is from a manuscript in the British Museum, written and illuminated in England in the middle of the fifteenth century. It is called *Fais et Gestes du Roi Alexandre*[1]. The picture (fig. 141) represents Alexander as a

Fig. 142. S. Luke writing his Gospel.

From the Dunois *Horæ*, a MS. in the possession of H. Y. Thompson, Esq.

[1] MSS. Mus. Brit. 15 E. VI.

little child, standing in front of his tutor, who is seated in one of the chairs I described above. On the learned man's right is his book-desk. A circular table with a rim round it to prevent the books falling off, is supported on a central pedestal, which contains the screw. The top of the said screw is concealed by the little Gothic turret in the centre of the table. This turret also supports the book which the reader has in use.

My next example is from a miniature in a volume of Hours known as the Dunois *Horæ*, also written in the middle of the fifteenth century. It has been slightly enlarged in order to bring out the details more clearly. The subject is S. Luke writing his Gospel, but the background represents a scholar's room. There is a bookcase of a very modern type, a table with two folio volumes lying upon it, and in the centre a hexagonal book-desk, with a little Gothic turret as in the last example. Round the screw under the table are four cylindrical

Fig. 143. A lady seated in her chair reading.
From a MS. written in France, early in the fifteenth century.

supports, the use of which I fail to understand, but they occur frequently on desks of this type. The whole piece of furniture rests on a heavy cylindrical base, and that again on a square platform.

I now pass to a variety of the screw-desk, which has a small book-rest above the table. The whole structure rests upon a prolongation of the solid platform on which the reader's chair is placed, so that it is really exactly in front of the reader. My illustration (fig. 143) is from " The booke of the noble ladyes in frensh," a work by Boccacio; it was written in France early in the fifteenth century[1].

Fig. 144. Screw-desk.
From a fifteenth century MS. in the Bibliothèque de l'Arsenal, Paris.

Fig. 145. Hexagonal desk, with central spike, probably for a candle.
From a French MS. of *Le Miroir Historial*.

These double desks are exceedingly common, and I might fill a large number of pages with figures and descriptions of the variety which the ingenuity of the cabinet-makers of the fifteenth century managed to impart to combinations of a screw

[1] MS. Mus. Brit. 20 C. v.

and two or more tables. I will content myself with one more example (fig. 144) which shews the screw exceedingly well, and the two tables above it. The uppermost of these serves as a ledge to rest the books on, as does also the hexagonal block above it which conceals the top of the screw[1].

We meet occasionally with a solid desk, by which I mean one the level of which cannot be altered. In the example here given (fig. 145) from a French MS. of *Le Miroir Historial*, there is a central spike which I suspect to have been intended to carry a candle[2].

In some examples of these book-desks the pedestal is utilized as a book-cupboard (fig. 146). The picture which I have selected as shewing a desk of this peculiarity is singularly beautiful, and finished in the highest style of art available at the end of the fifteenth century in France. It forms half of the frontispiece to a fine manuscript of Boccacio's *Livre des cas des malheureux nobles hommes et femmes*[3]. The central figure is apparently lecturing on that moving theme, for in front of him, in the other half of the picture, is a crowd of men exhibiting their interest by the violence of their gestures. On his left is the desk I mentioned; it stands on an unusually firm base, and one side of the vertical portion is pierced by an arch, so as to make the central cavity available for putting books in. From the centre of the table rises a tall spike, apparently of iron, to which is attached a horizontal arm, bearing a lighted lantern. On the table, in addition to three books, is an inkstand and pen-case. In front of the lecturer is a carved chest, probably one of those book-coffers which I have already mentioned. The chair and canopy are richly carved, and the back of the seat is partially covered by a piece of tapestry. Further, the lecturer is allowed the unusual luxury of a cushion.

I will next deal with the appliances for reading and writing directly connected with the chairs in which scholars sat, and I will begin with the desk.

[1] Paris, Bibliothèque de l'Arsenal, MS. 5193, fol. 311. Boccacio: *Cas des malheureux nobles hommes et femmes.*

[2] Paris, Bibl. Nat., MSS. Français. 50, *Le Miroir Historial*, by Vincent de Beauvais, fol. 340. Probably written in cent. XV.

[3] MSS. Mus. Brit. Add. 35321. MSS. Waddesdon, No. 12. Bequeathed by Baron Ferdinand Rothschild.

Fig. 146. A lecturer addressing an audience.

From a MS. of *Livre des cas des malheureux nobles hommes et femmes*, written in France at end of fifteenth century.

Fig. 148. The author of *The Chronicles of Hainault* in his study (1446).

Fig. 150. A writer with his desk and table.

From a MS. of *Le Livre des Propriétés des Choses* in the British Museum.

The simplest form of desk is a plain board, set at a suitable angle by means of a chain or cord extending from one of its corners to the back of the chair, while the opposite corner rests against a peg driven into the arm of the chair. This arrangement, variously modified, occurs very frequently; sometimes there are two pegs and two chains, but what I may term the

Fig. 147. S. Mark writing his Gospel.

From a MS. *Hours* written in France in the fifteenth century.

normal form is shewn in my illustration (fig. 147)[1]. It is difficult to understand how the desk was kept steady.

The author whose study I shall figure next (fig. 148) is engaged in writing the Chronicles of Hainault[2]. His desk rests securely on two irons fastened to the arms of his chair. On his

[1] MSS. Bodl. Lib. Oxf., MSS. Rawl. Liturg. e. 24, fol. 17 *b*.

[2] MSS. Bibliothèque Royale de Bruxelles, No. 9242. *Chroniques de Hainaut*, Pt. 1. fol. 2, 1446.

right is a plain lectern with an open volume on each side of it, and behind are two or more shelves set against the wall with books lying on their sides. On his left is a chest, presumably a book-chest, with books lying on its closed lid. One of these is open. He has prudently placed his chair near the window in such a position that the light falls upon his work from the left. It should be noted that the upper part of the window only is glazed, the lower part being closed by shutters. When these are thrown back, the lights are seen to be filled to half their height with a trellis, such as was ordered for the French king's library.

My third example of a chair fitted with a desk (fig. 149) is taken from *Les Miracles de Notre Dame*[1], a manuscript which belonged to Philip the Good, Duke of Burgundy, and was written for him at the Hague in 1456. The illustration represents S. Jerome seated in his study. From arm to arm of the chair extends a desk of a very firm and solid construction. The ends of this desk apparently drop into the heads of the small columns with which the arms of the chair terminate. The saint has in his left hand a pointed *stylus*, and in his right a pen, which he is holding up to the light. On the desk beside the manuscript lies an ink-horn. To the right of the saint's chair is a hexagonal table with a high ledge round it. There is no evidence that this table has a screw; but the small subsidiary desk above it seems to be provided with one. It will be observed that the support of this desk is not directly over that of the table beneath it. The desk is provided with two slits—an ingenious contrivance for dealing with a roll. On the table, besides an open book, are a pair of spectacles, four pens, a small box which may contain French chalk for pouncing, and what looks like a piece of sponge.

I now figure two different sets of library appliances. The first (fig. 150) is from a manuscript of the *Livre des Propriétés des Choses*, in the British Museum, written in the fifteenth century[2]. The writer is seated in one of those low chairs which

---

[1] MSS. Bibl. Nat. Paris, MSS. Fran. 9198. See *Miracles de Nostre Dame*, by J. Mielot, Roxburghe Club, 1885; with introduction by G. F. Warner, M.A.

[2] MSS. Cotton, Augustus, VI. fol. 213 *b*. There is a beautiful example of a table and desk on this plan in a MS. of *La Cité des Dames*, from the old Royal Library of France in the Bibl. Nat.. MSS. Fran. 1177.

Fig. 149. S. Jerome in his study.

From *Les Miracles de Nostre Dame*, written at the Hague in 1456.

occur very frequently in miniatures, and look as if they were cut
out of a single block of wood. His desk, which is quite
independent of the chair, is of the simplest design, consisting
of a piece of wood supported at an angle on two carved uprights.
On his left stands a very elegant piece of furniture, a table with
a desk at a considerable height above it—so high, in fact, that it
could only be used standing. This upper desk is fitted with a
little door as though it served as a receptacle for small objects.

Fig. 151. S. Luke writing his Gospel.
MSS. Douce, Bodl. Lib. Oxf., No. 381.

The second example (fig. 151) shews S. Luke sitting on a bench writing at a table[1]. The top, which is very massive, rests on four legs, morticed into a frame. In front of this table is a desk of peculiar form; the lower part resembles a reversed cone, and the upper part a second cone of smaller diameter, so as to leave space enough between the two bases for a ledge to rest books on. Round the base of the desk three quaint lions do duty as feet. These lions occur again beneath the frame of the picture, and may be connected with a former possessor of the manuscript. The pedestal of the desk is a twisted column, which, like the base, and indeed the whole structure, looks as though it were made of brass.

I now pass to a totally different way of fitting up a study, which seems to have been common in Italy, to judge by the number of paintings in which it occurs. It consists of a massive desk of wood, one part of which is set at right angles to the other, and is connected in various ways with shelves, drawers,

Fig. 152. S. Augustine at his desk.

From a painting by Fra Filippo Lippi at Florence.

[1] MSS. Bodl. Lib. Oxf., MSS. Douce, No. 381, fol. 159. A second example occurs in the same MS., fol. 160.

Fig. 153. S. Jerome reading.

From an oil painting by Catena, in the National Gallery, London.

Fig. 154. A writer at work.

From a French translation of *Valerius Maximus*, written and illuminated in Flanders in 1479, for King Edward IV.

pigeon-holes, and other contrivances for holding books and papers. In the example I here figure (fig. 152), from a painting by Fra Filippo Lippi (1412—1469) representing S. Augustine's vision of the Trinity, there are two small recesses above the desk on the saint's right, both containing books, and behind the shorter portion of the desk, three shelves also with books on them. Attached to the end of the desk is a small tray, probably to contain pens.

A similar desk occurs in the beautiful picture by Catena in the National Gallery[1], representing S. Jerome reading, of which I give a reproduction on a reduced scale (fig. 153). This picture also contains an excellent example of a cupboard in the thickness of the wall, a contrivance for taking care of books as common in the Middle Ages as it had been in Roman times[2].

Cupboards in the thickness of the wall are also to be seen in the frontispiece (fig. 154) to a copy of a French translation of Valerius Maximus[3], written in Flanders in 1479 for King Edward IV. The writer—probably intended for the author or the translator of the book—is seated at a desk, consisting of a plank set at an angle and capable of being turned aside by means of a central bracket, like that used by the Carmelite (fig. 136). Observe the two weights hanging over the edge of the desk and the ends of the two horns, intended to hold ink, projecting through it. The window, as in the picture representing the author of the Chronicles of Hainault at work, is glazed in the upper part only, while in the lower are two framed trellises of wire-work. Behind the writer are two cupboards in the thickness of the wall. One of these is open, and shews books lying on their sides, upon which are some pomegranates. I cannot suggest any reason for the introduction of these fruits, except that from their colour they make a pleasing variety; but I ought to mention that they occur very frequently in miniatures representing a writer at work. On the other side of the window is a small hanging cupboard. Here again a fruit is introduced on the lowest shelf. Round the room is a settle, raised above

---

[1] I have to thank my friend Sidney Colvin, M.A., for drawing my attention to this picture.

[2] See above, pp. 37, 38.

[3] MSS. Mus. Brit. 18 E. IV.

the floor on blocks at intervals. The seat is probably a chest, as in the settles described above in the Vatican Library.

The last picture (fig. 155) in this series of illustrations represents what I like to call a scholar's room, at the beginning of the fifteenth century[1]. The owner of the apartment is busily writing at a desk supported on a trestle-table. He holds a *stylus* in his left hand, and a pen in his right. The ink-horn he is using is inserted into the desk. Above it are holes for two others, in case he should require ink of different colours. Above the inkstand is a pen stuck in a hole, with vacant holes beside it. The page on the desk is kept flat by a weight. Above this desk is a second desk, of nearly equal size, on which lies an open book, kept open by a large weight, extending over two-thirds of the open pages. Behind the writer's chair is his book-chest. The background represents a well-appointed chamber. The floor is paved with encaustic tiles; a bright fire is burning on the hearth; the window, on the same plan as that described in the last picture, is open; a comfortable—not to say luxurious—bed invites repose. The walls are unplastered, but there is a hanging under the window and over the head of the bed.

With this simple room, containing a scholar's necessaries and no more, I will contrast the study of the Duke of Urbino.

This beautiful room, which still exists as the Duke left it, is on an upper floor of the castle, commanding from its balcony, which faces the south, an extensive view of the approach to the Castle, the city, and the country beyond, backed by the Apennines. It is of small size, measuring only 11 ft. 6 in. by 13 ft. 4 in., and is somewhat irregular in shape. It is entered by a door from the Duke's private apartment. The floor is paved with rough tiles set in patterns. The walls are panelled to a height of about eight feet. The bare space between the top of the panel-work and the ceiling was probably hung with tapestry. The ceiling is a beautiful specimen of the most elaborate plaster-work, disposed in octagonal panels. The decoration of the panel-work begins with a representation of a bench, on which various objects are lying executed in intarsia work. Above ·

---

[1] *Le Débat de l'honneur entre trois Princes chevalereux.* Bibl. Roy. Bruxelles, No. 9278, fol. 10. The MS. is from the library of the Dukes of Burgundy, and may be dated in the second third of the fifteenth century.

Fig. 155. A scholar's room in the fifteenth century.

From a MS. in the Royal Library at Brussels.

this bench is a row of small panels, above which again is a row
of large panels, each containing a subject in the finest intarsia,
as for example a portrait of Duke Frederick, figures of Faith,
Hope, and other virtues, a pile of books, musical instruments,
armour, a parrot in a cage, etc. In the cornice above these is
the word FEDERICO, and the date 1476.

Opposite the window there is a small cupboard, and on the
opposite side of the projection containing it there are a few
shelves. These are the only receptacles for books in the room.
From its small size it could have contained but little furniture,
and was probably intended for the purpose traditionally ascribed
to it, namely as a place of retirement for the Duke when he
wished to be alone.

Another specimen of a library so arranged as to provide
a peaceful retreat is afforded a century later by that of
Montaigne, of which he has fortunately left a minute description.

[My library is] in the third story of a Tower, of which the Ground-
room is my Chappel, the second story an Apartment with a withdrawing
Room and Closet, where I often lie to be more retired. Above it is a
great Wardrobe, which formerly was the most useless part of the House.
I there pass away both the most of the Days of my Life, and most of
the Hours of those Days. In the Night I am never there. There is
within it a Cabinet handsome and neat enough, with a Fire-place very
commodiously contriv'd, and Light very finely fitted. And was I not
more afraid of the Trouble than the Expence, the Trouble that frights
me from all Business, I could very easily adjoyn on either side, and on
the same Floor, a Gallery of an hundred paces long, and twelve broad,
having found Walls already rais'd for some other Design, to the requisite
height. Every place of retirement requires a Walk. My Thoughts sleep
if I sit still; my Fancy does not go by itself, as when my Legs move it:
and all those who study without a Book are in the same Condition.
The figure of my Study is round, and has no more flat Wall than
what is taken up by my Table, and my Chairs; so that the remaining
parts of the Circle present me a view of all my books at once, set up
upon five degrees of Shelves round about me. It has three noble and
free Prospects, and is sixteen paces[1] Diameter. I am not so continually
there in Winter; for my House is built upon an Eminence, as its Name
imports, and no part of it is so much expos'd to the Wind and Weather
as that, which pleases me the better, for being of a painful access, and a
little remote, as well upon the account of Exercise, as being also there
more retir'd from the Crowd. 'Tis there that I am in my Kingdom, as

---

[1] The original words are 'seize pas de vuide.' The substantive 'pas' must I think
mean a foot, the length a foot makes when set upon the ground. The word pace, the
length of which is 2 ft. 6 in. or 3 ft., is inapplicable here.

we say, and there I endeavour to make myself an absolute Monarch, and so sequester this one Corner from all Society both Conjugal, Filial, and Civil[1].

The notices of libraries which I have collected have brought me to the end of the sixteenth century, by which time most of the appliances in use in the Middle Ages had been given up. I hope that I have not exhausted the patience of my readers by presenting too long a series of illustrations extracted from manuscripts. I love, as I look at them, to picture to myself the medieval man of letters, laboriously penning voluminous treatises in the writing room of a monastery, or in his own study, with his scanty collection of books within his reach, on shelves, or in a chest, or lying on a table. We sometimes call the ages dark in which he lived, but the mechanical ingenuity displayed in the devices by which his studies were assisted might put to shame the cabinet-makers of our own day.

As the fashion of collecting books, and of having them bound at a lavish expense, increased, it was obvious that they must be laid out so as to be seen and consulted without the danger of spoiling their costly covers. Hence the development of the lectern-system in private houses, and the arrangement of a room such as the Duchess Margaret possessed at Malines. Gradually, however, as books multiplied, and came into the possession of persons who could not afford costly bindings, lecterns were abandoned, and books were ranged on shelves against the wall, as in the public libraries which I described in the last chapter.

There is still in existence, on an upper floor in the Palazzo Barberini at Rome, a library of this description, which has probably not been altered in any way since it was fitted up by Cardinal Francesco Barberini about 1630. The room is 105 ft. long by 28 ft. broad, and is admirably lighted by two windows in the south wall, and seven in the gallery. The shelves are set round three sides of the room at a short distance from the wall, so as to leave space for a gallery and the stairs to it. The cases are divided into compartments by fluted Ionic columns 5 ft. high. These rest upon a flat shelf 14 in. wide, beneath which are drawers for papers and a row of folios. This

---

[1] *Essays of Michael Seigneur de Montaigne.* Made English by Ch. Cotton, Vol. III. pp. 53, 54. 8vo. London, 1741. I have to thank my friend Mr A. F. Sieveking for this reference.

part of the structure is 3 ft. high from the floor to the base of the columns. Above the columns is a cornice, part of which is utilized for books ; and above this again is the gallery, where the arrangement of the shelves is a repetition of what I have described in the lower part of the room. Dwarf cases in a plainer style and of later date are set along the sides and ends of the room. Upon these are desks for the catalogue, a pair of globes, some astronomical instruments, and some sepulchral urns found at Præneste. The older woodwork in this library has never been painted or varnished, and the whole aspect of the room is singularly old-world and delightful.

Fig. 156. Dean Boys in his Library, 1622.

Another instance is afforded by the sketch of the library of John Boys, Dean of Canterbury, who died in 1625. It occurs on the title-page of his works dated 1622, and I may add on his tomb in Canterbury Cathedral also. He clung to ancient fashions so far as to set his books with their fore-edge outwards, but in other respects his book-shelves are of a modern type.

I have now reached the limit which I imposed upon myself when I began this essay. But before I conclude let me say a few last words. I wish to point out that collectors and builders in the Middle Ages did not guard their manuscripts with jealous care merely because they had paid a high price to have them written; they recognised what I may call the personal element in them ; they invested them with the senses and the feelings of human beings; and bestowed them like guests whom they delighted to honour. No one who reads the *Philobiblon* can fail to see that every page of it is pervaded by this sentiment; and this I think explains the elaborate precautions against theft; the equally elaborate care taken to arrange a library in so orderly a fashion that each book might be accessible with the least difficulty and the least delay; and the exuberant gratitude with which the arrival of a new book was welcomed.

In my present work I have looked at libraries from the technical side exclusively. It would have been useless to try to combine fire and water, sentiment and fact. But let me remind my readers that we are not so far removed from the medieval standpoint as some of us perhaps would wish. When we enter the library of Queens' College, or the older part of the University Library, at Cambridge, where there has been continuity from the fifteenth century to the present day, are we not moved by feelings such as I have tried to indicate, such in fact as moved John Leland when he saw the library at Glastonbury for the first time?

Moreover, there is another sentiment closely allied to this by which members of a College or a University are more deeply moved than others—I mean the sentiment of association. The most prosaic among them cannot fail to remember that the very floors were trodden by the feet of the great scholars of the past; that Erasmus may have sat at that window on that bench, and read the very book which we are ourselves about to borrow.

But in these collections the present is not forgotten; the authors of to-day are taking their places beside the authors of the past, and are being treated with the same care. On all sides we see progress; the lecterns and the stalls are still in use and keep green the memory of old fashions; while near them the plain shelving of the twentieth century bears witness to the ever-present need for more space to hold the invading hordes of books that represent the literature of to-day. On the one hand, we see the past; on the other, the present; and both are animated by full, vigorous life.

INDEX.

CAMBRIDGE: PRINTED BY J. AND C. F. CLAY, AT THE UNIVERSITY PRESS.